A Project Manager's Guide to Passing the Project Management (PMP®) Exam

Published by:
Sturgeon Publishing

Published by: Sturgeon Publishing & The Project Management Excellence Center, Inc

Email: info@pmexam.com

Library of Congress Control Number:

ISBN 0-9726656-7-6 (paperback)

Manufactured in the United States of America
10 9 8 7 6 5 4 3 2 1

Table of Contents

Chapter 1
PMP® Certification & Exam

What is the PMP® Certification?

The Project Management Institute (PMI®) offers certification as a Project Management Professional (PMP®). More detailed information is available from PMI® in a brochure called "Certification & Standards" and is available on the web at www.pmi.org.

PMI® conducts a certification program in project management. PMI's Project Management Professional (PMP®) certification is the project management profession's most globally recognized and respected certification credential. To obtain PMP® certification an individual must satisfy education and experience requirements, agree to and adhere to a Code of Professional Conduct, and pass the PMP® Certification Examination.

Worldwide there are more than 110,000 PMP®'s who provide project management services in 120 countries. Many corporations now require PMP® certification for individual advancement within the corporation or for employment.

Requirements for Earning PMP® Certification?

There are four main requirements for earning PMP® certification:

1. Having experience working in the field of project management—4,500 hours with a baccalaureate degree and 7,500 without a degree.
2. Signing a PMP® Candidate Agreement and Release form.
3. Completing the PMP® Certification Exam Application
4. Paying a fee of $555 for non-PMI® members and $405 for members.

Requirements for Maintaining PMP® Certification?

In order to maintain your PMP® certification, you must earn at least sixty Professional Development Units within a three-year cycle and adhere to PMI's PMP® Code of Professional Conduct. You may want to consult the PMI® Web site at http://www.pmi.org for more details.

Structure and Content of the PMP® Certification Exam

The PMP® exam consists of 175 multiple-choice questions that test your knowledge in the nine PMBOK® Guide knowledge areas of Integration, Scope, Time, Cost, Quality, Human Resource, Communications, Risk, and Procurement; the five PMBOK® process groups of Project Initiation, Project Planning, Project Execution, Project Control, and Project Closing; and the area of Professional Responsibility. The exam can be difficult, not because of the nature of the subject matter (which is actually quite basic), but because—

- Some questions are awkwardly worded and ambiguous; sometimes it is difficult to determine exactly what the test writer is asking.
- Some questions tend to test one's memory of specific language (that is, definition and terms) from the PMBOK® Guide, PMI® publications, and other reference materials.

Many questions take an activity that could legitimately be done many different ways and ask you to choose the "best way", or "what is the first step" you would take given a particular situation.

The exam is mostly qualitative, not quantitative, and many of the quantitative questions are not that difficult. However, most exam takers seem to find the most problems with questions that address quality, cost, and risk topics. The quality questions are difficult for many people because they have learned a philosophy and practice of quality in their organizations that are somewhat different from that espoused by PMI® even though PMI's approach is consistent with many of the "gurus" in the field. The questions that address cost topics tend to cover a breadth of material much more diverse than the average test-taker has previously been exposed to. For example, in addition to having to know all the earned-value formulas, one needs to know a variety of information from benefit-cost ratio to understanding the two methods of capital depreciation.

How to Prepare for the PMP® Exam?

Like most people, you have probably developed your own study habits through the years, and you know what works best for you. I am not suggesting that I have identified the only way to study for this rigorous undertaking. In fact, there are several ways to approach this, which when combined with individual study can have powerful results. But I have identified some approaches over the years that seem to produce good results:

- Do a little every day. Do not wait until the week before the exam to start studying. You are already too late.
- Prepare for the exam with other test-takers. Studying with other people provides a powerful advantage enabling you to learn more information faster. Plan on lunch-hour sessions, if convenient, or before or-after-work sessions.
- Within your group, you can create a division of labor where different persons are responsible for teaching the subject matter in specific sections of the PMBOK® Guide to others in the group.
- Perhaps the most powerful of all approaches is to review in your group every practice test question you received. The process of discussing among yourselves how you selected your answer and what rationale you used for each answer is an extremely productive one. We guarantee that this group study method will, in all likelihood, result in your learning more about project management concepts and practice than any individual study method.
- Ask people questions who have taken the exam. Get as much input as possible. Do not limit your questions to those who have passed the exam. If possible, ask those who have failed the exam what their experiences were.

One Month before the Exam

You do not have much time. You should be taking and retaking the practice test, studying the Simulated Test Bank, and working with a study group (if possible). Keep track of the questions and definitions you are answering right and those you are getting wrong. Make sure you are studying a little every day.

Concentrate on those areas in which you are having problems. Spend a minimum of one hour each day in your three weakest areas. Implement the study strategies you know work best for you (should you answer all the easy questions first, the harder ones, or skip around, or some other approach?) Write down your approaches and practice them. Using whatever format and approach you find helpful, go over at least ten new definitions every day.

One Week before the Exam

Continue to work through the practice questions and any practice test you may have. Also on a daily basis, start reviewing definitions.

Exam Day

Think confidently! Do not dwell on your weaknesses; concentrate on your strengths. You have been studying very hard, you are prepared, and you know what to expect.

Tips for Taking the PMP® Exam

- Make sure you have everything you need remember that pencils and calculators are usually provided. You will not be allowed to bring any additional items in with you.
- Listen carefully to the proctor's directions and comments as you do not want to make any procedural errors; it can result in lost time and possibly wrong answers.
- Review the exam, reading the directions carefully. Do not start answering the questions before you read the directions on the screen.
- Try and budget your time as you have a little more than a minute for each question. Realistically, you can answer some questions in a few seconds, and others will take several minutes to answer. Be mindful of the time you are spending in each section, but do not be obsessed with it. Very few people run out of time.
- Write down important formulas, facts, and statistics in the margin or on scratch paper as soon as you sit down. This can be done during the computer tutorial. This safeguard will ensure that you do not forget certain information if you become too nervous.
- Look for "qualifying" words in the stem of the question or in the answers. For example, words such as, rarely, often, seldom, many, always, and so on will determine the correct answer.
- Answer the easy questions first. A good way to reduce anxiety is to answer the easy questions first. This will build your confidence as you proceed through the rest of the exam section. If you attempt the more difficult questions initially, you will tend to feel uninformed, unprepared, and "unhappy."
- If you do not know the answer, mark (electronically or otherwise) the question and complete it later. There will be many questions for which the answer will not be immediately apparent. Rather than struggle with the question, move on to the next one. Return to those unanswered questions later. Chances are your memory will return, and you will be able to make a better educated guess the second or third time you read the question.
- Guess aggressively. Never leave a question blank. You are scored on the number of correct answers; points are not deducted for wrong answers.
- Use all the time allowed. If you finish early, check for errors. Review the directions once again to ensure that you have followed them correctly.
- Try not to think about your score while taking the exam. Thinking about your score will not raise it; thinking about the answers will!

What you need to know for the Exam

Project Integration Management

The Project Integration Management section on the PMP® certification exam addresses critical project management functions that ensure coordination of the various elements of the project. As the PMBOK® Guide explains the processes in integration management are primarily integrative. Project integration management involves making trade-offs among competing objectives in order to meet or exceed stakeholder needs and expectations and addresses develop project charter, develop project management plan, direct and manage project execution, monitor and control project work, integrated change control and close project. These seven processes not only interact with each other but also interact with processes in the other eight knowledge areas. Noting PMI's view that integration occurs in other areas also is important. For example, project scope and product scope need to be integrated; project work needs to be integrated with the other work of the ongoing organization, and deliverables from various technical specialties need integration.

The Project Integration Management questions are straightforward. In the past, most people find them to be easy. Nevertheless, because they cover so much material, you do need to study them carefully to become familiar with PMI's terminology and perspectives. PMBOK® Guide Figure 4.1 provides an overview of the structure of Project Integration Management.

The Project Integration knowledge area is concerned with coordinating all aspects of the project and is highly interactive. Project planning, project execution, and change control occur throughout the project and are repeated continuously while working on the project. Project planning and execution involve weighing the objectives of the project against alternatives to bring the project to a successful completion. Change control impacts the project plan, which, in turn, impacts execution, so you can see that these three processes are very tightly linked. The processes in this area also interact with other processes in the remaining knowledge areas.

Project Scope Management

The Project Scope Management questions on the PMP® exam cover a diverse, yet functional set of project management topics: project planning, work breakdown structures, project charter, scope statement, scope verification, scope management plan, and the scope changes are among the topics covered.

PMI® views project scope management as a five-step process that consists of scope planning, scope definition, create WBS, scope verification, and scope control. In the PMBOK® Guide figure 5.1 provides an overview of the structure.

The project scope management questions on the exam are straightforward. In the past most people have found them to be easy; do not be lulled into a full sense of security by past results. These questions cover a wide range of material, and you must be familiar with the terminology and perspectives adopted by PMI®.

Project Scope Management is concerned with the work of the project. All of the processes involved with the work of the project, and only the work that is required to complete the project are found in this knowledge area. All of the scope management processes involve detailing the requirements of the project and the activities that will eventually comprise the project plan, verifying those details using measurements techniques, and controlling changes to these processes.

Project initiation occurs when an individual or group recognizes that a project should begin. Although project initiation is not always a clearly defined process, it frequently includes determining what the project should accomplish, defining the goal of project, and developing a project charter. These actions might vary depending on the organization for which the project is done.

PMI® defines initiation as the process that formally recognizes the beginning of a new project or the continuation of an existing project into its next phase. Note that projects are authorized in different ways in different organizations. PMBOK® Guide section 5.1 lists typical reasons to authorize projects, including market demand, business needs, customer request, technological advance, or social need.

The PMBOK® Guide notes the importance of relating the product description to the business need or other stimuli that gave rise to the product. The PMBOK® Guide states that the product description will generally have fewer details in early phases and more details in later phases as the product characteristics are progressively elaborated. The PMBOK® Guide also notes the need for projects to support an organization's strategic plan. In the initiation process, the PMBOK® Guide identifies the identification and assignment of the project manager as a key output and suggests that the project manager be assigned as early as possible in the project but always before project plan execution begins.

Initiation is where we get our work. This is a concept that is important, since it is where the project manager is assigned and where he/she can point to the beginning of the project. This is challenging, since many projects might be born out of thin air and do not often have a clear beginning point.

Project Time Management
The Project Time Management questions on the PMP® exam focus heavily on the Critical Path Method (CPM) and the Precedence Diagramming Method (PDM), and the differences between these techniques. The exam tests your knowledge of how these networks are constructed, how schedules are computed, what the critical path is, and how networks are used to analyze and solve project scheduling, and resource allocation and leveling issues.

The exam may also contain some scheduling exercises. There is a focus on fast tracking as a method to accelerate the project schedule. You must know the advantages offered by networks over bar charts and flow diagrams and understand the two ways in which networks can be represented (activity-on-arrow and activity-on-node). You should also understand the notion of float (or slack) and how it presents challenges and opportunities to project schedulers.

In the PMBOK® Guide, the functions of Project Time Management are separated into six phases: activity definition, activity sequencing, activity resource estimating, activity duration estimating, schedule development, and schedule control. Review PMBOK® Guide figure 6.1.

This knowledge area is concerned with estimating the duration of the project plan activities, devising a project schedule, and monitoring and controlling deviations from the schedule. Collectively, this knowledge area deals with completing the project in a timely manner.

In many cases, all of the activity processes described here along with schedule development are completed as one activity. Sometimes, only one person is needed to complete these six processes, and they're all worked on at the same time. Time management is an important aspect of project management as it concerns keeping the project activities on track and monitoring those activities against the project plan to assure the project is completed on time.

As you go through this section of the exam, you do not want to spend quite as much time as you might anticipate studying the calculations associated with the whole network. Instead, what you want to look at are some unusual relationships—start-start, finish-finish, and lag and lead times, and examining the issues associated with the classical representations of schedules. That includes CPM, PDM, AOA (activity-on-arrow), and AON (activity-on-node).

Project Cost Management

Project cost management includes the processes required to ensure that the project is completed within the approved budget. It is primarily concerned with the cost of the resources required to complete project activities.

A broader view of project cost management is often referred to as life-cycle costing. It involves including acquisition, operating, and disposal costs when evaluating various project alternatives. A creative approach used to optimize life cycle costs, save time, increase profits, improve quality, expand market share, use resources more effectively, and solve problems is called value engineering.

Life cycle costing and value engineering techniques are used together to reduce cost and time, improve quality and performance, and optimize the decision-making. In many application areas, predicting and analyzing the prospective financial performance of the project's product is done outside the project.

In some areas such as capital facilities projects, project cost management includes predicting and analyzing the prospective financial performance of the project's product. In these situations, project cost management will include general management techniques such as:

- Return on investment
- Discounted cash flow
- Payback analysis

Should consider the information needs of the project stakeholders and the different ways and times stakeholders measure project cost. For example, the cost of a procurement item may be measured when committed, ordered, delivered, incurred, or recorded for accounting purposes. When project costs are used as a component of a reward and recognition system, controllable and uncontrollable costs should be estimated and budgeted separately to ensure that rewards reflect actual performance.

The ability to influence cost is greatest at the early stages of the project. Early scope definition and requirements identification are critical to reducing costs in a project.

Project Quality Management

The Project Quality Management questions on the PMP® exam are straightforward. The exam reflects the current emphasis on customer satisfaction and continuous improvement through quality tools such as Pareto analysis and cause-and-effect diagrams. You must know the difference among quality planning, performing quality assurance, and performing quality control.

PMBOK® Guide includes all quality-related activities under the term Project Quality Management, which compromise the three quality processes mentioned above. Review PMBOK® Guide figure 8.1 for an overview of the Project Quality Management structure.

The Project Quality Management knowledge area assures that the project meets the requirements that the project was undertaken to produce. These processes measure overall performance, monitor the project's results, and compare them to the quality standards set out in the project planning process to assure that the customer will receive the product or service they thought they purchased.

Project Quality Management is composed of the following three processes:

- Quality Planning - involves defining quality standards and deciding how to achieve them.
- Perform Quality Assurance - consists of measuring project progress to ensure the product meets quality standards.
- Perform Quality Control - involves supervising project activity completion and correcting any errors.

The purpose of quality management during the project management process is to identify customers' needs, to develop goals based on those needs, and to identify factors that impede achievement of project goals. Another aim of quality management is to keep a project on schedule, which helps avoid sacrificing quality in the interest of time and cost.

Before beginning a project, it is important for you the project manager to have a solid understanding of quality management and how its components are integrated into the project management process.

The components of quality management fit into these steps of the project management process:

- Quality planning is part of the planning step of the project management process.
- Quality improvement is part of the executing step of the project management process.
- Quality control is part of the controlling step of the project management process.

The PMBOK® Guide defines quality as the totality of characteristics of an entity that bears on its ability to satisfy stated or implied needs.

Stated and implied needs are the inputs to developing project requirements. A critical aspect of quality management in the project context is turning implied needs into requirements through Project Scope Management.

It is important to recognize the difference between quality and grade. Grade is a category or rank given to entities having the same functional use but different technical characteristics. Low quality is always a problem; low grade may not be. For example:

- A software product may be of high quality (very few defects, a readable user's manual) but of low grade meaning it has a limited number of features.
- Or, a software product may be of low quality but of high grade meaning it has many defects but lots of customer features.

The project manager and team must determine and deliver the required levels of quality and grade.

One important area that is emphasized in the PMBOK® Guide is the growing attention to customer requirements as the basis for managing quality. Another concept that may appear on the test, which is not specifically mentioned in the PMBOK® Guide, is "gold-plating." Simply defined, gold-plating gives the customer more than what was required. Exceeding the specified requirements is a waste of time and money, with no value added to the project. The customer should expect and receive exactly what was specified. This is the underlying philosophy of project quality management espoused by PMI®; it is the process required to ensure that the project will satisfy the needs for which it was undertaken.

Project Human Resource Management

The Project Human Resource Management section of the PMP® exam focuses heavily on organizational structures, roles and responsibilities of the project manager, team building, and conflict resolution.

In contrast to other areas of the PMBOK® Guide in which commonly known terms are used, much of the terminology developed for Project Human Resource Management seems peculiar to PMI®. In spite of the unfamiliarity of some terminology, most people do find the human resource questions to be difficult.

Project Human Resource Management involves all aspects of people management and personal interaction including leading, coaching, dealing with conflict, and more. Some of the project participants whom you'll get to practice these skills on include stakeholders, team members, and customers. Each requires the use of different communication styles, leadership skills, and team-building skills. A good project manager knows when to enact certain skills and communication styles based on the situation.

The PMP® exam is heavily weighted toward team development (that is, behavioral topics). In the past only a few questions have appeared on administrative issues, and they should be relatively easy to answer, given familiarity with general corporate—personnel policies governing your everyday work life. The questions predominantly focus on forms of organization, project manager roles and responsibilities, types of power, project conflict, conflict management, and team building.

Project Communications Management

The Project Communications Management questions on the PMP® exam are basic and are taken primarily from the PMBOK® Guide and other PMI® published materials. Common sense and your own expertise will play a large role in your ability to answer the questions on this topic.

PMI® considers management style to be an essential component of how a project manager communicates, and thinks of the kickoff meeting as one of the most effective mechanisms in

Project Communications Management. The questions on the exam about this focus on formal and informal communication, verbal versus written communication, conflict resolution, and management styles.

The processes that make up the Project Communications Management knowledge area are as follows: Communications Planning, Information Distribution, Performance Reporting, and Manage Stakeholders.

The processes in the Project Communications knowledge area are related to general communication skills but aren't the same thing. Communication skills are considered general management skills that the project manager utilizes on a daily basis. The processes in the Communications knowledge area seek to ensure that all project information including project plans, risk assessments, meeting notes, and more is collected and documented. These processes also ensure information is distributed and shared with appropriate stakeholders and project members. At project closure, the information is archived and used as a reference for future projects. This is referred to as historical information in several project processes.

Communication Skills

The general management skill of communicating is related to, but not the same as, project communications management. Communicating is the broader subject and involves a substantial body of knowledge that is not unique to projects.

Communicating consists of using sender receiver models which includes both feedback loops and barriers to communication. Note that you will want to create internal and external feedback loops to help evaluate the effectiveness of communications. Feedback is considered either positive or negative based on the effect it has, not on its content. Research suggests that, amongst the many reasons why information fails to be communicated, the following are the main barriers:

- Different status of the sender and the receiver - (e.g. a senior manager sends a memo to a production supervisor - who is likely to pay close attention to the message. The same information, conveyed in the opposite direction might not get the attention it deserves).
- Use of jargon - employees who are "specialists" may fall for the trap of using specialist language for a non-specialist audience (e.g. the IT technician who cannot tries to explain how users should log onto a network, in language that sounds foreign to most users of the network).
- Selective reporting - where the reporter gives the recipient incorrect or incomplete information.
- Poor timing - information that is not immediately relevant (e.g. notice of some deadline that seems a long way off) is not always actioned straightaway.
- Conflict - where the communicator and recipient are in conflict; information tends to be ignored or distorted.
- Choice of Media - Choice of media is when to communicate in writing versus orally, when to write an informal memo versus a formal report, and when to communicate face-to-face, or via e-mail. The media chosen for communication activities will depend upon the situation.
- Writing Style - Writing style deals with grammar issues such as voice structure (active versus passive), sentence structure, and proper word selection.

- Presentation Techniques - This area includes both body language and presentation of material. It also includes such things as agenda preparation and dealing with conflict.

The Communications Model

According to PMI®, the communications model consists of four major parts, as indicated below:

- Sender - The originator of the message.
- Message - Thoughts, feelings, or ideas, reduced to "code" that are understandable by both sender and receiver.
- Medium - The vehicle or method used to convey the message. The choice of medium will color and influence the effect of the message. The most common media are visual, audio, and tactile.
- Receiver - The person for whom the message is intended. He or she must accept and understand the message before communication has taken place.

The receiver may filter the information, that is, selectively reduce its quantity or quality. If the receiver is actively listening, he or she is attentive and asks for clarification or repetition of ambiguous messages. The sender should request feedback to ensure the message has been received in its entirety.

Project Risk Management

On past exams many people find the project risk management questions demanding because they address many concepts that some project managers have not been exposed to in their work or education. However, the questions correspond closely to the PMBOK® Guide material so you should not have much difficulty if you study the concepts and terminology found in the PMBOK® Guide. Although the questions included do not contain mathematically complex work problems, they do require you to know certain theories, such as expected monetary value (EMV) and decision-tree analysis. Additionally, you are likely to encounter questions related to levels of risk faced by both buyer and seller based on various types of contacts.

Project Risk Management contains six processes: Risk Management Planning, Risk Identification, Qualitative Risk Analysis, Quantitative Risk Analysis, Risk Response Planning, and Risk Monitoring and Control.

As the name of this knowledge area implies, these processes are concerned with identifying and planning for potential risks that may impact the project. Organizations will often combine several of these processes into one step. The important thing about this process is that you should strive to identify all the risks and develop responses for those with the greatest consequences to the project objectives.

In order to manage project risk, you must first understand what constitutes risk. First, risks are generally associated with uncertain outcomes or a lack of knowledge of future events. Second, risks are measured according to the probability of their occurrence and the consequences of not achieving project goals. Finally, project risk compares actual project and product results to the project's quality standards. Know the concept of risk versus reward.

A risk is any factor that may potentially interfere with successful completion of the project. A risk is not a problem—a problem has already occurred; a risk is the recognition that a problem or opportunity might occur. By recognizing potential problems, the project manager can attempt to avoid or minimize a problem through proper actions.

The procedure that the team will use to manage project risks is defined in the Planning Phase, documented in the Project Plan, and then executed throughout the Execution Phase of the project.

The Risk Management Plan, documents the parameters used to manage risk throughout the project. In addition to documenting the results of the risk identification and analysis steps, it must cover who is responsible for managing various areas of risk, how risks will be tracked throughout the project, how contingency plans will be implemented, and how project contingency reserves will be allocated to handle risk.

Project reserves are resources (people, dollars, and commodities) that are available to the project if needed. Reserves can come in two types -- contingency reserves (known unknowns) and management reserves (unknown unknowns). Contingency reserves are developed based on the results of risk planning, and are usually available for release at the project manager's discretion to address risks that materialize, and to ensure the project succeeds even if the risk occurs. Management reserves are developed at the discretion of management, and are put in place when the ability to obtain additional budget may compromise the success of the project. Management reserves are typically part of project budgeting, and not part of risk planning.

Project risks are identified, monitored and carefully managed throughout the life of the project. It is particularly important in the Planning Phase to document risks and identify contingency reserves that have been applied to the risks.

There are various areas that can affect a project's risk level:

- The technology used on the project
- The environment in which the project is executed
- The relationships between team members
- How well the project fits the business area or strategic objectives of the organization
- How great of a change will result from the project

Risks are documented so that contingency measures can be taken to mitigate their effects. Risks to both the internal and external aspects of the project should be tracked. Internal risks are those items that the project team can directly control (e.g., staffing), and external risks are those events that happen outside the direct influence of the project team.

As stated before, risk identification begins early in the Planning Phase of the project. A Risk Management Plan is started during the Planning Phase. Then, as scheduling, budgeting, and resource planning occur, the plan is updated to reflect further risks identified throughout the Planning Phase.

Project Procurement Management

The Project Procurement Management questions on the PMP® exam tend to be more process oriented than legally focused. The exam requires you to know the differences between the two categories of contracts (fixed-price and cost-reimbursement) and the risks inherent in each category for both the buyer and seller. Several questions will also test your knowledge of the various types of contracts within each category.

The processes in the Project Procurement Management knowledge area are as follows: Plan Procurements, Conduct Procurements, Administer Procurements and Close Procurements.

Project procurement management is the process required to acquire the goods and services necessary to attain project scope. Goods and services typically are referred to as a product and are obtained from outside the performing organization.

PMI® discusses Project Procurement Management from the perspective of the buyer in the buyer-seller relationship but notes that the buyer-seller relationship can exist at many levels on one project. On the exam the seller may be called a subcontractor, vendor, or supplier. The seller generally manages work as a project in and of itself. The buyer may also be referred to as the customer. The terms and conditions of the contract are a major input to the seller's processes. The terms and conditions may actually contain the input as it may describe key milestones, deliverables, or objectives, or they may serve as a constraint since they may limit the project team's options (for example, requiring buyer approval of staffing decisions or staffing changes).

PMI® further discusses project procurement management from the perspective of the seller being external to the organization but notes that the discussion is also applicable to formal agreements entered into with other units in the performing organization. If informal agreements are used, then processes in Human Resource Management and Communications Management are more likely to apply. Apply extra caution when answering questions in this area: make sure you know whom the question refers to when you see the words buyer and seller. In most cases, the buyer is the project manager.

Procurement planning is the process in which the project manager identifies those needs of the project that can be met by purchasing products or services from outside the organization.

Procurement planning deals with the following:

- What to procure
- When to procure
- How to procure
- How much to procure

It is very uncommon for an organization to be able to create or supply all the products necessary to complete a project internally. In those circumstances where it is necessary to go outside the organization, the response is to purchase the product or service from an external source or enter into a contract with an outside vendor to perform a service or develop the product for the organization. Whatever choice is made, there is definitely a considerable amount of forethought and planning that needs to go into such a decision.

Professional Responsibility

Professional Responsibility will focus on the following tasks:

- Ensuring integrity and professionalism
- Contributing to the project management knowledge base
- Enhancing individual competence
- Balancing stakeholders' interests
- Interacting with team and stakeholders in a professional and cooperative manner
- Specific knowledge areas and skills have been identified in the Role Delineation Study for each of these tasks.

These questions will be based on situations or scenarios that require an understanding of the Project Management Professional Code of Conduct and the importance of professional ethics, awareness of legal issues, cultural sensitivity, and managing conflict of interest.

Chapter 2
Fundamentals of Project Management

What is the Project Management Body of Knowledge (PMBOK® Guide)?

The Guide to the Project Management Body of Knowledge (PMBOK® Guide) is a term that describes the sum of knowledge within the profession of project management. The body of knowledge rests with the professionals and academics that apply and advance it.

The Guide to the Project Management Body of Knowledge (PMBOK® Guide) describes what is generally accepted, meaning that the knowledge and practices are applicable to most projects most of the time, and there is a widespread consensus about their value and usefulness. The text is published by the Project Management Institute, which is recognized as one of the authoritative association for project managers. Based on stringent requirements for project management experience, academic education, and a rigorous testing program, PMI® certifies individuals as Project Management Professionals (PMP®), the most recognized certification for project managers in the business world today.

What is a Project Management Framework?

A project management framework provides standard, structured guidelines for conducting information technology projects in a disciplined, well-managed, and consistent manner. The ultimate goal of a project management framework is to promote the delivery of quality products on time and within budget.

A Framework is a broad management structure adaptable to meet the unique requirements of information technology projects of all types, regardless of complexity, scope, visibility and risk. A Framework acknowledges that large, complex projects require a more rigorous application of management processes than small, well-defined projects with readily achievable goals. The project manager must assess the characteristics of their specific project and determine the project management processes that are required.

A project management framework is not intended to be a step-by-step recipe or cookbook for managing a project nor does it eliminate the need to apply professional experience, expertise and judgment on every project. Most projects contain far too many variables and specifics to support a prescriptive structure.

What is Project Management?

A project is initiated when an individual or group recognizes a problem or opportunity and decides to take action. The action results in some kind of deliverable either a product, which might be a political campaign or a new automobile, or a unique service. After an idea is developed, time and effort must be invested to develop the concept into a deliverable. Initiating a project begins the project's life cycle.

Project management involves using specific knowledge, processes, tools, and methods to make sure a project meets or exceeds stakeholders' requirements. A stakeholder can be anyone interested or invested in the project, anyone who can influence the project, or anyone who is affected by the project.

The goal of project management is to achieve predetermined objectives for the scope, quality, time, and cost of a project. Project management also involves striving for participant satisfaction. For project management to be successful, it requires a group of individuals dedicated to achieving the project goal. In striving for participant satisfaction, project managers must address the needs of team members and stakeholders.

Most of the knowledge and skills that a project manager needs are unique to the project management process. For example, general managers do not ordinarily need to complete a critical path analysis or diagram network functions. However, some aspects of general management and project management overlap, such as planning, staffing, setting expectations, and organizing people and information.

Project management may be informally defined as "The art of directing and coordinating human and material resources to achieve stated objectives within limits of time, budget, and stakeholders' satisfaction." Or more formally defined as "The application of modern management techniques and systems to the execution of a project from start to finish, to achieve predetermined objectives of scope, quality, time and cost, to the equal satisfaction of those involved.

There are two different models of approaching the study of project management:

- Product-oriented processes are concerned with specifying and creating the final product. A methodology for product-oriented processes describes how to develop and implement IT products, e.g. how to do requirements specifications, how to design a network, and how to develop an acceptance test plan.
- Project management processes are concerned with describing and organizing the work of the project. The methodology described in this book is built around five standard project management processes (initiation, planning, execution, controlling, and closing) that are independent of the product being developed and the product development and implementation methodology.

What is a Project?

A project is a temporary sequence of tasks with a distinct beginning and an end that is undertaken to create a unique product or service. In addition, a project must have defined objectives in order to clearly indicate when the project has been completed. There are some necessary features that characterize all projects:

- Projects follow an organized process in order to meet specific goals.
- Project goals are based on specific quality standards.
- Projects use time, money, resources, and people that are allocated to the project.
- Projects have a distinct beginning and end.
- Projects generally have time and cost constraints.
- Projects are usually completed by a team of people.

There are several attributes that characterize a project:

- Projects are unique. The product or service being produced by the project is different and involves doing something that has not been done before.
- Projects have a purpose. Projects have a well-defined set of desired results. They can be divided into smaller tasks in order to achieve the overall project goal.
- Projects have a life cycle. Projects progress from an idea through the planning, executing, and controlling steps, and finally to a close. The project life cycle also indicates that projects are temporary, with a definite beginning and a definite end.
- Projects have interdependencies. The various tasks of a project interact with one another, while at the same time interacting with the parent organization.

Projects are temporary in nature, while operations are ongoing. Projects have definitive start dates and definitive end dates. Operations involve work that is continuous without an ending date and most often repeat the same process.

Typically, a team assigned to a project will spend time, money, and other resources allocated specifically for the project. Projects run under time and cost constraints, but project managers and teams must overcome them to meet the project's goals, which are based on quality standards. Examples of projects include moving to a new office location, writing a book, developing a new product or service, and implementing a new payroll system.

Project Management Process Groups

The image at the right is a graphical depiction of the five project management phases of a project life cycle. All projects regardless of size, type and complexity go through the five project management phases. Small, uncomplicated projects may progress through the phases very quickly while larger, more complex projects may spend a great deal of time completing each phase.

Although the diagram depicts project management phases as separate entities, in reality most projects will traverse back and forth between phases several times throughout the course of the project. As shown on the diagram, projects frequently revisit the planning phase as they execute and control the project.

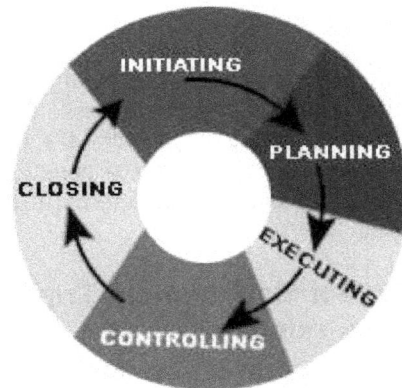

Figure 1 – Project Management Process Groups

Each project phase is defined as follows:

1. **Project Initiation**. Project Initiation activities occur before the project actually begins and answers the questions why, what and how. Why the project needs to occur, what the project will produce and how the desired product will be developed. At this point in the project life cycle, the product and the project work to produce the product are typically still very high level concepts, or strategies. The details of the work to be performed are still to be defined.
2. **Project Planning**. Project Planning activities translate the high level concepts defined during Project Initiation into product requirements that in turn establish the scope of the project. Once the project scope is defined, project planners develop the project schedule

and estimate project cost. Project Planning also involves defining the project organization and communication structures and developing the management processes that will be used throughout the project.

3. **Project Execution**. Project Execution involves coordinating and authorizing people or other resources to carry out the plan.

4. **Project Monitoring and Control.** Project Monitoring and Control involves ensuring the project objectives are met by monitoring and measuring progress against the plan and taking corrective action when needed. The sooner problems or variances from the plan are detected the easier it is to take corrective action. Therefore, it is better to provide early warning of potential problems than to wait until the problems have grown to the point that corrective action is difficult or even impossible. Open, honest and early communications between project team members, project manager, and the stakeholders are the key ingredient of all successful projects.

5. **Project Closeout**. Project Closeout activities include obtaining formal acceptance of the project, documenting lessons learned throughout the project and organizing project documentation for archiving. For a project to be successful; several variables must be addressed as part of the five project management process groups. These variables include scope, time, quality, communication, and management issues related to risk, cost, budget, human resources, contracts and procurement, and integration.

For a project to be successful; several variables must be addressed as part of the five project management process groups. These variables include scope, time, quality, communication, and management issues related to risk, cost, budget, human resources, contracts and procurement, and integration.

The separate processes for these issues are linked to the five process groups within the overall project management process. For example, to manage a project's scope, you need to use initiation processes, which are part of the initiating process group. Scope management also involves scope definition processes, which are part of the planning process group. To understand the overall project management process, you need to understand how the processes from each group interact.

Project Management Triple Constraints

The basic goal of project management is to deliver an acceptable product, typically referred to as project scope, on schedule and within budget. Invariably, scope, schedule and budget (cost) are also fundamental constraints in every project. Constraints are factors that could restrict product or project options, setting limits to what can be achieved, how it can be achieved, in what timeframe, or at what cost.

Figure 2 – Project Management Triple Constraints

Scope, schedule and cost are inherently interrelated. Increasing one constraint automatically increases at least one of the other two constraints. For example, if project scope cannot get completed on schedule, resources must be employed for longer than anticipated to complete project work. Additional resources translate to additional cost. Alternatively, if the planned project schedule must be adhered to, it may be necessary to reduce project scope.

Because project scope, project schedule and project cost are correlates of each other, they are often referred to as the Project Management Triple Constraints. They are often depicted as a triangle as shown.

Once the triple constraints of project scope, schedule and cost have been defined, they must be continually monitored to ensure that their delicate balance is maintained throughout the project.

Project Roles and Responsibilities

It is important to have a defined structure for the project team. To ensure the successful accomplishment of project activities, each individual should have a clear understanding of their authority and the responsibilities for which they are accountable. Project team members should be accountable for the effective performance of their assignments.

A successful project requires that project participants contribute to the planning process, that they accept and support the project plan, and that they become responsible for completion of assignments.

Project Management Knowledge Areas

Listed below are the nine project management knowledge areas:

1. **Project Integration Management** - Integration Management skills are used to integrate the work in other core areas. The primary focus of integration management is the creation of a cohesive, comprehensive, and well-designed project plan and the execution of that project plan. Another skill is the overseeing of the change control process, both as it is developed in the plan and as it is executed throughout the life of the project.
2. **Project Scope Management** - Scope Management is the skill project managers use to define the work that needs to be done on any given project. This entails making sure that all the work required is included and that no unneeded work is added. It includes formal project and phase initiations, developing the written scope statement (with scope exclusions), and listing major and intermediary project deliverables. It also includes the formal agreement by major players to the scope as defined and scope control (the ongoing process of evaluating project changes).
3. **Project Time Management** - Time Management is the skill that most people associate with project management because it is crucial for keeping on schedule. It includes creating or refining the project work breakdown structure, determining dependency relationships among the project tasks, estimating the effort and duration of the tasks, and creating a project schedule. It also includes the control component of monitoring and updating the project progress and making changes to estimates and schedules. A commonly misunderstood facet of project management is that, by the nature of projects, estimates and schedules will change. As long as the project manager stays on top of these changes, this should not affect the final target completion date.
4. **Project Cost Management** - Cost Management includes determining the project cost categories, estimating the use of each resource in each category, budgeting for that estimated cost and getting it approved, and then controlling the cost as the project progresses. Both fixed costs (such as equipment and software purchases) and variable

costs (such as team member time) are included in the planning and estimating and are then monitored and controlled.

5. **Project Quality Management** - Quality Management has three subsets, generally referred to as Quality Planning, Quality Assurance, and Quality Control. In Quality Planning, a project manager defines what represents quality and how quality will be measured. In Quality Assurance, the project manager watches the overall quality of a project to see that standards will be met. In Quality Control, the project manager examines actual project outputs to evaluate their conformance to the standards set in the plan.

6. **Project Human Resource Management** - Human Resource Management addresses the people involved in a project. It includes the planning components of determining what skills are needed to perform the various project tasks, defining the participants' roles and responsibilities, and selecting potential candidates for those tasks. It also includes acquiring the appropriate resources (internally, from external departments, or even external companies or independent contractors) and any professional development that the team members may need to improve their project performance.

7. **Project Communications Management** - Communication Management is the often neglected, yet perhaps most important, component of project management. It includes deciding who needs what information, to what level of detail, and in what media and time period. These needs are documented in the communication plan subsection of the project plan so that parties can review them and then follow them. The communication plan may also specify the format to be used for each communication, as well as turnaround times for each communication. Once the plan is approved, project managers then use their communication management skills to make sure the information is gathered and distributed according to the plan.

8. **Project Risk Management** - Risk Management starts with identifying the potential risks to a project and then determining the likelihood of each risk happening and how that risk would impact the project if it occurred. From this list and ranking, contingencies are developed for the highest risks. As the project is executed, one can use these contingencies to regain control of a project if a potential risk does occur.

9. **Project Procurement Management** - Procurement Management involves developing, executing, and monitoring contracts with service and product vendors. It also includes deciding what must be procured, soliciting bids for the products or services, selecting the appropriate vendor, and closing the contract once the project has been completed.

Organizational Influences

Most projects are a smaller part of a larger organization, and this organization will have significant influence on the conduct and success or failure of the project. There are three primary organizational influences that can affect project management:

1. The organizational values, beliefs, and expectations can either be adopted or rejected by the project team, having a direct effect on the management of a project.
2. The structure of an organization can affect project management because it can dictate the availability of resources such as money and staff.
3. The organization's project philosophy can affect project management, since a project-based organization would reward different actions than a non-profit-based organization.

Project-based organizations operations are primarily projects. This would include organizations whose main source of revenue is projects (consultants, contractors) and organizations that manage by projects.

Non-project based organizations are more focused on operations, and seldom have management systems to facilitate project needs efficiently. This complicates the project management effort.

Obviously, each organization has developed its own culture and style, and the project teams must consider this. For example, a team suggesting a high—risk approach will more likely receive sponsorship in an entrepreneurial organization that may not have an established style. A project manager's approach should reflect the organization style, meaning a participative style will clash with a rigidly hierarchical organization, and an authoritative style will clash with a participative organization.

Key General Management Skills

General management deals with every aspect of managing an ongoing enterprise and includes finance and accounting, sales and marketing, research and development, manufacturing and distribution; strategic, tactical and operational planning; human resources issues and work relationships and personal time and stress management. Possession of these skills is also essential to a project manager. (It is practically impossible for a project manager to retain the full spectrum of technical skills necessary on a large project, but rather, they should focus on the project management skills required to effectively administer the project.)

There are five key abilities required for being an effective manager:

1. **Leading** - Leading is differentiated from managing in that managing is primarily concerned with consistently producing key results expected by stakeholders while leading involves establishing direction, aligning, motivating, and inspiring people.
2. **Communicating** - The successful transmission or exchange of information is essential so that the recipient understands what the sender intends. This includes verbal, nonverbal, and written communication. A key here is listening as well as communicating, and communications may be external or internal, formal or informal, vertical or horizontal.
3. **Negotiating** - This involves conferring with others to reach an agreement. It may involve scope, cost and schedule objectives, or changes to these; contract terms and conditions; assignments and resources.
4. **Problem Solving** - Problem solving involves a combination of problem definition (distinguishing between causes and symptoms) and decision-making (analyzing problems to determine viable solutions and then making a selection). Note that project decision-making is not limited to project managers. Customers, project team members, functional managers, or other project stakeholders may be involved in decision making.
5. **Influencing the Organization** - The ability to get things done is the mark of a great project manager. This requires the ability to identify political realities both inside and outside the organization, as well as having an understanding of the mechanics of power and politics. Power is the potential ability to influence behavior, change the course of events, and overcome resistance. It is the ability to get people to do something they wouldn't necessarily do. Politics involves getting a collective effort from a group of people with differing interests.

Four Functions of the Project Manager

It is widely held that a project manager has these four main functions:

1. **Planning** - The project manager determines the time, cost, and personnel resources needed to complete the work, which would include team assembly, development of work schedules, and human resource requirements.
2. **Organizing** - Assembling the personnel, financial, and physical resources to complete the project.
3. **Leadership** - This is necessary in order to combine resources and administer the project.
4. **Control** - Execution of the project plan, and continuous monitoring and measurement of progress as it relates to time, cost and quality.

Chapter 3
Characteristics of a Project

Every project is made up of three fundamental components:

- The project environment
- The project manager
- The project team

A healthy project environment is vital to successful project management. Several environmental and socioeconomic issues can affect a project, and these issues must be managed. Organizational structure can also have a major impact on a project's success.

Internal environment

A project manager must create a positive internal environment for a project. The internal environment can influence the attitudes of the project's team members and enhance or diminish their desire to achieve the project goal. For a project to succeed, team members must be dedicated, invested, and committed. A positive internal environment should include:

- A corporate culture that acknowledges and appreciates the efforts of team members
- Good working relationships among team members
- Open lines of communication
- An environment of trust
- A willingness to take risks
- Recognition for effort and achievement

External environment

The project's external environment is also critical because it can influence the project's internal climate. For example, suppose there's a political conflict among managers in an organization. The managers' attitudes can affect the attitudes of their direct reports, and some of them might be part of your team. The external environment encompasses all components outside the project, including:

- The parent organization, whose policies and procedures can influence a project
- The political environment, which can affect a project if government policies change
- The current business climate, which can decrease the effectiveness of a project's output
- The geographical setting, which can delay a project if an environmental issue arises
- Social commitments, which can influence a project due to responsibilities such as reduced environmental risks

Knowledge of these and other issues in the external environment can help you anticipate and plan for changes and events that can affect your project.

Project Stakeholders

Another factor that can influence a project is its stakeholders. A project stakeholder can be an individual, group, or organization involved in a project or with interests that influence the project. Stakeholders can be either formal or informal. Formal stakeholders have a direct interest or investment in a project; informal stakeholders are those who might be affected by a project's result.

During the initiation and planning phases of a project, you and your team should identify both types of stakeholders and their expectations. This will help you manage their expectations and minimize conflicts over project deliverables. Formal stakeholders in a project typically include:

- The project manager, who is ultimately responsible for the success or failure of a project
- The project team members, who are directly responsible for completing project tasks
- The parent organization, which provides project personnel and resources
- The customer that requests the end product or service

Stakeholders have varying levels of influence on a project:

- Some stakeholders have specific requirements they want the project to meet, and their stake in the project is significant.
- Less critical stakeholders might also have specific requirements for the project, and it's up to the project team to decide if their requirements can be fulfilled.
- Some stakeholders need to feel involved and might want to provide input and feedback throughout the project.

The project team should modulate the effort invested to meet the stakeholders' needs based on the stakeholders' levels of influence.

Socioeconomic Issues

In addition to addressing stakeholder concerns, you must monitor and manage various socioeconomic issues that can affect your project. The following socioeconomic issues are often relevant to a project:

- Government standards and regulations — When planning your project, determine the standards and regulations that can influence project deliverables.
- International issues — As organizations span international boundaries, international issues might be pertinent to your project.
- Social and cultural influences — Make sure your project does not pose a threat to social concerns or violate cultural norms.

Suppose that your project involves going into a small community to build a dam. You would need to consider how the project could affect the lives of those in the community. Cultural influences are important if you manage a project at a new geographic location, especially a different country or continent. What might be acceptable in one culture can be considered rude or insensitive in another.

Other factors, such as wages, working conditions, and management styles, depend on the culture and are often government regulated. Your project plan must take these factors into consideration and incorporate provisions related to special cultural needs.

Organizational Issues

A project's parent organization can also affect how you manage a project. In particular, you should be aware of the following organizational issues:

- Values, beliefs, and expectations — A project team can either adopt or reject the organization's values, beliefs, and expectations. Their attitude toward these issues directly affects the project environment.
- For example, suppose that a parent organization expects employees to work from 8:00 A.M. to 5:00 P.M. If a project requires long work hours and work over the weekends, the project manager might decide to give team members an occasional day as a holiday to make up for the additional work hours. This situation can create conflict with functional managers and can be seen as special treatment for project team members.
- Structure — The structure of the parent organization can dictate resource availability as well as your authority as a project manager. For example, if the parent organization is organized to facilitate project management, you can exercise more authority than if the parent organization has a functional structure.
- Project philosophy — A project-based organization rewards different actions than does a non-project-based organization. For example, a project-based organization rewards its teams based on team rather than individual achievement to promote teamwork. This kind of organization might also reward teams for meeting targets despite constraints.

When you are aware of the issues that can affect a project environment, you can prepare for those issues as you plan. This preparation can help you avoid conflicts that can derail a project and help ensure that the project stakeholders benefit from the project's success.

Organizational Structures

The term organizational structure refers to the parameters within which you and your project team operate. Before you choose a structure, consider these factors:

- The nature of the project
- The characteristics of different organizational structures
- The structure that best fits with the parent organization
- Whether the quality of the project deliverables can be improved by team effort
- How team synergy can benefit the project
- The requirement for full-time commitment of resources
- The number of project constraints

You can help determine the organizational structure for your project. For example, for a large and complex project, you might ask for a full-time team dedicated to the project. However, with small or simpler projects, the structure is more likely to be determined by the existing organizational structure.

Generally, you can determine the appropriate organizational structure for a project by following these steps:

1. Define the project's objectives.
2. Determine the key tasks for each objective.
3. For each task, establish the functional departments within the parent organization.
4. Identify the personnel who will work on the project, and identify the customers' needs and expectations.
5. Define any special characteristics associated with the project, such as the need for a specific technology.
6. Analyze the pros and cons of the functional, project, and matrix structures, and choose the one that best suits the project.

Functional Project Organizational Structure

One option when creating a project team is to keep it within a functional division of the organization. Usually, a project is assigned to the functional department that can add the maximum resources, provide the maximum support in implementing the project, or ensure the project's success.

Advantages of using a functional project organizational structure include the following:

- Experts from functional departments can assist when necessary.
- The functional departments define a path of professional growth and advancement for the project team members.
- The functional department offers high flexibility to use personnel from the department.
- Individuals within a functional department are likely to share knowledge and expertise freely, enhancing creativity and problem solving within the project team.

Some disadvantages of using a functional project organizational structure include the following:

- Sometimes no team member is given complete responsibility for the project, and a lack of clear accountability can increase the probability of failure.
- The project is not the central focus because the functional department's focus might differ from the project focus. The lack of focus on a project can lead to slow response to stakeholders' needs, as well as other problems.
- Project team members tend to be less motivated because the project is often their second focus after their functional duties.
- The team is more likely to ignore project issues that are external to its functional department.

Project Organizational Structure

A project organizational structure forms when the project is detached from the rest of the parent organization and functions as a self-contained unit. Depending on the parent organization, you and the project team might have total autonomy or might use some of the same administrative and financial resources as the parent organization.

Advantages of using a project organizational structure include the following:

- Communication between dedicated team members is more efficient and effective than communication between partially dedicated team members working in different departments.
- Team members report only to the project manager instead of reporting to both the project and functional managers.
- The project manager has complete authority over the project.
- A project team can develop a strong sense of commitment.
- Decision making is more efficient because it does not need to involve the entire organization.

Some disadvantages of using a project organizational structure include the following:

- Pure project teams tend to conform inconsistently to policies and procedures because, unlike the parent organization, pure project teams do not follow a process that tests and reinforces procedures.
- Rivalry or competition between team members and the parent organization can result in an unhealthy work atmosphere that impedes project success.
- Uncertainty about team members' futures after project completion can adversely affect their work. This uncertainty arises primarily when a project nears completion and the team members are not assigned to another project.
- When several projects run simultaneously, a duplication of effort can result. Resources can be used more effectively if teams share them across projects.

Matrix Organizational Structure

The matrix organizational structure merges the functional and project organizational structures to combine their advantages and overcome their disadvantages. Because organizations differ in many ways, no two organizations use the same matrix design. One of the greatest benefits of using a matrix structure is that responsibility is shared between project and functional managers. Both maintain a degree of authority, responsibility, and accountability to the project.

In a matrix organization, the project manager controls the project team's activities and schedules, but the functional managers control assignment of team members to projects and the use of technology and other requirements.

Weak and Strong Matrix Organization

A strong matrix is similar to a project organizational structure. However, unlike a project organization, in which a project is a stand-alone entity, a strong matrix organization does not separate the project from the parent organization. In a strong matrix, the project manager has a high level of authority over resources assigned to the project.

A weak matrix is similar to a functional organizational structure. When a project uses a weak matrix form, the project manager might be the only full-time team member, and the functional departments might only supply services to the project. For example, if a project is to create a database, the functional department that handles administrative systems might be required to develop the database. In a weak matrix, the functional manager retains authority over resources.

Advantages of using the matrix structure for a project include the following:

- The project manager has access to the resources within each functional department, enabling the sharing of key resources. This reduces duplication of effort and minimizes costs.
- Team members still have their functional "home" after the project is complete, reducing anxiety and stabilizing motivation levels.
- Matrix organizations are flexible and can respond rapidly to change, conflict resolution, and project needs.
- Policies and procedures can be developed independently for a project. However, because representatives from administrative units of the parent organization are involved, these policies are consistent with those of the parent organization.
- When several projects run simultaneously, company-wide resources can be shared.
- Authority and responsibility for achieving the overall project goal are shared.
- It's easier to develop a good balance between time, cost, and personnel.

Disadvantages of using the matrix structure for a project include the following:

- Project team members have two supervisors: the project manager and the functional manager. This structure might result in confusion, split loyalties, division of authority, and possible project failure.
- There is a high possibility of role ambiguity for managers and team members.
- Project managers might be accountable for project success but lack the authority necessary to achieve success.
- Sharing team members across multiple projects and a functional area can result in low levels of commitment and focus. A lack of commitment and focus can cause projects to take longer and cost more than planned.
- The volume of information and workflow can lead to confusion and complicate communication.
- Conflicts can arise if a functional manager's goals differ from the overall project goals.

The Project Manager

As a project manager, you need to take charge of a project. In this role, you perform four basic functions:

1. Planning the project, which includes developing the scope statement
2. Organizing resources
3. Overseeing the execution of the project plan
4. Controlling project variables until project completion

Project managers should have the ability to focus on task accomplishment and should understand business management principles. Project managers also should be versatile, be able to communicate well, and understand the critical issues related to their projects.

Your primary responsibility as a project manager is to plan the project. If you complete all the planning steps effectively, the project should run smoothly. When planning a project, include the following:

- A statement of project objectives, deliverables, expectations, and constraints
- A list of the resources needed to complete the project
- A definition of all the tasks needed to achieve the project goal
- A timetable with milestones
- A definition of quality standards for the product or service

Functional managers are responsible for resource allocation, utilization, and performance within specialized departments as well as for direct technical supervision. Project managers are process facilitators who are responsible for ensuring that projects achieve specific goals.

The relationship between the functional manager and the project manager depends on the organizational structure. In a weak matrix structure, a functional manager frequently handles manpower and materials. Therefore, it's important to maintain good working relationships. The best relationship between functional and project managers is one with minimal conflicts, where both parties work toward achieving the organization's goals. In this scenario, the matrix structure is balanced.

Senior management involvement in a project is often necessary and usually takes the form of a steering committee or a "sponsor" role. The main functions of a steering committee are to make major project decisions, approve scope changes, and give input about corporate objectives that affect the project, such as overall corporate technology strategies.

A senior manager often performs the role of a sponsor for large, complex, or highly visible projects. The sponsor provides you with guidance and support, often in the form of resolving resource conflicts with functional managers, appearing before the steering committee as a project advocate, approving the budget and plan, and reviewing status reports.

Project Management Skills

Successful project management requires that certain infrastructure elements be in place. Among these are basic skills in people management, established processes for organizational planning and communication, availability of tools that support management processes and a culture that values cooperation, teamwork, and planning.

Project management requires overall management knowledge. The principles, practices, concepts, techniques, tools, and skills of general management are the foundation for project management. Core management competencies include the ability to work well with people, to take responsibility, to lead a group, and to make decisions.

Project management requires leadership skills. A leader is a person of influence. According to leadership expert John Maxwell, a leader is one that "knows the way, goes the way, and shows the way." A leader will have a well rounded set of skills that include oral and written communication, team building, coaching, mentoring and a desire to help individuals and organizations become successful.

Project Management Responsibilities

Project managers have several responsibilities. When managing projects, you must try to keep tasks on schedule, stay within budget, and manage priorities to produce high quality products and services.

Integrated within the time, cost, and quality-related responsibilities are issues relating to professionalism. As a project manager, you interact with several people, and the manner in which you conduct yourself and your projects will make an impression. As the project manager, you have responsibilities to:

- The parent organization
- Stakeholders
- The project team
- Other project managers
- Yourself

A project manager has several responsibilities to the parent organization. For example, you need to report for work on time and make appropriate use of resources. You must also give the parent organization timely, accurate information about your projects and work toward making them successful. You must also work in conformance with the parent organization's culture, which involves abiding by the organization's rules and standards. During projects, you should follow these rules and standards to make decisions and guide your teams.

Project managers might also need to travel to other locations to manage projects. In such cases, you must learn about the work culture and environment inside and outside the organizations, as well as the laws and customs that can affect the project. You must be aware of and abide by government laws and regulations and use sound ethical practices when managing projects. Operating in conformance with the laws and regulations not only protects parent organizations from unnecessary liabilities but also protects stakeholders from any potential harm or losses.

You must strive to meet the information needs of project stakeholders. Two unfortunate situations can occur as a direct result of inadequate communication between a project manager and a stakeholder:

- The stakeholders' needs or expectations for the project change, and you are unaware of these changes and therefore unable to address them.
- The stakeholders' goals conflict with the project goals, but the stakeholders are not aware of the discrepancy.

As the project manager, you can avoid these situations by maintaining steady communication with stakeholders. When stakeholders' needs and expectations change, you can work with the stakeholders to adjust the project to make sure the end results are acceptable. When conflicting goals exist, you can collaborate with stakeholders to find an appropriate solution.

Communication helps you build trust with stakeholders and increases your credibility. Another way to foster trust and bolster your credibility is to behave ethically in all phases of your work life.

Project managers are also responsible to the project team. Responsibilities vary according to the nature of a project, but the common responsibilities include providing a safe and positive environment, establishing communication channels, and resolving problems and conflicts.

In addition to the responsibilities to the parent organization, stakeholders, and project team, project managers also have responsibilities to each other. Project managers must:

- Exhibit professional conduct. The manner in which you manage projects and conduct business creates an impression on those around you. Conducting yourself in a professional manner can help you gain respect among your peers as well as among your team members and supervisors.
- Promote project management. As a project manager, you should try to help others understand the value of project management and advocate project management practices.
- Exchange information. Project managers should share their knowledge and experience. Project management has experienced rapid growth due largely to the efforts of experienced professionals who have published their research and lessons learned.

As a project manager, you also have responsibilities to yourself. You should participate in continuing education to enhance your skills and learn new tools and methods that can help you manage projects more efficiently. You should strive to grow as a professional, behave ethically and responsibly, and encourage the same behavior from your team members.

Review Questions

1. During the planning phase of your current project, you prepare a detailed financial plan. For this process, you are using:

   (A) An industry specific skill
   (B) A project management skill
   (C) A skill that is common to general management and project management
   (D) A general management skill

2. The ability of the stakeholders to influence the final characteristics of the project's product and the final cost of the project is highest when?

   (A) During the writing of the project charter
   (B) While constructing the work breakdown structure
   (C) During scope definition
   (D) At the beginning of the project

3. You are one of four full-time project managers in your organization. You all share an administrative person and there are generally 8-10 projects per year that involve about 25% of the organizations employees, however, these employees do not report to you. Your organization can best be classified as?

   (A) Functional
   (B) Strong matrix
   (C) Projectized
   (D) Balanced matrix

4. In a balanced matrix the project manager has what level of authority?

   (A) Low to moderate
   (B) Moderate to high
   (C) Little or none
   (D) Limited

5. Weak matrices maintain many of the characteristics of what type of organization?

   (A) Projectized
   (B) Functional
   (C) Balanced matrix
   (D) Strong matrix

6. In a projectized organization the project manage has what level of authority?

   (A) Moderate
   (B) High
   (C) Little
   (D) Low

7. The first topic you should address as project manager in a project kick-off meeting is?

   (A) Project plans and budgets
   (B) Project scope and schedules
   (C) Roles and responsibilities
   (D) Resource plans and schedules

8. The conclusion of a project phase is generally marked by a review of both key deliverables and project performance to date to determine if the project should continue into its next phase and?

   (A) Obtain customer approval before continuing into next phase
   (B) Detect and correct errors cost effectively
   (C) Monitor actual performed against the scope statement
   (D) Monitor actual work performed to the work breakdown structure

9. Strong matrices have many of the characteristics of a _____ organization?

   (A) Projectized
   (B) Weak matrix
   (C) Strong matrix
   (D) Functional

10. You have began working on a subsequent phase of your project before approval of the current phase of deliverables because you felt the risk involved were acceptable. This practice of overlapping phases is often called?

    (A) Fast tracking
    (B) Leveling
    (C) Crashing
    (D) Reverse resource allocation

11. In a matrix organization, which of the following is not a responsibility of the project manager?

    (A) Complete task definitions.
    (B) Resource requirement definitions.
    (C) Major timetable milestones.
    (D) Personnel performance measurements.

12. In what type of organization are the team members often collocated and most of the organization's resources are involved in project work.

    (A) Projectized
    (B) Functional
    (C) Balanced matrix
    (D) Strong matrix

13. Project execution is very much an integrative process whereby all the work that was planned is actually accomplished. During this integrative process, what is the area that the project manager will spend the least amount of time on?

    (A) Documentation and planning
    (B) Trade off among schedule, cost and scope
    (C) Prioritization and removal of road blocks
    (D) Conflict resolution

14. You are responsible for the communication controls for the X-Star series of government satellites. Your current assignment is:

    (A) Project management
    (B) Functional management
    (C) Facility management
    (D) Program management

15. In a weak matrix organization, functional managers are usually responsible for which of the following?

    (A) Approval for changes to the project schedule.
    (B) Monitoring personnel performance.
    (C) Changes that impact their team member participation.
    (D) Monitoring their project team member's deliverables.

16. Phase end reviews are often called all of the following except?

    (A) Stage gates
    (B) Stage points
    (C) Kill points
    (D) Phase exits

17. You have been assigned as project manager for a complex project in your organization. You know that this project will fit best in what type of organization?

    (A) Cross-functional
    (B) Functional
    (C) Balanced
    (D) Matrix

18. In a weak matrix the project manager's authority is likely to be?

    (A) Limited
    (B) Non-existent
    (C) Medium to high
    (D) Low

19. Team members want to work for a project manager that can provide them with career path planning. In which organizational form is career path planning difficult for project employees?

    (A) Pure project
    (B) Project expediter
    (C) Project coordinator
    (D) Matrix

20. The state of being totally answerable for the satisfactory completion of a specific assignment is called:

    (A) Accountability
    (B) Fiduciary
    (C) Responsibility
    (D) Authority

21. You have been assigned as a project manager on a job replacing 20 miles of sewer pipe, part of your job is to determine if there are changes to the scope of the project, the schedule, the budget and the technical requirements. These responsibilities are part of which process?

    (A) Planning
    (B) Closing
    (C) Executing
    (D) Controlling

22. You are getting to start on the life cycle model of the typical project for your company; you realize that which of the following stages below is expected to experience the highest resource usage?

    (A) Intermediate phase(s)
    (B) Closing phase(s)
    (C) Phase IV
    (D) Staffing phase(s)

23. In a functional organization the project manager _____ authority and his role is usually _____.

    (A) Moderate, full-time
    (B) Limited, part-time
    (C) Little or none, part-time
    (D) High, full-time

24. You have been promoted to manager, continuous process improvement. Your new position:

   (A) Is a project because the work will be performed by people.
   (B) Is not a project because continuous process improvement will continue indefinitely.
   (C) Is a project because it is constrained by limited resources.
   (D) Is a project because improvements must be planned, executed, and controlled.

25. The "triple constraint" philosophy involves which project attributes?

   (A) Time, Cost, and Quality
   (B) Product, Price, and People
   (C) Time, Quality, and Contracts
   (D) Scope, Cost, and Communication

Answers

1. C
2. D
3. D
4. A
5. B
6. B
7. C
8. B
9. A
10. A
11. D
12. A
13. A
14. D
15. B
16. B
17. D
18. A
19. A
20. A
21. D
22. A
23. C
24. B
25. A

Chapter 4
Initiating Process Group

The Initiating Process Group is the conceptual element of project management—the basic processes that should be performed to get the project started. This starting point is critical because those who will deliver the project, those who will use the project, and those who have a stake in the project need to reach an agreement on its initiation. Stakeholders may be able to exert influence that can positively or negatively affect the Project Team's ability to successfully complete the project, so it is very important to involve and manage, to the extent possible, all stakeholders in the Process Group activities. By garnering the buy-in and shared ownership of the project by the stakeholders, it generally improves the probability of satisfying customer requirements.

The basic processes for the Initiating Process Group are:

- Selecting the project
- Determining business needs
- Considering Enterprise Environmental Factors (e.g., historical data, marketplace conditions, organization structure, industry standards)
- Considering Organizational Process Assets (e.g., policies, procedures, plans, guidelines)
- Determining objectives
- Developing the Project Charter
- Developing the Preliminary Project Scope Statement
- Determining high level deliverables and estimates
- Developing a product description
- Identifying the qualifications of the Project Manager that would be best suited for the particular project
- Determining high level resource requirements
- Obtaining project initiation approval

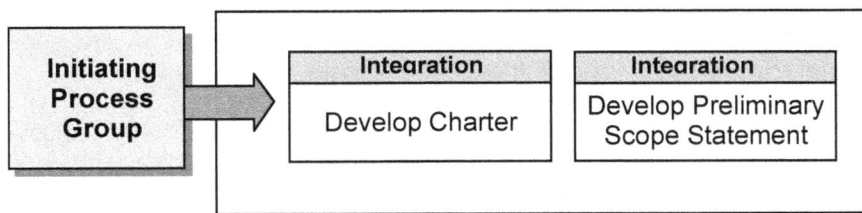

Initiating Process Group	Integration	Integration
	Develop Charter	Develop Preliminary Scope Statement

Figure 3 - Initiating Process Group Processes

For the project to get started "right," it is essential that all stakeholders participate in this critical Process Group. The success of the organization and the Project Team depends upon starting with complete and accurate information, management support, and the authorization necessary to manage the project. According to the PMBOK®, in order to have an effective project management team, the team needs to understand and use knowledge and skills from at least five areas of expertise. These areas are (1) The PMBOK®, (2) Application area knowledge, standards and regulations, (3) Understanding the project environment, (4) General management knowledge and skills and (5) Interpersonal skills.

The image above depicts the Initiating Process Group process flow. The figure below illustrates the project Initiating Process Group stakeholder participation.

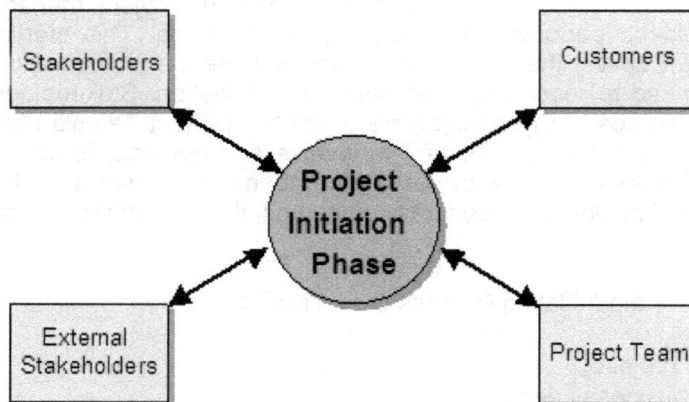

Figure 4 - Initiating Process Group Stakeholders

Develop Project Charter (4.1)

A Project Charter announces that a project has begun. The purpose of the charter is to demonstrate management support for the project and the project manager. It is a simple, powerful tool.

As an announcement it has classically taken on many forms--anything from a memorandum, to a letter, to an e-mail, to the template that is advocated at the end of this subsection. The charter is then sent to everyone who may be associated with the project to give notice of the new project and new project manager.

Because the Project Charter is created to formally communicate the existence of the project, it is issued at the end of the Project Initiation Phase and is looked upon as the beginning of the Planning Phase of a project. It is used as the basis to create the Project Plan.

Inputs to developing the Project Charter include contracts (when applicable), project statement of work, enterprise environmental factors (such as marketplace conditions, available resources and infrastructure), and finally organizational process assets such as risk control procedures, standardized templates or change control procedures. These documents identify a need and establish senior management commitment.

Note of caution - there are typically two ways that a project charter may be interpreted. One is the way that has been described in this subsection; as a formal recognition that a new project has begun. The other way refers to what many have come to know as the Statement of Work. Both uses will probably continue to be widespread, and this note is a reminder of that fact.

The Project Charter contains the following attributes:

- General Information
- Project Purpose / Objective
- Project Scope
- Project Authority
- Roles and Responsibilities
- Management Checkpoints
- Signatures

"Why are we doing this project?" is the question that the purpose statement attempts to answer. As part of the project charter, it is the first element that announces why this project is being undertaken. The purpose statement is of paramount importance, especially when significant amounts of time and money are involved. Knowing the answer to this question will allow the project team to make more informed decisions throughout the project.

And although there are many "whys" in the context of a project, the charter does not attempt to answer them all. Neither the purpose statement nor the project charter itself should be used as the venue on which to build a business case or a cost benefit analysis.

Consequently, project objectives are used to establish performance goals—planned levels of accomplishment stated as measurable objectives that can be compared to actual results. Performance measures should be derived for each goal. These measures can be quantified to see if the project is meeting the organization's objectives. Project performance can then be traced directly to the organization's goals, mission, and objectives, enabling participants to correct areas that are not meeting those objectives.

Project scope is documented at a high level in the Project Charter. The level documented must be sufficient to allow for further decomposition within the Project Plan. For example, the requirement for training may be identified within the Project Charter. Decomposition within the Project Plan will document the types of training to be delivered, procurement or development of course materials, and so on. Project objectives within the Project Charter projects are executed to meet the strategic goals of an organization. Objectives are communicated in the Project Charter to ensure that all stakeholders understand the organization's needs that the project addresses.

Because of a project's complexity, many difficult decisions must be made to keep it on track. For this reason the Project Charter defines the authority and mechanisms to resolve potential problems. Three areas must be addressed. First, the organization's senior management must issue the Project Charter. A level of management is required that can provide organizational resources to the project and have control over the elements that affect it. Second, the Project Charter must establish a project manager who is given authority to plan, execute, and control the project. Finally, the Project Charter must establish a relationship between the project and senior management to ensure that a support mechanism exists to resolve issues outside the authority of the project manager.

In this way, the Project Charter becomes a contract between senior management and the project manager; both have duties and obligations to the project. The Project Charter should have a signature page, which all appropriate parties should sign.

The roles and responsibilities for initiating, planning, executing, controlling, and closing out a project are divided among many individuals of the project team. These roles and responsibilities are a result of various contributing factors:

- The size and nature of the organization
- The size and nature of the project
- The number of projects already underway
- The capabilities of the project team members
- The maturity of the project management function within the organization

Allocating roles and responsibilities for various phases, tasks, and activities of a project is essential to ensuring that work is done on time. From this perspective then, it becomes necessary to unambiguously identify work required, to clearly identify dependencies, to accurately estimate durations, to clearly define quality standards, to succinctly describe deliverables, and to develop measurable performance criteria for tasks.

Another manner to detail roles and responsibilities on a project would be to develop a responsibility matrix. In essence, a responsibility matrix lays out the major activities in the project. This matrix can help avoid communication breakdowns between individuals, departments, and organizations because everyone involved can see clearly who to contact for each activity.

A responsibility matrix can be as simple as a spreadsheet, or as intricately drawn from a graphics software application. The matrix can be pasted to a text document for inclusion as part of the project documentation. The image below shows an example of a Responsibility Matrix.

To ensure that the project progresses satisfactorily, management checkpoints or milestones should be clearly defined with planned dates to measure progress. Checkpoints are high-level milestones. Senior management uses them to approve the completion of a phase or milestone and as go/no-go decision points to proceed with the project. The checkpoints ensure that the products and services delivered meet the project objectives in the time frame established by senior management in the Project Charter.

Artifact	Project Owner	User	Project Manager	System Analyst	Software Architect	Use Case Specifier	Developer Roles	Test Roles	Administrator Roles
Vision	A	C	C	W	C		C		C
Use Case Model	A	C	C	W					
Software Architecture Document	A				W		C		C
Use Case Specification	A	C		C	C	W		C	
Use Case Realization					C	C	W		
Component					C		W	C	

W = Write / responsible for   C = Contribute / review   A = Formally Accept

Figure 5 - Responsibility Matrix

There are eight major sections of the Project Charter:

- General Information
- Project Purpose
- Project Objective
- Project Scope
- Project Authority
- Roles and Responsibilities
- Management

After establishing the Project Charter, the project team begins the process of devising and maintaining a workable scheme to accomplish the business needs that the project was undertaken to address.

Because the Project Charter is an announcement, and because its purpose is to formally announce the project, it is not meant to manage changes that occur. The charter is intended as a one-time document; therefore, if a change occurs that is significant enough to outdate the charter's original purpose and scope then a new charter should be issued.

Project Selection Methods

PMI® feels strongly that organizations should have a formal process for deciding projects to sponsor and for ensuring that projects are supportive of the organization's strategic objectives. In many organizations, some type of senior management steering committee or Program Management Office (PMO) performs this project-evaluation and -selection process. Project-selection methods are the techniques used to execute this process, and they are organized into two major categories: benefit measurement methods and constrained optimization methods.

The project-selection method(s) used by an organization should be relevant to the objectives of the company and its managers and should be consistent with the capabilities and resources of the organization. The two methods of project selection are benefit measurement (comparative approach) and constrained optimization (mathematical approach).

Listed below are the key points of these two method types.

1. **Benefit Measurement** (comparative approach) - Scoring models, cost-benefit analysis, review board, economic models. Benefit measurement is the most common approach.
2. **Constrained Optimization** (mathematical approach) - Linear programming, nonlinear programming, integer programming, dynamic programming, multi-objective programming. Constrained optimization makes use of math models and complex criteria and is often managed as a distinct project phase.

Expert Judgment

Expert judgment is mentioned in this chapter because develop project charter is the first PMBOK® process that lists expert judgment as a primary tool or technique. In this case, as in most, expert judgment is used to evaluate the inputs into the process. Specifically, expert judgment is used to assess the product description, the project-selection criteria, and the validity of the historical information. In addition, expert judgment could be used to identify key assumptions and constraints. Anyone with specialized knowledge and/or experience relevant to the goals of the project can be used as a source of expert judgment.

Project Planning Methodology

Be familiar with the use and purpose of a project planning methodology, that is, any structured approach to help prepare the project plan. It may be simple, consisting of forms and templates. Or it may be complex, such as required simulations to perform schedule or cost risk analysis. PMI® makes the distinction between "hard" tools in a methodology, such as project management software, and "soft" tools, such as a facilitated kickoff meeting.

When it comes to project planning, the key issue you need to understand here is that organizations should have some kind of methodology that they follow as to project planning, something that lends a little consistency to the processes they are using internally. This process should be a good blend of hard and soft tools. Make sure you have that distinction down as well.

Project Management Information System (PMIS)

A Project Management Information System (PMIS) facilitates project information to flow within an organization. The software application is a core component of the overall PMIS and is considered to represent the tools and techniques used to gather, integrate, and distribute output of the other project management processes (e.g. project management outputs such as the overall Project Management Plan and subsidiary plans).

Note that the PMIS is a tool used by each of the project integration management processes used to gather, integrate, and distribute the outputs of other project management processes. It is simply an information system that stores all of the information related to your project. The PMIS is used from the beginning of the project through closeout. It may be software such as Microsoft Project, Microsoft Access or it may be a manual system.

Knowing what a project management information system is used for is key. There will be several questions about the project management information system on the exam. They are not just looking for software tools. Tools such as computer software may be used as part of the information system, but the system is not exclusively made up of those components. It is made up of software, forms, templates, memos, and the processes that go into funneling information through your project.

Develop Preliminary Project Scope Statement (4.2)

The inputs into developing this process are the project Charter, project statement of work, enterprise environmental factors, and organizational process assets according to the PMBOK®. The Charter has been described previously. The project statement of work, or SOW, is created at this stage and contains narrative that describes the products or services that will be the output of the project. The SOW shows the business need for the project, which links it closely to the Charter. In addition, the scope definition gives the product requirements. Finally, the Charter has a clear link to the strategic plan of the organization. Because all projects support the organization's overall strategic vision, the strategic plan (or at least the main points in the strategy) should be part of the development of the early project scope statements.

One of the techniques of managing an organization or project is to manage the variance between what was planned and what actually occurs. This is also one of the tools and techniques found in project management methodology. We have already encountered one of the techniques used in project management through the use of earned value (EV), as discussed in Chapter 4. This technique measures the variance in projects and is an accounting form that is not often seen in general management. In Project Integration Management, the term used to describe the process of managing by variance is called Earned Value Management (EVM). EVM is a project integrating methodology, whereas EV is the technique. EVM is the way project management uses variance management to assess the state of the project. It measures performance against the project plan.

The output of developing a preliminary Scope Statement is the document itself. Remember that everything is preliminary until you lock the Scope Statement under version control. As you do preliminary work, you look for as many inputs as you can find in order to finalize your baseline Scope Statement.

The development of a written statement, known as the Project Scope Statement, provides the basis for future project decisions. This statement is of singular importance to the project, as was previously stated, because it sets the overall guidelines as to the size of the project. The content of this statement, at a minimum, will include the following:

- **Project Results/Completion Criteria**: What will be created in terms of deliverables (and their characteristics) and/or what constitutes a successful phase completion.
- **The Approach to be Used**: What type of process or technology will be used, whether the project will be done internally or externally, etc.
- **Content of the Project**: What is and is not included in the work to be done.

The following documents may be helpful in developing a preliminary project scope statement:

- Project Work Statement
- Project Objectives (including identified constraints and assumptions)

- Project Feasibility Document
- Project Concept Document
- Project Charter

Note that during subsequent process phases the development of the preliminary project scope statement process validates and refines, if required, the project scope defined for that phase.

Review Questions

1. Which of the following statements best describes why stakeholders are necessary on a project?

    (A) They determine the project schedule, deliverables, and requirements.
    (B) They help to determine the project constraints and product deliverables.
    (C) They supply the resources and resource constraints on the project.
    (D) They help provide assumptions, the WBS, and the management plan.

2. Which statement about project deliverables is correct?

    (A) They are described during project planning and improved over time.
    (B) They are determined by the project sponsor.
    (C) They are defined at project onset with the input of project stakeholders.
    (D) They are determined after the work is completely defined.

3. A person is writing a document identifying the business need for a project and is including a description of the product created by the project. She provides objectives and goals for the project in his document. What is the role of this person on the project?

    (A) A member of the project core team working at the direction of the project manager.
    (B) A manager or executive in the organization who is higher in the corporate hierarchy than the project manager.
    (C) The sponsor.
    (D) The project manager for the project.

4. Which of the following would be the best project to select?

    (A) A project that will take three years to complete and has an NPV of US $85,000.
    (B) A project that will take six years to complete and has an NPV of US $45,000.
    (C) A project that will take 10 years to complete and has an NPV of US $60,000.
    (D) A project that will take eight years to complete and has an NPV of US $30,000.

5. You are beginning a new project that has been attempted, but unsuccessful, several times in the past few years. Previous projects were cancelled because of "politics," (differing views and direction by key stake holders of the project). This is an example of:

    (A) Stakeholder analysis.
    (B) Project charter.
    (C) Historical information.
    (D) Risk identification.

6. Which type of organization is best for managing complex projects involving cross-disciplinary efforts?

   (A) Line
   (B) Matrix
   (C) Projectized
   (D) Functional

7. Benefit measurement and constrained optimization are examples of:

   (A) variable costs.
   (B) benefit cost ratios.
   (C) project selection methods.
   (D) types of depreciation.

8. All the following are general characteristics of a project with the exception of which of the following?

   (A) A project is temporary.
   (B) A project has a definite beginning and end.
   (C) A project is made up of interrelated activities.
   (D) A project repeats itself every month.

9. Who determines the requirements of a new project?

   (A) Customer
   (B) Stakeholders
   (C) Project manager
   (D) Senior management

10. When entering into a contract, it is best to assume that there will be disputes about the performance of the work as specified, and to:

    (A) include a procedure in the contract describing the means for dispute resolution.
    (B) track claims to ensure the best position during litigation.
    (C) make sure disputes are never brought to public knowledge.
    (D) include a change order provision in the contract.

11. Your company can accept three possible projects. Project A has an NPV (net present value) of US $30,000 and will take six years to complete. Project B has an NPV of US $60,000 and will take three years to complete. Project C has an NPV of US $90,000 and will take two years to complete. Based on this information, which project would you pick?

    (A) Project A
    (B) They all have the same value.
    (C) Project C
    (D) Project B

12. A project may be selected based on all of the following except:

    (A) net present value.
    (B) benefit measurement.
    (C) value analysis.
    (D) the number of resources used.

13. You have created the project charter but could not get it approved. Your manager and his boss asked that the project begin immediately. Which of the following is the best thing to do?

    (A) Set up an integrated change control process.
    (B) Push to get the charter signed.
    (C) Perform an impact analysis.
    (D) Start work on only the critical path tasks.

14. The project charter is created during which life-cycle phase?

    (A) Planning
    (B) Execution
    (C) Initiation
    (D) Closeout

15. The best time to assign a project manager to a project is during:

    (A) Execution.
    (B) Closure.
    (C) Initiation.
    (D) Planning.

16. Your customer requested that the new railroad cars you are building for his company be constructed from heavy grade aluminum. After reviewing the requirements, two of your experts inform you that the customer would be better off with steel cars. You meet with the customer to discuss the issue, and he informs you to go ahead with the aluminum cars. What should you do?

    (A) Provide aluminum cars that meet the customer's requirements.
    (B) Meet with your experts to find another proposal for the customer.
    (C) Meet with the customer again to ensure that he understands the expert opinions about using steel instead of aluminum.
    (D) Find a way to cut other costs and upgrade the cars to steel.

17. Your management has decided that all orders will be treated as a "project" and that project managers will be used to update orders daily, resolving issues and ensuring that the customer formally accepts the product within 30 days of completion. The revenue from the individual orders can vary from US $100 to US $150,000. The project manager will not be required to perform planning or provide documentation other than daily status. How would you define this situation?

    (A) This is program management since there are multiple projects involved.
    (B) Because each individual order is a "temporary endeavor," each order is a project. This is truly project management.
    (C) Orders incurring revenue over US $100,000 would be considered projects and would involve project management.
    (D) This is a recurring process.

18. A market demand, a customer request, and a technological advance are examples of:

    (A) components of a WBS.
    (B) claims to the project.
    (C) changes to the project.
    (D) reasons to initiate a project.

19. There are two projects to choose between: Project A with an NPV of US $45,000; or Project B with an NPV of US $85,000. What is the opportunity cost of selecting project B?

    (A) US $40,000
    (B) US $130,000
    (C) US $45,000
    (D) US $85,000

20. A project manager can best resolve the differences between the requirements of one stakeholder and those of another by saying which of these statements?

    (A) Let's look at why there is a difference of opinion on the requirements.
    (B) There are many points on which we agree. I am certain if we focus on them, we will find a solution.
    (C) I have made the decision to resolve the problem this way.
    (D) This discussion is getting too heated. Let's regroup to solve the problem tomorrow.

21. Who issues the project charter?

    (A) Project manager
    (B) Management
    (C) Stakeholders
    (D) Project team

22. Your boss, the vice president of research at your electronic system development firm, defines success on the project as providing "state-of-the-art" development. The vice president of marketing defines it as "world-class practices." The vice president of engineering, who is the customer for this project, is primarily concerned with new features. Which of the following best describes what you should do?

    (A) Make sure the requirements are defined in measurable terms.
    (B) Concentrate on new features.
    (C) Identify additional stakeholders that want new features to shift the balance in that direction.
    (D) Concentrate on making the project state-of-the-art.

23. The policies, methodologies, and templates for managing projects within the organization should be supplied by the:

    (A) functional department.
    (B) project manager.
    (C) project office.
    (D) project sponsor.

24. Identifying project performance criteria, defining project strategy, and determining product description are all part of which project management phase?

    (A) Planning
    (B) Initiation
    (C) Monitoring and Control
    (D) Execution

25. Your customer has asked for a 2000 call capacity for the new call center project. However, one of your company's technical experts believes a 3000 call capacity can be reached. Another thinks that based on the technical needs of the customer, the capacity needs to be only 1500 calls. What is the best thing to do?

    (A) Set the goal at 3000 calls.
    (B) Meet with the customer to better understand the reasons behind the 2000 call capacity.
    (C) Set the goal at 2000 calls.
    (D) Meet with the technical experts and help them to agree on a goal.

26. In which of the following forms of organization do projects receive the least attention?

    (A) Matrix
    (B) Coordinator
    (C) Expeditor
    (D) Functional

27. The amount of funds available for a company to invest in projects is called:

    (A) working capital.
    (B) sunk costs.
    (C) value analysis.
    (D) direct cost.

28. Your company has just presented its new five-year strategic plan. You have received a new product request from a customer that is in line with the previous five-year strategic plan, but it does not meet the objectives of the new plan. The product description seems to have a valid business driver and to be a straightforward development effort. As project manager, what is the best course of action?

    (A) Submit the product to management for review and approval before proceeding.
    (B) Do a cost benefit analysis of the project and submit it for management approval.
    (C) Request a project charter from management and begin a WBS.
    (D) Inform the customer of the change in corporate direction and ask him/her to take another look at the project.

29. In order to complete initiation, a project manager needs the project charter and:

    (A) work breakdown structure.
    (B) scope management plan.
    (C) scope statement.
    (D) constraints.

30. Who has the power in a strong matrix?

    (A) Senior management
    (B) Project manager
    (C) Functional manager
    (D) Sponsor

31. Which of the following is true for a project that was originally scheduled for completion in six months but has been ongoing for two years?

    (A) The project needs only one project sponsor.
    (B) A project is something that is temporary.
    (C) The WBS is a good way to determine project tasks.
    (D) Too many tasks can mean the project never is completed.

32. A project manager is planning a project when he discovers that the project has many different phases, and each phase must be done in a sequence. What of the following is the best option for the project manager?

    (A) Make sure the WBS has tasks that include extra team meetings.
    (B) Obtain a charter for each phase.
    (C) Make sure the communication plan addresses interdependencies.
    (D) Make sure each team member knows how their tasks interact with other tasks.

Answers

1. B
2. C
3. B
4. A
5. C
6. B
7. C
8. D
9. B
10. A
11. C
12. C
13. B
14. C
15. C
16. B
17. D
18. D
19. C
20. A
21. B
22. A
23. C
24. B
25. B
26. D
27. A
28. A
29. D
30. B
31. B
32. B

Chapter 5
Planning Process Group

The Planning Process Group is considered the most important Process Group in project management. Time spent up front identifying the proper needs and structure for organizing and managing a project saves countless hours of confusion and rework during the

Project planning defines project activities that will be performed, the products that will be produced, and describes how these activities will be accomplished and managed. Project planning defines each major task, estimates the time, resources and cost required, and provides a framework for management review and control.

Planning involves identifying and documenting scope, tasks, schedules, cost, risk, quality, and staffing needs. This planning process:

- Identifies specific work to be performed and the goals that define the project
- Provides documented estimates regarding schedule, resources and cost for planning, tracking, and controlling the project
- Obtains organizational commitments that are planned, documented, and agreed upon
- Continues the development and documentation of project alternatives, assumptions, and constraints
- Establishes a baseline of the plan from which the project will be managed.

The result of the Planning Process Group, the Project Management Plan, will be an approved, comprehensive document that allows a Project Team to begin and complete the work necessary to achieve the project goals and objectives (product/process). The Project Management Plan will address how the Project Team will manage the project elements, including the Project Management System (i.e., set of tools, techniques, methodologies used to manage a project). The Plan will provide a high level of confidence in the organization's ability to meet the scope, timing, cost, and quality requirements by addressing all aspects of the project.

The Planning Process Group is comprised of a number of constituent project management processes that will estimate the project's size, technical scope, and the required resources. It will produce a schedule, Work Breakdown Schedule (WBS), WBS Dictionary, identify and assess risks, and negotiate commitments. Completing these processes is necessary to establish the entire, comprehensive Project Management Plan. Typically, several iterations of the planning processes are performed before the plan is completed and approved.

The image on the next page depicts the Planning Process Groups as a series of activities and steps to be completed that result in a complete Project Management Plan. These process activities will:

1. Produce a plan that will define how the project objectives will be achieved – scope, schedule, resources and cost.
2. Establish subsidiary management plans that will define how specific aspects of the project will be managed to make certain the objectives are met.

The Planning Process Group will result in the development of the subsidiary management plans which are:

- Cost management plan
- Human Resource management plan
- Scope management plan
- Schedule management plan
- Quality management plan
- Procurement management plan
- Communications management plan
- Risk management plan
- Integration management plan

Planning Process Group Activities

Figure 6 - Planning Process Group Activities

Project Management Plan (4.3)

The Project Management Plan is the controlling document to manage a project. The Project Management Plan will address how the Project Team will manage the project elements, including the Project Management System (i.e., set of tools, techniques, methodologies used to manage a project). The Plan will provide a high level of confidence in the organization's ability to meet the scope, timing, cost, and quality requirements by addressing all aspects of the project.

The Project Management Plan describes the:

- Purpose, scope, and interim and final deliverables of the project
- Schedule and budget for the project
- Project assumptions and constraints
- Managerial and technical processes necessary to develop the project deliverables
- Resources required to deliver the project deliverables

The project management plan is a key integrative document that uses the outputs of the other planning processes and strategic planning to create a consistent, coherent document that can be used to guide both project execution and project control. Be familiar with what the project management plan is used for and what items are often included in a project management plan. Also, you should realize that although the project manager is responsible for seeing that the project management plan is accomplished, the entire project team must make important contributions to the various pieces of the plan.

When it comes to project management plan, what you really need to know is, what, do we use a project management plan for? It is used to guide project execution, to document the planning assumption and to document planning decisions regarding some alternatives that have been chosen. We use it to simplify communication between the project team and stakeholders and define key management reviews as to content, expense, and time. It is a baseline for progress management and project control. Is the WBS the project management plan? NO. The Work Breakdown Structure is not the project management plan—it is a key component of the project management plan, but it is not the project management plan. Also realize the project schedule is not the project management plan. The schedule lists planned dates for performing activities and meeting milestones identified in the project management plan.

Although the project manager is responsible for seeing that the project management plan is accomplished, all stakeholders, including the entire project team, must make important contributions to the various pieces of the plan. Note also that the project management plan is not the performance measurement baseline. The project management plan is expected to change throughout the project as more information becomes available, whereas the performance measurement baselines for technical scope, schedule, and cost are expected to change only intermittently and then, generally, only in response to an approved scope of work or deliverable change. PMI® stresses planning as a key success factor in projects.

Configuration Management System

The configuration management system describes the change control procedures used with an organization. It identifies the process for changes, including the use of any change order forms and the people involved in review and approval. Define the criteria for changes. What are the triggers for the need for a change request? (e.g. If a particular project is a day late, is the whole project plan readjusted or is the day absorbed in another section?

In short a configuration management system:

- Describes the required change management approach. Change happens and documentation of the reason (need or benefit), impact (cost and/or schedule), must be maintained.
- Describes how a change request is made (after each incident or only when a threshold is reached). Outline how the change request should be disposed (approval or rejected), and outline the number of business days after submittal. This disposal needs to be in writing and is typically 3 or 5 business days and rarely more than two weeks.
- Describe criteria for change.
- Change is the request to adjust any portion of the SOW, approved deliverable or approved change request.
- Change can be (and should be) more than an adjustment to scope.
- Change may be "compliance" or "non-compliance." A compliance change request adjusts something agreed to. A non-compliance change request defines something that did not happen as planned. Examples include system not being available (lost time) or people not performing their duties per R&R and the project plan.
- Change may be an incident of a risk.
- Change can also be time extensions to the project.

Change Control Systems

A change control system is a collection of formal, documented procedures that defines the steps by which official project documents may be changed. It includes the paperwork, tracking systems, and approval levels necessary for authorizing changes. The change control system must also include procedures to handle changes, which may be approved without prior review (e.g., changes that occur as the result of an emergency). These changes must still be documented and captured so that they do not cause problems later in the project.

Note that in short change control is the following:

- Influencing the activities that create changes to ensure that those changes are beneficial
- Determining that a change has occurred
- Managing the actual changes when they occur

Change control is not the prevention of changes. It is concerned with identification and management of possible changes to the project.

Management of the changes includes the administrative management, tracking, review, and assessment of proposed changes; the organized and timely review and decision on change approval; and the administrative process to ensure that the project team is informed of changes when they are approved.

Scope Planning (5.1)

Scope planning is the process during which the scope statement is prepared. The scope statement is important because it serves as the basis for future project decisions and includes the criteria to determine whether the entire project or a particular phase of the project has been completed successfully. Furthermore, the scope statement forms the basis for an agreement between the project team and the customer by identifying the project objectives and deliverables.

It is important to realize that there are both intermediate and end deliverables. An end deliverable is the final product of the project. For example, a document that identified the technical specifications for a new software program is an intermediate deliverable, while the actual software program is considered the end deliverable. In order to clearly show how the work of the project will actually be completed, all deliverables should be defined in terms of a tangible, verifiable product or service.

Expert Judgment

Expert judgment is mentioned throughout the PMBOK® Guide but in scope management as a tool and technique in the scope planning process. Any group or individual with specialized knowledge applicable to the specific project may provide expertise—people in other units within the performing organization, outside consultants, stakeholders (including customers), professional and technical associations, and industry groups.

Project Deliverables

Project deliverables identify what the project is supposed to produce. For example, the purpose of a project might be to create a new service or to fix a current product defect. The term deliverables is used too frequently in project management because the focus is on the outputs. Focusing on outputs helps define the boundaries of the project and keeps the team focused on the project goal.

Project Charter

You should know what a project charter is and what it does for the project manager. The project charter officially does the following:

- Establishes the project
- Authorizes the project manager to use organizational resources to accomplish project activities
- Provides a general description of project objectives

You should also know that the charter should be created during the concept phase of a project, and it is normally created by upper management. The project manager may or may not be personally involved in creating the project charter (this practice varies among companies). It is a key output of in project integration management and normally is issued by a manager external to the project at a level in the organization appropriate to the needs of the project. Without a charter, it is difficult for the project manager to operate with the level of authority required, especially in a matrix environment.

This is a document that has gained much importance over the last few years; thus, you can expect to see at least a couple questions about it. It does establish the project and is only valid if it is signed. There needs to be a signature on a project charter. Know that it also establishes the authority for the project manager.

Tools and techniques for scope planning include expert judgment and templates, forms and standards.

The PMBOK® Guide strongly recommends a written scope statement even if its elements have been included in other documents, such as the project charter. Elements that comprise the scope statement (project justification, project product, project deliverables, and project objectives) are discussed in the PMBOK® Guide.

The PMBOK® Guide also recommends that a scope management plan be prepared. The scope management plan should include a clear description of how scope changes will be identified and classified. This is particularly difficult, but it is absolutely essential when the product characteristics are still being elaborated. This may be a stand-alone document, or it may be part of the project plan.

If we have a good statement of work, do we need a scope statement? The answer is yes. We have a detailed project requirements document; do we need a scope statement? The answer is yes.

When don't we need a scope statement? The short answer is virtually never. PMI® is very big on the scope statement. It is a foundation document. It is a major component of the way business is done. It clarifies and guides; it is fundamental.

Scope Definition (5.2)

Scope definition is taking the project deliverables and the work required to create those deliverables and breaking all of the major project deliverables into smaller elements. This process should be completed for each of the project deliverables listed in the scope statement. It is important to understand that scope definition is a component of the project scope variable and that it is also part of the second step in the project management process–planning.

Product Analysis

Product analysis is used to develop a better understanding of the project's product. You should be familiar with some of the product analysis techniques:

- **Product Breakdown** - Involves developing a better understanding of the product by breaking it down into constituent parts.
- **Value Engineering** - Examines each element of a product or system to determine whether there is a more effective and less expensive way to achieve the same function.
- **Value Analysis** - Focuses on optimizing cost performance. Systematic use of techniques to identify the required functions of an item, establish values for those functions, and provide the functions at the lowest overall cost without loss of performance.
- **Functional Analysis** - Examines the project's high-level requirements statements, identifying specific functions and estimating total costs based on the number of functions to be performed.

Defining Project Scope

There is often confusion in project teams regarding the difference between project objectives and project scope. The term "project scope" refers to the magnitude of the effort to complete a project. Conversely, the term "project objectives" refers to a description of the desired outcome of the project. For example, the objective could be to build a new five-story building on the location of the back parking lot by next December. The scope could be to build the building with a prefabricated metal frame with a cement floor. Consequently, it is imperative that the project objectives and the project scope be clear to everyone to ensure project success.

Project Scope Statement

The development of a written statement, known as the Project Scope Statement, provides the basis for future project decisions. This statement is of singular importance to the project, as was previously stated, because it sets the overall guidelines as to the size of the project. The content of this statement, at a minimum, will include the following:

- Project Results/Completion Criteria: What will be created in terms of deliverables (and their characteristics) and/or what constitutes a successful phase completion.
- The Approach to be Used: What type of process or technology will be used, whether the project will be done internally or externally, etc.
- Content of the Project: What is and is not included in the work to be done.

To ensure that the project scope is completed correctly and in its entirety, it is imperative that a Project Scope Statement be completed and signed by the key stakeholders. Some of the major items included in the project scope statement include:

- **Project Objectives** - Project objectives are those criteria within the project that will determine whether the project is a success or a failure. If the product or process designed does not meet the objectives as laid out by the project stakeholders, then customer satisfaction will be jeopardized. Remember that objectives should be set at an acceptable level with the intent of delivering product or process that meets the objectives. The objectives should be documented and agreed upon in order to deliver a suitable product. Objectives can be described in two different ways:
  - o **Hard Objectives** - These relate to the time, cost, and operational objectives (scope) of the product or process.
  - o **Soft Objectives** - These relate more to how the objectives are achieved, and which may include attitude, behavior, expectations, and communications.
- **Project Scope Description – See above.**
- **Project Requirements** - Describes the conditions or capabilities that must be met or possessed by the deliverables of the project to satisfy a contract, standard, specification, or other formally imposed documents.
- **Project Boundaries** - Identifies generally what is included within the project. It states explicitly what is excluded from the project, if a stakeholder might assume that a particular product, service, or result could be a component of the project.
- **Project Deliverables** - Project deliverables include both the outputs that comprise the project, as well as project management reports and documentation. Depending on the project scope statement, the deliverables may be described at a summary level or in great detail.
- **Project Acceptance Criteria** - Acceptance criteria define what must exist in order to secure customer approval. This may include creating (and securing approval) of a template or a pilot. This should reduce or eliminate judgmental approval or rejection. It is not necessary to delay completion of the SOW while determining acceptance criteria for every deliverable. Those acceptance criteria not readily determined should be defined through another deliverable. However, the key is to have acceptance criteria approved before creation of the deliverable.

- **Project Constraints** - All projects have constraints, and these need to be defined from the outset. Projects have resource limits in terms of people, money, time, and equipment. While these may be adjusted up or down, they are considered fixed resources by the project manager.
- **Project Assumptions** - Similarly, certain criteria relevant to a project are assumed to be essential. For instance, it is assumed that an organization will have the foresight to make the necessary budget appropriations to fund internal projects. Project assumptions need to be defined before any project activities take place so that time is not indiscreetly utilized on conceptualizing and initiating a project that has no basis for funding.
- **Schedule Milestones** - A summary-level schedule, which easily identifies the major milestones for the customer or project team.
- **Fund Limitations** - Any restrictions that may be placed upon funds for the project, whether in total value or over specified over a certain time frame, such as monthly or quarterly.
- **Cost Estimates** - Estimating the cost of the resources needed to complete project activities.

Creating WBS - Work Breakdown Structure (5.3)

If you were to take a car trip to a town less than 100 miles away, you may not need to do a lot of planning. Just hop in the car and go. However, if you were driving from New York City to Miami and then Los Angeles, you would most likely spend some time looking at maps and researching your route. Somehow, you would break the big trip down into smaller pieces, like miles per day or geographic borders such as states. Nevertheless, whatever approach you use, the only way to accurately plan a trip of this size is to break it down into smaller parts.

The same is true for projects. You may understand a project well enough to balance its cost-schedule-quality equilibrium, but you also need to be able to break it down–to understand the whole project by understanding it parts. The work breakdown structure (WBS) is the tool for breaking down a project into component parts. It is the foundation of project planning and one of the most important techniques used in project management. If done well, it can become the secret to successful project management.

The work breakdown structure identifies all the tasks in a project; in fact, a WBS is sometimes referred to simply as a task list. It turns one large, unique project, into many small manageable tasks. The WBS uses outputs from project definition and risk management and identifies the tasks that are the foundation for all subsequent planning.

A WBS is a technique for breaking down a project into its component elements. It is a graphic picture of the hierarchy of the project, broken down level by level into subprojects and finally into tasks. It organizes the project by defining all the tasks that must be performed in the conception, design, development, fabrication, and test of the project hardware, software, or service. As the levels become lower, the scope, complexity, and cost of each subproject become smaller, until the tasks that are completely capable of accomplishment are reached. These smallest tasks, called work packages, must be identified as manageable units that can be planned, budgeted, scheduled, and controlled. Work component descriptions often are collected in a WBS dictionary that will include work package descriptions as well as planning information, such as schedule dates, cost budgets, and staff assignments. The WBS indicates the relationship of the organizational structure to the project objectives and tasks, and so provides a firm basis for planning and controlling the project.

The WBS is first and foremost a technical data gathering structure, deployed so that the achievement in technical progress can be measured and analyzed against a formal baseline plan. The WBS aids the customer in understanding the status of the project as time elapses. The WBS aids the customer's customer in understanding the status of the project. All managers, internal and external need to use the planning and status information within the WBS structure to aide in the adjustment to the current program paths and for maximizing the attainment of short-term and long-term goals.

There are no hard-and-fast rules for preparing a WBS; good judgment is the only criterion. However, the size of these work packages is very important because they must be small enough in terms of cost and labor to permit realistic estimates to be made, and to simplify control. Many believe that the "80-hour rule" can be of tremendous help in formulating the WBS and keeping it under control. This rule states that each task should be broken down into work packages that require no more than 80 hours of work for completion. At the end of each 80-hour-or-less period, the work package is reported simply as either completed or not completed. "By means of such periodic check-ins, drifting of a project can be controlled early" (Stuckenbruck, The Implementation of Project Management). Other writers have mentioned the use of other "rules" for work package durations. However, PMI® has used the 80-hour rule in its exam for many years. So be on the lookout for it.

Figure 7 - Sample Work Breakdown Structure

Benefits of Using a WBS
- Builds the project team
- Provides a framework to identify projects separately from organizations, accounting systems, and funding sources
- Clarifies responsibilities
- Focuses attention on project objectives
- Forces detailed planning and documentation
- Identifies specific work packages for estimating and assigning work

Uses of the WBS
- Planning and budgeting
- Funding
- Estimating & Scheduling
- Performance measurement
- Configuration management
- Integrated logistic support
- Test and performance evaluation

Development of the WBS
- Use Work Breakdown Structure templates
- Decomposition - This requires subdividing the major project deliverables into smaller, more manageable components until the deliverables are defined in sufficient detail to support development of project.
- Identifying the major deliverables of the project, including project management
- Deciding whether adequate cost and duration estimates can be developed in sufficient detail for each deliverable. If not, then identify constituent components of the deliverable in terms of tangible, verifiable results. When adequate detail exists, the last step is to verify the correctness of the breakdown. To do this, you need to determine whether: (1) the lower-level items are both necessary and sufficient for the broken down item; (2) each item is clearly and completely defined; and (3) each item can be appropriately scheduled, budgeted, and assigned to an organizational unit.

You need to understand the Work Breakdown Structure for this exam. PMI® currently emphasizes the product orientation to the work breakdown structure—the deliverable as orientation. Most important, you should know the Work Breakdown Structure is a decomposition of the project work that has to be done. Know how they are numbered and be able to read the numbering system and how it contributes to understanding the project. Also, be aware of the 80-hour rule. Know all of the uses, benefits, and be familiar with the fact that the Work Breakdown Structure contributes to customer communication.

Work Breakdown Structure Templates

All projects are unique; however, many projects are similar at a high level. Organizations that implement similar projects should develop templates to assist in the planning process. A WBS template, a generic definition of project scope, provides an excellent starting point to tailor the specifics of a unique project. Templates should be at a relatively high level and in an automated format to allow for ease of use. Because of the many types of projects that may exist in a single organization, different templates should be created. If tailoring a template requires extensive work, create your own WBS. It may be useful as a template for a later project.

Work breakdown structure templates provide the following:

- A generic structure for elements understood throughout the organization, allowing for consistent communication.
- The ability to ensure that the entire scope for a project is defined by starting with a template that breaks down WBS elements typically found in similar projects.
- A reduction in the amount of time spent developing a WBS.

Decomposition

In order to define the scope of a project, you must decompose the project deliverables. Decomposition is the process of breaking a project into manageable chunks of work, resulting in smaller deliverables that make up the final product. When decomposing a project, you begin with large chunks of work and break them down into smaller chunks so they are easy to plan, manage, and schedule. The lowest level of decomposed item is considered a work package. The following are some advantages to decomposition:

- Estimates for cost, time, and resources are much more accurate.
- The smaller deliverables are more manageable, resulting in fewer changes being made once the project begins.
- Each project deliverable can be clearly assigned to a team member, resulting in a greater level of accountability.
- The project manager can measure team members' performance against completion of these smaller deliverables.
- Control of the project is easier, since you are dealing with smaller pieces of the overall project.

The WBS is decomposed into discrete products and services to be delivered during the project. Higher level elements represent groupings of products and services to be delivered. Decomposition identifies discrete products and services. Elements are decomposed in the following way:

- A discrete product or service is identified
- Responsibility to deliver the product or service is assigned to one individual or functional area
- Scope is clearly understood
- Cost is reasonably estimated
- The element is manageable
- Higher risk or more critical elements are decomposed to a lower level

After the WBS is decomposed to the lowest level, responsibility is assigned to all elements. Assignment at the higher level ensures that management is responsible for the entire project scope. Individuals assigned to the lower level elements are responsible for planning, controlling, and delivering the product.

WBS Dictionary

Once defined, an element's scope is described. This description is often referred to as a "Work Breakdown Structure Dictionary". The purpose of the work breakdown structure dictionary is to clearly describe what scope is to be delivered within each element so that the functional area responsible for delivery can accept it, plan it, and manage the delivery. The work breakdown structure dictionary also provides boundaries and hand-offs between functional areas responsible for delivery. The WBS Dictionary is often a separate document that the WBS references. Senior management within the project reviews and approves the WBS and its supporting dictionary. Those personnel who are assigned responsibility should accept the responsibility to deliver the scope of each element. This step is essential in assuring management commitment to the project.

Scope Baseline

Once the deliverables are confirmed in the scope statement, they need to be developed into a work breakdown structure (WBS) of all the deliverables in the project. The scope baseline includes all the deliverables produced on the project, and therefore identifies all the work to be done. These deliverables should be inclusive. Building an office building, for example, would include a variety of deliverables related to the building itself, as well as such things as impact studies, recommendations, landscaping plans, etc.

Activity Definition (6.1)

The purpose of activity definition is to clarify the main project activities, which are outlined on the work breakdown structure. The purpose of activity sequencing is to arrange activities in a logical order for completion. As you define the project's main activities from the WBS, you should compile those activities into an activity list. The finished activity list then becomes a guide you can use during activity sequencing. Before starting activity definition, you should choose the duration estimating technique you'll use, so you know the detail level of activity definition needed for that technique.

Activity definition and sequencing are important because it ensures that no activity is omitted or left unfinished. It is also important because it includes specifying the order in which activities are to be executed. The primary input to this process is the WBS in which each work package is broken down into the activities that need to be completed to produce the deliverable.

PMI® points out that typically the WBS and the activity list are developed sequentially. The activity list should be organized as an extension to the WBS. Note that as the activity list is developed, the project team may identify missing deliverables or may decide that the deliverable descriptions need clarification. These updates are known as refinements.

Decomposition

Decomposition as it relates to activity definition, is the process of breaking a project into manageable chunks of work, resulting in smaller deliverables called schedule activities. This process (activity definition) defines the smaller deliverables (outputs) as schedule activities rather than deliverables which is done when creating the work breakdown structure.

Rolling Wave Planning

Rolling wave planning is a phased iterative approach to project development, applicable to new product development, information systems and other technical development environments. It is based on the premise that you should only plan in detail as far ahead as is sensible at the time. It is an excellent formal project development approach for inventive work. When done well, it balances structured process with flexibility. It is appropriate for project life cycle models/methods that allow incremental development (spiral, evolutionary prototyping, etc.).

Planning Components

Be aware of the following two planning components:

- **Control Account** – The focal point for planning, monitoring, and controlling tasks. The Control Account represents work within a single WBS element, and it is the responsibility of a single organizational unit.
- **Planning Package** – A future segment of work within a Control Account that is not yet broken down into work packages. A planning package has a firm budget, estimated start and complete dates, and Statement of Work.

Activity List

The activity list must include all activities which will be performed on the project. It should be organized as an extension to the WBS to help ensure that it is complete and that it does not include any activities which are not required as part of the project scope. As with the WBS, the activity list should include descriptions of each activity to ensure that the project team members will understand how the work is to be done.

Milestone List

The milestone list is used to provide a series of indicators regarding project progress to date and achievements or goals yet to be reached. It gives management a clear sense of specific levels of accomplishment (or consumption). The milestone list affords team members the same information, but more as a gauge of their own levels of achievement. The milestone list is generated after the planning process is sufficiently complete that critical process steps have been identified. It is used in management meetings as a simple checklist to clarify which accomplishments have been met and which have not.

Because milestones are binary (either met/complete or not), they present information to management or stakeholder's in a clear, comprehensible form. For team members, milestones provide both a history of accomplishment as well as a set of goals for the future. Every milestone checked brings the project one step closer to fruition.

Activity Sequencing (6.2)

Now that we have a list of activities, we need to put them into some sort of logical order, which is called activity sequencing. Many factors influence how you order your activities, such as the product characteristics, dependencies that can be mandatory, discretionary, or external, and milestones that have been agreed upon in activity definition.

Mandatory dependencies are called hard logic. Mandatory dependencies often occur because of physical limitations. An example of this would be in construction, where you must complete the framing before you can hang the drywall. However, in IT, there are fewer of these dependencies than you might think at first glance. Most project managers confuse these mandatory dependencies with discretionary dependencies out of habit. Let's discuss the differences.

Discretionary dependencies are preferred sequence of activities, sometimes called "Best Practices." In Information Technology, most project managers plan to wait until design is complete before starting coding. But in reality, you can start coding about half way through design. Discretionary dependencies are also known as preferred, preferential, or soft logic.

Project Time Management – CPM & PDM

The exam tests your knowledge of the differences between CPM and PDM. The following notes highlight the individual characteristics of each of the network systems on which you will be tested.

Critical Path Method (CPM)

- Emphasis on controlling cost and keeping the schedule flexible
- One time estimate per activity
- Activity oriented (float)-activity-on-node

Precedence Diagram Method (PDM)

A method of constructing a project network diagram using nodes to represent the activities and connecting them with arrows that show the dependencies. This technique is also called activity-on-node (AON) and is the method used by most project management software packages.

PDM includes four types of dependencies or precedence relationships:

1. Start-to-Start - relationship in a precedence diagramming method network in which one activity must start before the successor activity can start.
2. Start-to-Finish - relationship in a precedence diagramming method network in which one activity must start before the successor activity can finish.
3. Finish-to-Start - relationship in a precedence diagramming method network in which one activity must end before the successor activity can start. This is the most commonly used relationship in the precedence diagramming method.
4. Finish-to-Finish - relationship in a precedence diagramming method network in which one activity must end before the successor activity can end.

You need to know what CPM and PDM are. Will regards to CPM, you will want to know a little shared of history here–that this came from the 1950s and was part of the Polaris Program was U.S. Navy based and under took the task of trying to launch missiles from submarines. The critical path method (also from the 1950s–remember that for the exam) works on a single data point, but it still works from the activity-on-arrow approach. Finally, the precedence diagramming method, the one you are most familiar with, comes from Stanford University in the 1960s. Know what the different relationships mean: start-to-start, start-to-finish, finish-to-start, and finish-to-finish.

Arrow Diagramming Method (ADM)

This is a method of constructing a project network diagram using arrows to represent the activities and connecting them at nodes to show the dependencies This technique is also called activity-on-arrow (AOA) and, although less prevalent than PDM, is still the technique of choice in some application areas. ADM uses only finish-to-start dependencies.

Leads and Lags

Leads and lags are delays that are imposed in the relationship between the independent and dependent activity. Leads and lags can help to shorten schedules as well as allow for delays between activities. Leads and lags are designated by adding a plus for lags and a minus for leads and the number of periods that the lead or lag adds to the schedule.

- **Leads** - In a network diagram, the minimum necessary lapse of time between the start of one activity and the start of an overlapping activity.
- **Lag** - The amount of time after one task is started or finished before the next task can be started or finished.

Activity on Arrow (AOA)

Activity sequencing concerns the order in which activities are performed and how many sets of activities can be under way at the same time (known as parallel paths). Sequencing is important because we often need to accomplish the project as quickly as possible, yet the schedule we develop must be realistic and achievable. Activity sequencing uses the following types of dependencies:

- **Mandatory Dependencies** (hard logic) - Mandatory dependencies are restrictions specific to an activity. Mandatory dependencies require that one activity be completed before another can begin. For example, when building a house, the foundation must be finished before raising the walls. Mandatory dependencies are static, which mean that they never change.
- **Discretionary Dependencies** (soft logic) - Discretionary dependencies, which are restrictions outlined by the project team, are based on two factors. First, if there are multiple methods of doing an activity, team members choose the best method. For example, if a team has an option to use one of two software programs, they can use the program they think best suits their needs for activity completion. Secondly, if there are many activity sequences, team members pick the one most desirable for achieving the project goals. It is important to use discretionary dependencies only after careful consideration, since they can affect the activity sequence throughout the entire project.
- **External Dependencies** - External dependencies that involve a relationship between project and non-project activities. Examples: testing activity in a software project may be dependent upon arrival of hardware; may need environmental hearings before site preparation can begin on a construction project.

Milestone events also need to be part of activity sequencing so that requirements for meeting the milestones are met. You need to realize that all activities in a network diagram have at least one predecessor and one successor activity, with the exception of the start and end activities. If this convention is followed, then the sequence is relatively straightforward to identify. When you establish a project schedule, you need to compute two schedules: the early schedule, which we calculate using the forward pass; and the late schedule, which we calculate using the backward pass.

Early Start / Forward Pass

The early schedule is simply the earliest time at which an activity can start and finish. These are calculated numbers that are derived from the dependencies between all the activities in the project.

Late Schedule / Backward Pass

The late schedule consists of the latest times at which an activity can start and finish without delaying the completion date of the project. These are also calculated numbers that are derived from the dependencies between all of the activities in the project.

By using these two types of schedules you will determine the window of time within which each activity must be started and finished for the project to complete on schedule; and the sequence of activities that determines the project completion date. The sequence of activities that determine the project completion date is called the critical path. The critical path can be defined in several ways: 1) the longest duration path in the network diagram; 2) the sequence of activities whose early schedule and late schedule are the same; and 3) the sequence of activities with zero slack or float. All of these definitions say the same thing: what sequence of activities must be completed on schedule in order for the project to be completed on schedule.

The activities that define the critical path are called critical path activities. Any delay in a critical path activity will delay the completion of the project by the amount of delay in that activity. This is a sequence of activities that will warrant the project manager's special attention.

The earliest start (ES) time for an activity is the earliest time at which all of its predecessor activities have been completed and the subject activity can begin. The ES time of an activity with no predecessor activities is set to 1, the first day on which the project can begin production. The ES time of activities with one predecessor activity is determined from the earliest finish (EF) time of the predecessor activity. The ES time of activities having two or more predecessor activities is determined from the latest of the EF times of the predecessor activities. The EF of an activity is calculated as [(ES + duration) - one time unit]. The reason for subtracting the one time unit is to account for the fact that an activity starts at the beginning of a time unit (hour, day, and so forth) and finishes at the end of a time unit. In other words, a one-day activity, starting at the beginning of a day, begins and ends on the same day. For example, take a look at the figure below titled Forward Pass Calculations. Note that activity E has only one predecessor, activity C. The EF for activity C is the end of day 3. Because it is the only predecessor of activity E, the ES of activity E is the beginning of day 4. On the other hand, activity D has two predecessors, activity B and activity C. When there are two or more predecessors, the ES of the successor, activity D in this case, is calculated based on the maximum of the EF dates of the predecessor activities. The EF dates of the predecessors are the end of day 4 and the end of day 3. The maximum of these is 4, and therefore the ES of activity D is the morning of day 5.

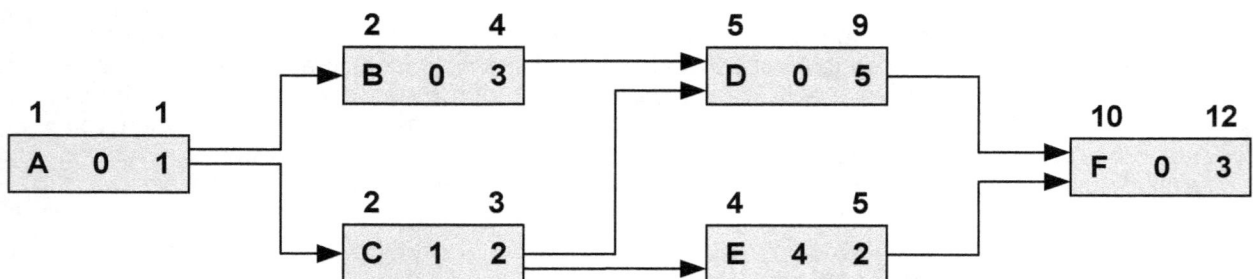

Figure 8 - Forward Pass Calculations

The latest start (LS) and latest finish (LF) times of an activity are the latest times at which the activity can start or finish without causing a delay in the completion of the project. Knowing these times is valuable for the project manager, who must make decisions on resource scheduling that can affect completion dates. The window of time between the ES and LF of an activity is the window within which the resource for the work must be scheduled or the project completion date will be delayed.

In order to calculate these times, you have to work backward in the network diagram. First set the LF time of the last activity on the network to its calculated EF time. Its LS is calculated as (LF - duration) + one time unit). Again, you add the one time unit to adjust for the start and finish of an activity within the same day. The LF time of all immediate predecessor activities is determined by the minimum of the LS, minus one time unit, times all of its successor activities.

Let's calculate the late schedule for activity E. (see image above) Its only successor, activity F, has an LS date of day 10. The LF date for its only predecessor, activity E, will then be the end of day 9. In other words, activity E must finish no later than the end of day 9 or it will delay the start of activity F and delay the completion date of the project. The LS date for activity E will be, using the formula, 9 - 2 + 1, or the beginning of day 8. On the other hand, consider activity C. It has two successor activities, activity D and activity E. The LS dates for them are day 5 and day 7, respectively. The minimum of those dates, day 5, is used to calculate the LF of activity C, the end of day 4. The complete calculation for the backwards pass is shown in the image on the next page.

Figure 9 - Backward Pass Calculations

The Critical Path

The critical path is the longest path through the network. But it represents the shortest amount of time in which the project can be completed. Keep in mind that it is possible to have more than one critical path. The critical path drives the completion date of the project. Any delay in the completion of any one of the activities in the critical path sequence will delay the completion of the project. The easiest way to identify the critical path in a network diagram is to identify all possible paths through the network diagram and add up the durations of the activities.

Dummy activities are only required in activity-on-arrow networks and their purpose is to show multiple relationships or dependencies among project activities that otherwise are not in sequence. See the image below for an explanation on figuring the critical path. Dummy activities consume no time or resources; they are present only to show that a dependency exists between two activities. Relationships among activities are "finish-to-start."

Figuring the Critical Path using the image on the next page and assuming all duration in days:

Path 1:   A-D-H-J   Length = 1+4+6+3 = 14 days

Path 2:   B-E-H-J   Length = 2+5+6+3 = 16 days

Path 3:   E-F-J   Length = 2+4+3 = 9 days

Path 4:   C-G-I-J   Length = 3+6+2+3 = 14 days

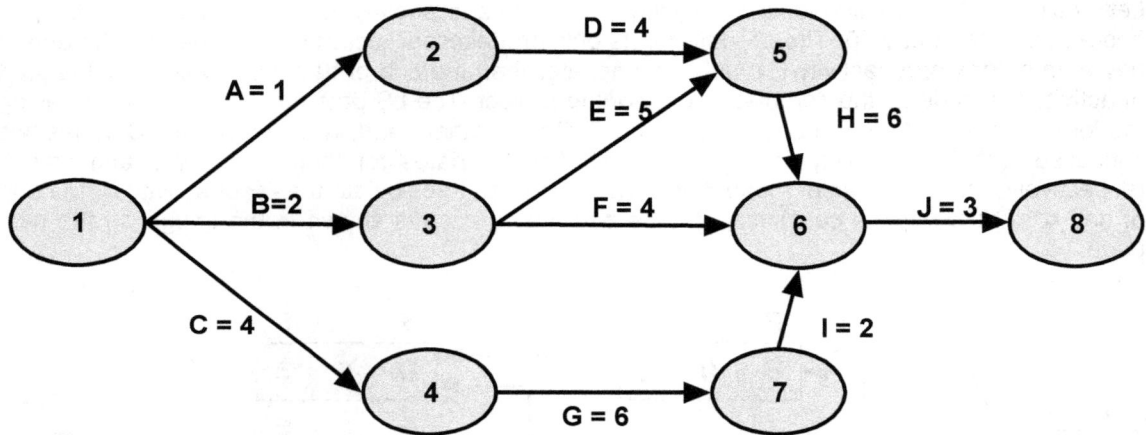

Figure 10 - Critical Path Example

Since the critical path is the longest path through the network diagram, Path 2, B-E-H-J, is the critical path for the project.

Activity-on-node Networks

No dummy activities are required. Activity-on-node networks incorporate lag-which is defined as waiting time between activities in a network; for example, we order something and must wait for it to arrive or we paint something and must wait for it to dry-and lead, which is defined as an acceleration of the successor task.   For example, we can clean up after painting; we do not need to wait for the paint to dry.

Slack

Slack (also called float) is the amount of time that a particular activity can be delayed without delaying the project. Activities on the critical path usually have zero slack. Slack is a calculated number and it is the difference between the late finish and the early finish (LF - EF). If the result is greater than zero, then the activity has a range of time in which it can start and finish without delaying the project completion date. There are two types of slack:

- **Free Slack** - This is the span of dates in which an activity can finish without causing a delay in the early schedule of any activities that are its immediate successors. Free slack can be equal to but never greater than total slack. When you choose to delay the start of an activity, possibly for resource scheduling reasons, first consider activities that have free slack associated with them.   Notice in the figure below that activity C has an early start (ES) of the beginning of day 2 and a late finish (LF) of the end of day 4. Its duration is two days and it has a 3-day window in which to be completed without affecting the early start (ES) of any of its successor activities. It therefore has free slack of only one day. If an activity's completion stays within the free slack range, it can never delay the early start date of any other activity in the project.
- **Total Slack** - This is the range of dates in which an activity can finish without delaying the project completion date. In reviewing the diagram below look at activity E and notice that it has a free float of four days as well as a total float of four days. If Activity E were completed more than three days later than its early finish (EF) date, it would delay completion of the project. All activities on the critical path must be done on their earliest schedule or the project completion date will suffer. If an activity with total slack greater than zero was delayed beyond its late finish (LF) date, it would become a critical path activity and cause the completion of the project to be delayed.

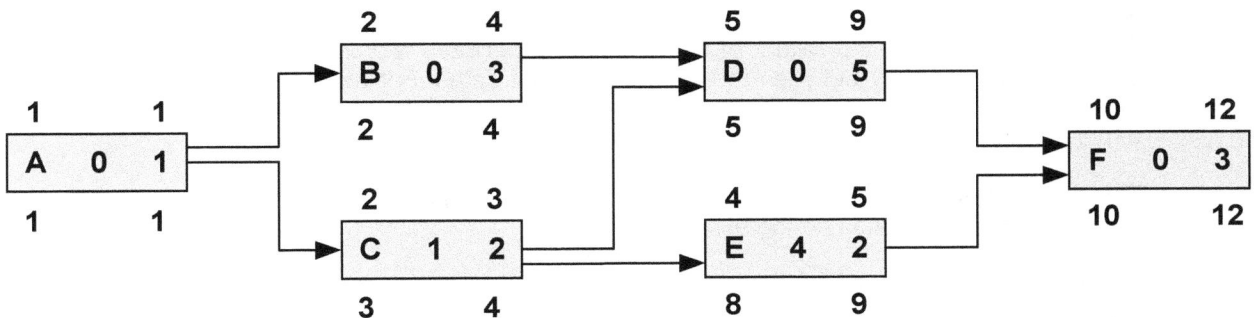

Figure 11 - Critical Path Diagram

Activity Relationships

You must know the definitions of these four terms:

1. **Finish-to-Start** - The finish to start (FS) dependency says that activity A must be completed before activity B can begin. This is the most commonly used relationship in the precedence diagramming method. For example, activity A can represent purchasing paint for a house and activity B can represent the painting of the house. To say that the dependency between A and B is finish-to-start means that once we have finished buying the paint we may start painting the house. The finish-to-start dependency is displayed with an arrow emanating from the right edge of the predecessor activity and leading to the left edge of the successor activity.
2. **Start-to-Start** - The start-to-start (SS) dependency says that activity B may begin once activity A has begun. Remember that there is a no-sooner than relationship between activity A and activity B. Activity B may begin no sooner than activity A begins. Altering the example used previously we could say that as soon as we begin buying the paint for

the house (activity A) we may begin painting the house (activity B). We don't need all the paint for the house in order for activity B to commence. In this case there is a start-to-start (SS) dependency between activity A and B. As seen in the illustration below, the start-to-start dependency is displayed with an arrow emanating from the left edge of the predecessor (A) and leading to the left edge of the successor (B).

3. **Finish-to-Finish** - The finish-to-finish (FF) dependency states that activity B can't finish sooner than activity A. For example, painting the house (activity B) can't finish until purchasing all the paint for the house (activity A) is completed. In this case, activity A and B have a finish-to-finish dependency. The finish-to-finish dependency is displayed with an arrow emanating from the right edge of activity A to the right edge of activity B.

4. **Start-to-Finish** - The start-to-finish (SF) dependency is a little more complex than the finish-to-start and the start-to-start dependencies. Here activity B can not be finished sooner than activity A has started. For example, suppose your business organization has adopted a new computer network. You wouldn't want to eliminate the old system until the new system is operable. When the new network starts to work (activity A) the old system can be discontinued (activity B). The start-to-finish dependency is displayed with an arrow emanating from the left edge of activity A to the right edge of activity B as seen in the illustration on the next page.

Task Dependencies

Task dependencies is the nature of the relationship between two linked tasks. You link tasks by defining a dependency between their finish and start dates; For example, the "contact caterers" task must finish before the start of the "determine menus" tasks. There are four kinds of task dependencies.

This material is extremely important and most likely you will see at least six or seven questions relating to this information on the exam.

We will start with activity-on-arrow, which works with activity sequencing. It is always a finish-to-start relationship. Activity A must finish before Activity B can start. In activity-on-arrow diagrams, there are sometimes "dummy" activities.

The critical path is an important element here, and you will have a couple of questions on it. The critical path is the shortest time in which the project can possibly be accomplished. It is also referred to as the longest path through a network. It is the shortest period in which the project can be completed. Thus, it is the longest path through the network.

Activity-on-node networks also allow you the latitude of putting in lag. Know that slack is a synonym for float. However, float and slack are not the same thing as lag. Lag is something we assign when we want a delay. Slack or float describes what the function of a network is. **Memorize the relationships in the task dependency diagram.**

Task dependency	Example	Description
Finish-to-start (FS)		Task (B) cannot start until task (A) finishes
Start-to-start (SS)		Task (B) cannot start until task (A) starts
Finish-to-finish (FF)		Task (B) cannot finish until task (A) finishes
Start-to-finish (SF)		Task (B) cannot finish until task (A) starts

Figure 12 - Task Dependencies

Activity Resource Estimating (6.3)

Activity resource estimating is the process of defining resources (people, equipment, material) needed for the schedule activities. This includes what, when, and how many resources are needed for the various project activities. The activities attributes are the main input for this information.

Activities attributes, an output of activity definition, are descriptive terms and definitions used to describe codes, predecessors, successors, constraints, person responsible, geographical location, level of effort, lead and lag, imposed dates, assumptions, and so on. Organizational process and environmental factors influence resource estimating by limiting and controlling how you acquire and use resources.

Most project managers will use a combination of techniques to develop the resource estimates. Two of the most used are bottom-up estimating and expert judgment. Bottom-up takes the lowest level of the decomposed WBS and rolls up these tasks to the next level. For example, if you have only two tasks on a lower level that both take two days to complete, the summary task at the next higher level will take four days because it sums the numbers below it. Mature industries may have published estimating data that contains extensive data on all sorts of metrics for capabilities, type of machines, different tools, and so on. Some examples are feet of pipe laid per hour or the standard time it takes to do a brake job for a Ford Taurus. Of course, most project managers use some type of project management software to help with this estimating because it can help organize all the resource inputs.

The resource estimates are useful for identification and documentation of resource requirements used for each activity and any specialized knowledge and level needed. Resource calendars describe resource availability and allocation allowed. Resource Breakdown Structure (RBS) is a hierarchical structure of the identified resource by category and type (PMBOK®, p. 138).

Activity Duration Estimating (6.4)

When developing a duration estimate for an activity, we are primarily concerned with identifying how many "work periods" the activity will take and its elapsed time. The estimate is based on the following:

- Number of resources assigned
- Capability of those resources to do the job
- Prior results

The person or group that is most familiar with the work should develop, or at least approve, the estimate.

During the estimating process, the project team also must consider information on identified risks. This involves the extent to which the effect of risks is included in the baseline duration estimate for each activity, including risks with high probabilities for impact.

You should be familiar with the tools and techniques used to estimate activity durations:

- Expert judgment
- Analogous or top-down estimating
- Quantitatively based durations: Quantities to be performed for each work category multiplied by the productivity unit rate
- Reserve time (contingency). Note that PMI® states that project teams may choose to incorporate an additional time frame, reserve contingency, or buffer that can be added to the activity duration or elsewhere in the schedule as recognition of the schedule risk. Later, when more information about the project is available, this reverse time can be reduced or eliminated.
- Parametric estimate – A mathematical model that uses parameters, or project characteristics, to forecast project costs.

PMI® recommends that duration estimates always include some indication of the range of possible results (for example, 2 weeks plus or minus 2 days or 85 percent probability that the activity will take less than 3 weeks). This is called range estimating.

Schedule Development (6.5)

Schedule development is the process by which a project manager incorporates the project's main activities from a network diagram into a schedule. The purpose of project scheduling is to ensure that effective time management occurs during the project and that a project is completed within a reasonable amount of time. During schedule development, the project manager assigns a start and end date to each activity. It is critical to consider such things as activity relationships, activity duration, and resource availability when developing a project schedule.

Critical inputs are the project network diagram and the activity duration estimates. Project calendars (which affect all resources) and resource calendars (which affect only a specific resource or category of resources) must be considered when developing the schedule. Be familiar also with two categories of time constraints: imposed dates and key events or major milestones.

Imposed Dates

A project completion date might be imposed by an outside entity. For example, if a judge orders a landlord to make repairs at an apartment complex, the judge can dictate a date by which time all repairs must be made. If the repairs are not made by that date, the landlord might have to pay fines.

Key Events / Milestones

The second constraint to consider during development is the time frame expectations of project stakeholders. Since stakeholders expect to see progress, it is valuable to include milestones on project network diagrams and schedules. The milestones enable stakeholders to verify that progress has been made. Other key inputs are the risk management plan and activity attributes, including responsibility and geographic area.

Critical Path Method (CPM)

Critical path method calculates a single, deterministic early start, late start, early finish, and late finish date for each activity (ES, LS, EF, and LF). The dates are calculated based on specified, sequential network logic and a single duration estimate. The focus is on calculating float to determine which activities have the least amount of scheduling flexibility.

Early start and early finish dates for all activities are calculated using a forwards pass. Late start and late finish dates for all activities are calculated using a backwards pass. Float, slack, total float, and path float all refer to the amount of time that an activity may be delayed from its early start without delaying the project finish date. Free float refers to the amount of time that an activity may be delayed from its early start without delaying the early start of any immediately succeeding activities.

Schedule Compression

Both crashing and fast-tracking are ways to speed things up when schedule pressures exist or when the project is falling behind schedule. The focus is always on critical path activities because it is those activities that determine the length of the project.

Crashing

Crashing involves adding more resources to activities on the critical path in order to accomplish the work faster. As you shorten the time, what happens to costs? Often, they go up. It is important to remember that, when you have to crash a project, you must take time to estimate the increased costs and get approval.

The following is the recommended approach to crashing a network:

- Compute the critical path and establish an objective total duration.
- Identify the crash time and crash cost for each activity on the critical path.
- Prioritize the activities on the critical path that can be shortened at minimum cost.
- Shorten the highest priority activity by one time period and compare total duration with objective.
- Verify the critical path and continue activity reduction until crash time is reached.
- Select next priority activity and continue reduction.

Fast-Tracking

Fast-tracking involves analyzing the critical path to see which activities could be done in parallel (as opposed to sequential execution). It also involves more aggressive use of such PDM activity relationships as start-to-start so that subsequent activities can begin before the prior activity has been completed. This overlapping also reduces the project schedule. It is similar to crashing in that it usually requires more resources to make it happen. Fast-tracking often results in rework. This approach usually increases risk, because of the greater coordination required to monitor and control multiple, concurrent activities.

When it comes to these two issues, you need to be able to differentiate between the two besides knowing the process. The difference between crashing and fast-tracking is that crashing compresses the time on given activities on the critical path. Fast-tracking looks at doing activities in parallel. Also, you need to know the difference between fast-tracking and concurrent engineering. Fast-tracking is when you do tasks in parallel. When you do concurrent engineering, you are doing whole phases and tasks in parallel.

Resource Leveling

The goal of resource leveling is to optimize the use of people and equipment assigned to the project. It begins with the assumption that, when possible, it is more productive to have consistent, continuous use of the fewest resources possible. In other words, it seeks to avoid repeatedly adding and removing resources throughout the project. Resource leveling is the last step in creating a realistic schedule. It confronts the reality of limited people and equipment, and adjusts the schedule to compensate.

Let us consider a few of the problems faced by project managers in the process of leveling resources. As you are aware, every project faces the reality of limited people and equipment. The idea is to avoid both over and under allocation.

Project managers need to remember that whether its people or equipment, there are rarely a bunch of spares sitting around waiting to be used. Those over-allocation problems can become especially acute if project managers imagine that they have a large supply of rare resources, such as unlimited time of the only subject matter expert.

The other side of the problem is under allocation. If the project team is not busy on your project, it will likely be reassigned to other projects and be unavailable when the next peak comes.

A further problem arises if people working on this project are also working on several others at the same time. If every project in the firm has wild swings in its resources, it is almost impossible to move people smoothly between projects. Instead, people are yanked off one project to help another catch up, only to be thrown at another that is even further behind.

Project managers must do their best to avoid resource peaks and valleys, and try to use a consistent set of people on the project at a consistent rate. This is not only more realistic, it is more efficient, because every upswing in resources has a cost, whether it comes from procuring additional equipment or transporting new team members to a site. The learning cost can be the steepest. On knowledge projects, the learning curve can be so long that adding additional developers for only a few weeks can actually result in negative productivity.

Resource leveling involves scheduling the project in a way that uses resources most effectively. By using positive float available on non-critical paths through the project, the project planner can arrange a schedule of work that accomplishes the same result in the same time while smoothing or leveling the peaks and valleys in the resources to be consumed. Float, then, is considered a "project resource." Resource leveling generally results in a schedule that is longer in duration than the preliminary schedule. The reason for this stems from the fact that when most people develop a preliminary schedule, they assume that each resource required to complete any activity is available at the early start date, and that the number of resources is also required. Thus, when a resource leveling exercise is undertaken, the actual number of resources, and their availability, is factored into the schedule, which generally results in a schedule that is longer in duration than the preliminary one.

Two types of constrained scheduling techniques are:

1. **Resource-Constrained Schedule** - The network schedule is allowed to change, based on the availability of identified resources.
2. **Time-Constrained Schedule** - The network schedule is fixed. The absence of required resources per activity is indicated by negative float.

Additionally, you should be familiar with the following approaches:

- **Resource-Based Method** - One in which resources are reallocated from non-critical to critical activities in order to bring the schedule back, or as close as possible, to its original intended overall duration.
- **Reverse Resource Allocation** - Used on projects that have a finite and critical project resource that must be scheduled in reverse from the project's end date.
- **Critical Chain** - A technique popularized by Eli Goldratt that is used to modify the project schedule to account for limited resources and to incorporate buffers to reduce schedule risk. Because random events occur that cause some project activities to be late, activity buffers are introduced. They do not solve the problem, so a project buffer is required. Then another problem occurs: paths that feed into the critical path may be late; and this in turn may cause the critical path to be delayed. Feeding buffers now must be used. However, still there may be a problem because a scarce resource may be used by the critical path and by feeding paths. The approach to follow, therefore, is to set up a schedule to allocate scarce resources by an equivalent to the minimum slack heuristic, except that the slack includes all the relevant buffers. The critical chain is the sequence in which the scarce resource activities are processed.

Be familiar with the intended use of each of the following four resource planning tools:

- **Responsibility Assignment Matrix** - Used to identify who does what. A matrix that lists what work must be done on one side and who is responsible for doing it on the other side.
- **Resource Spreadsheet** - Quantifies how much effort is needed from each resource on the project during each time period.
- **Resource Gantt Chart** - Borrows the Gantt chart concept to identify the precise periods of time when a particular resource is working on a particular task.
- **Resource Histogram** - A vertical bar chart that shows the total number of resources needed during each time period of the project. When compared to the number of

resources that will actually be available, this planning tool is designed to identify any time periods for which insufficient resources are available. The idea is to work out these problems ahead of time so they do not cause problems or surprise the project manager during the course of the project. When it comes to resource leveling, remember that it is the reduction of the over-commitment of resources. That is what you are trying to do. You are trying to use resources most effectively. Resource smoothing involves roughly the same thing. Leveling involves, easing up on the commitment of resources, and smoothing involves trying to create some equilibrium among resources. In a resource-constrained schedule, leveling means that the network schedule is generally going to be extended. If you are cutting back on your resources' hours, generally it is going to take longer to complete the project. By contrast, in a time-constrained schedule, often leveling will result in a negative float. It will result in us moving out past the schedule due date, which means that we have a negative float. We have to make some kind of network correction to go back and resolve the conflict that is involved.

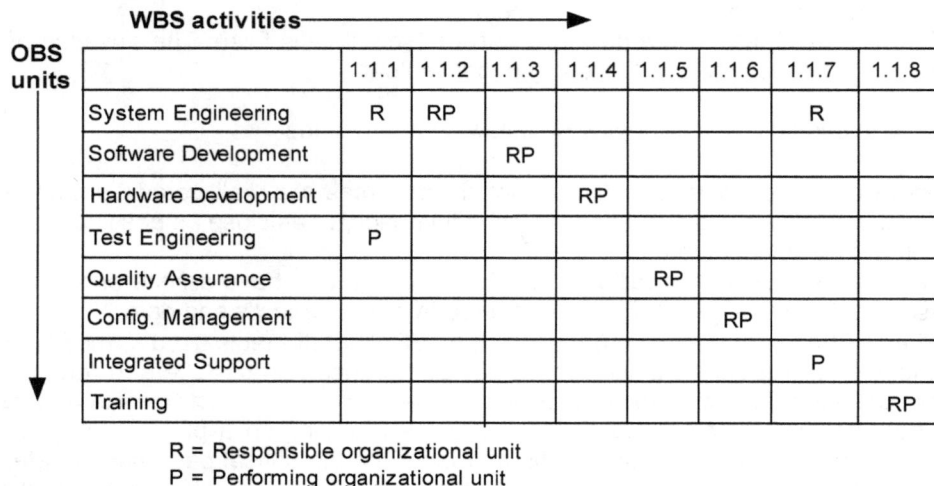

WBS activities ———————————————▶

OBS units		1.1.1	1.1.2	1.1.3	1.1.4	1.1.5	1.1.6	1.1.7	1.1.8
	System Engineering	R	RP					R	
	Software Development			RP					
	Hardware Development				RP				
	Test Engineering	P							
	Quality Assurance					RP			
	Config. Management						RP		
	Integrated Support							P	
	Training								RP

R = Responsible organizational unit
P = Performing organizational unit

Figure 13 - Resource Histogram

- **Monte Carlo Analysis** - Monte Carlo Analysis uses the power of a computer to simulate the project outcomes many times. It yields a range of possible outcomes (cost and schedule are usually of particular interest) and provides the probability for each outcome. This process gives a project manager much better information for planning a project. Note that PMI® considers the Monte Carlo Analysis the most popular form of what-if scenario analysis.
- **Heuristic Scheduling** (Rule of Thumb) - Heuristics are rules of thumb or guidelines that have been learned through experience and trial and error. An example of a heuristic is the PERT process, which has modified some statistical approaches to create a simpler but useful scheduling process; for example, the PERT formula for standard deviation is a heuristic (simple to use but yields good results). Heuristics, as defined by Webster's Dictionary, is learning by discovery. It is simple trial and error. We use heuristics in scheduling when we are trying to work from past experience. PERT is a good example of a heuristic, because it looks at the worst case, the best case, and the most likely, and works with those parameters to establish some standard deviation.

Advantages of Scheduling Tools

There are particular advantages to each tool. If you are working with networks, they are going to give you a sense of the relationships between activities–which ones comes first, how they interact, and how they are related. Networks also give you the critical path.

Bar Chart (Gantt Chart)

- Weak planning tool but effective progress reporting tool
- Easy to read
- No logical relationships between or among activities

Milestone Chart

- Shows significant events on the project
- Identifies only scheduled start or completion of major deliverables
- Good for communicating status with customers and upper management
- Milestones have zero duration

Networks (CPM, PDM)

- Show how project activities and events are related
- Identify critical path, project duration, and activity sequences

PMI® tends to think of the Gantt chart as this terrible useful tool, but for the exam you need to be aware that the bar chart or Gantt chart is considered an extremely weak planning tool. It is not a good planning tool, although you may use it every day. It is a fine progress-reporting tool. It works very well for reporting progress but not very well in terms of planning.

Milestone charts are good for the high-level perspective. They show significant events, and remember that a milestone is an activity of zero duration. It has no duration. They may try and trick you into believing that there is some reason you might want a milestone to have some duration.

The best way to know if it is a milestone - could it be expressed in the past tense in one way or another? If it can't–if it involves some activity or some time passing–it is not a true milestone.

Critical Chain Method

The Critical Chain Method (CCM) is an outgrowth of the Theory of Constraints (TOC) developed by Eliyahu Goldratt to scheduling and managing manufacturing. TOC focuses on identifying and fixing bottlenecks in order to improve the throughput of the overall system. Likewise, Critical Chain focuses on bottlenecks. For example, one pharmaceutical company was experiencing significant delays with drug approvals. After investigation, it found that the bottleneck was statisticians to analyze clinical trial data. The cost of hiring statisticians was more than offset by the revenue from getting products to market sooner.

Using the Critical Chain Method, projects can be completed more quickly and with greater scheduling reliability. The difference between traditional and Critical Chain scheduling is in how uncertainty is managed. In traditional project scheduling, uncertainty is managed by padding task durations, starting work as early as possible, multi-tasking, and focusing on meeting commitment dates. The following bullet points illustrate some of the problems associated with traditional project scheduling:

- Padding task durations (providing worst-case estimates) is done to ensure a high probability of task completion. The knowledge that there is so much safety time built into tasks results in various time wasting practices, e.g., waiting until the last moment to complete a task. As a result, all the safety time can be wasted at the start of the task so that, if problems are encountered, the task over-runs.
- Starting work as early as possible, even when not scheduled, is a response to worst-case estimates. When workers give worst-case estimates, they don't expect to stay busy with just one task – so they multi-task, working on several tasks at once by switching between them. The result is that everything takes a long time to complete and very little completes early.
- With the focus on meeting commitment dates (start and finish), output from a task completed early will rarely be accepted early by the next person needing this output. So, any effort spent in finishing early will be wasted. Early delivery of one task can't be used to offset lateness on another. Lateness, however, is always passed on and the lost time can't be made up without cutting the specifications or increasing resources allocated to subsequent tasks, if possible.

In Critical Chain scheduling, uncertainty is primarily managed by (a) using average task duration estimates; (b) scheduling backwards from the date a project is needed (to ensure work that needs to be done is done, and it is done only when needed); (c) placing aggregate buffers in the project plan to protect the entire project and the key tasks; and (d) using buffer management to control the plan. The key tasks are those on which the ultimate duration of the project depends, also known as the Critical Chain. The specific steps to identify and manage a Critical Chain schedule are as follows:

- Reduce activity duration estimates by 50%. Activity durations are normal estimates, which we know to be high probability and contain excessive safety time. We estimate the 50% probability by cutting these in half. (The protection that is cut from individual tasks is aggregated and strategically inserted as buffers in the project.
- Eliminate resource contentions by leveling the project plan. The Critical Chain can then be identified as the longest chain of path and resource dependencies after resolving resource contentions.
- Insert a Project Buffer at the end of the project to aggregate Critical Chain contingency time (initially 50% of the critical chain path length)
- Protect the Critical Chain from resource unavailability by Resource buffers. Resource buffers are correctly placed to ensure the arrival of Critical Chain resources.
- Size and place Feeding Buffers on all paths that feed the Critical Chain. Feeding buffers protect the Critical Chain from accumulation of negative variations, e.g. excessive or lost time, on the feeding chains. This subordinates the other project paths to the Critical Chain.
- Start gating tasks as late as possible. Gating tasks are tasks that have no predecessor. This helps prevent multitasking.
- Ensure that resources deliver Roadrunner performance. Resources should work as quickly as possible on their activities, and pass their work on as they complete.

- Provide resources with activity durations and estimated start times, not milestones. This encourages resources to pass on their work when done.
- Use buffer management to control the plan. Buffers provide information to the project manager, for example, when to plan for recovery and when to take recovery action.

Critical Chain approach is perhaps the most important new development in project scheduling in the last 30 years. Used properly, the Critical Chain approach is an extremely powerful means of gaining more predictability, productivity and speed from your project plans.

Project Schedule

The project schedule provides information regarding the overall project duration as well as each activity's duration. It reflects the project schedule baseline and is used to present that baseline information to team members, management, and the customer. The schedule may consist of a project-length timeline, as well as the specific activity information, including the activities:

- Working duration
- Effort hours
- Elapsed duration
- Earliest possible start date
- Earliest possible finish date
- Latest possible start date
- Latest possible finish date
- Available total float
- Available free float
- Relationships with other activities

As a complete set of project activities it can reflect all of the work in the project. As a subset of those activities, or fragnet (a self-contained subset of a project schedule), the project schedule can reflect a time-sensitive window of project activity.

Schedule Management Plan

Project managers cannot arbitrarily make changes to a schedule. A schedule management plan provides guidelines for project managers to follow when making changes to a project schedule. Schedule management plans are not necessarily formal or highly detailed, but should give enough detail to provide guidance when scheduling changes arise.

Cost Estimating (7.1)

Cost estimating is the process of developing an approximation (estimate) of the costs of the resources needed to complete project activities. In approximating cost, the estimator considers the causes of variation of the final estimate for purposes of better project management. Cost estimating includes identifying and considering various costing alternatives.

Where possible, estimates should be done prior to budget request rather than after budgetary approval is provided. Care must be taken to distinguish between cost estimating and pricing, especially for projects performed under contract.

Recognize that cost estimating is not pricing. Cost estimating involves developing an assessment of the likely quantitative result thus determining how much it will cost the performing organization to provide the product/service. Pricing is a business decision which determines how much the performing organization will charge for the product or service. The cost is taken into consideration along with other factors.

Work Breakdown Structure

The PMBOK® Guide indicates that the WBS identifies project activities that will need resources and will, therefore, require expenditures. The WBS also identifies all the work that must be scheduled and that will require expenditures. You will recall that the lowest level of project activity is known as the work package. A cost account or a control account is one level above the work package and is used for monitoring and controlling purposes. PMI® explains that a control account plan (CAP) is a management control point at which the integration of scope, budget, and schedule takes place, and at which performance is measured. CAPs are placed at selected points on the WBS. The chart of accounts is provided to describe the coding structure, used by the organization, to report financial information to its general ledger. Project cost estimates must be assigned to the correct accounting category. The project team should consider the extent to which the effect of risk is included in the cost estimates for each activity.

Chart of Accounts

Once all the cost approximations are complete for a project, these costs must be arranged correctly according to the organization's accounting department. A chart of accounts is a list of codes that are assigned to the various costs of a project. Each individual cost account generally represents a specific work package in the WBS, making it easy to monitor performance on a daily, weekly or monthly basis.

Expert Judgment and Estimating

The tools used in estimating are varied and are all likely to be used on the same project. Some activities can best be estimated using one method, some another. Expert judgment involves the use of people who have an expert understanding of the activity and are guided by historical information. In estimating a previous similar activity is used as a model for estimating future duration. It is a form of expert judgment and requires that the previous activity be truly similar to be accurate.

Analogous Estimating / or Top-Down Estimating

Analogous estimating is based on historical data and comparisons with similar projects within the group or company. Analogous estimating uses the actual cost of a previous similar project as the basis for estimating the cost of the current project. Is frequently used to estimate total project costs when there is a limited amount of detailed information about the project. (e.g., in the early project phases) Generally less costly than other estimating techniques, but it is also generally less accurate. Most reliable when 1) the previous projects are similar in fact and not just in appearance, 2) the individuals or groups preparing estimates have the needed expertise. Considered a form of expert judgment.

Parametric models are often used to extrapolate data from one project to fit another. It is most appropriate to use analogous estimating for top level planning and decision making. This type of estimate is accurate to within -10 percent and +25 percent. It should be noted that analogous estimating is good enough for planning, but not good enough for a final estimate.

Parametric Modeling

This type of estimating relies on knowledge of mathematical relationships between two or more characteristics of a project. Parametric modeling uses project characteristics (parameters) in a mathematical model to predict project costs. Models may be either simple or complex. Simple example of parametric modeling: Model the cost of constructing a residential home based on square footage of living space. A Complex example: Model software development costs using thirteen adjustment factors, each of which has five to seven points. Most reliable when 1) the historical information used to develop the model was accurate, 2) the parameters used in the model are readily quantifiable, and 3) the model is scaleable.

A commonly used statistical technique for modeling such relationships is known as regression analysis. The relationship is graphically represented on a scatter diagram. The regression line on the diagram estimates the average value for the dependent variable corresponding to each value of the independent variable.

A real-world example of a parametric model that sometimes relies on regression analysis is called the learning curve. The learning curve mathematically models the intuitive notion that the more times we do something; the faster we will be able to perform the task. Specifically, learning curve theory says that each time we double the number of times we have done something; the time it takes to perform the task will decrease in a regular pattern. The regression modeling process is able to determine the rate at which the decrease occurs.

Bottom-up Estimating

The bottom-up estimating method is the most accurate of the three methods. It is based on the work package level (lowest level) of the work breakdown structure and requires costing each package or task. Estimates are determined by the person who performs the task and the project manager should contact the person who will actually complete the task and ask him how long it will take to do the task and what the cost will be.

Accuracy of Estimates

PMI® offers the following guidelines for the accuracy of cost estimates:

- Order-of-magnitude estimates are approximations without detailed data, often done early in a project when a "ballpark guesstimate" is needed. Such estimates have an accuracy range of -25 percent to +75 percent.
- Budget estimates are based on slightly better data and are often used to establish initial funding and gain project approval. The range of accuracy is -10 percent to +25 percent.
- Definitive estimates are prepared from well-defined, detailed data. A bottom-up estimate would be an example of a definitive estimate, which is the most accurate (with a range of -5 percent to +10 percent).

Memorize these three types of estimating before taking the exam. When it comes to cost estimating, you can anticipate a number of questions specifically focusing on the idea that the WBS is still the best way to go, and the best tool you have when it comes to cost estimating. Why? Because the WBS supports bottom-up estimate. The WBS is critical to cost estimating because we estimate the activities, how much they are going to cost at the work package level, and then we roll them up to the cost accounts. PMI® also feels that this is the best method.

Analogous estimates are equally important. You will need to know what they are for the exam and that they are referred to as a type of top-down estimate. For the exam, think of analogous estimates as being top-down estimates.

Parametric estimating uses a variety of functions and tools that, in the end, come up with an estimate. Specifically, it is a formula used to express a mathematical relationship between the project and the dollars that are going to be invested in that project.

Accuracy of estimates will show up on the exam. You can anticipate a number of questions associated with the accuracy levels of the different types of estimates. Specifically, what you can expect is order of magnitude estimates to be described as +75/-25 percent. Budget estimates have a greater accuracy rate: +25/-10 percent. Budget estimates, remember, are also known as top-down estimates. Definitive estimates are bottom-up estimates. They are the WBS estimates. Definitive estimates have an accuracy range of +10/-5 percent.

Reserve Analysis

The word reserve is often used with a modifier (for example, contingency reserve or management reserve) in order to provide further detail on what types of risk are being mitigated. The PMBOK® Guide defines contingency reserve as the amount of money or time needed above the estimate that reduces the risk of overruns of project objectives to a level acceptable to the organization. For example, rework is certain; the amount of rework is not. Contingency reserves may involve cost, schedule, or both. Contingency reserves are intended to reduce the impact of missing cost or schedule objectives. They are normally included in the project's cost and schedule baselines. Management reserves are separately planned quantities used to allow for future situations that are impossible to predict (sometimes called "unknown unknowns"). Management reserves may involve costs or schedules. They are intended to reduce the risks of missing costs or schedule objectives. The use of a management reserve requires a change to the project's cost baseline. The purpose of a reserve is to reduce the chances of a cost-to-time overrun when risks turn into problems. Remember, in some application areas the definitions of management reserves and contingency reserves are exactly the opposite of those presented above. The important point for test-taking purposes is that you know what a reserve is and why one exists. The risk management plan often includes cost contingency, which can be determined on the basis of the expected accuracy of the estimate so the risk management plan serves as an input to cost budgeting.

Triangular Distribution

Triangular distribution is used only when we know the minimum, maximum and most likely values. It leads to a less conservative estimate of uncertainty. The triangular distribution is useful for stochastic modeling rather than statistical analysis because of its artificial nature. Distribution Formula: Probability (cost < most likely) = (most likely - min) ÷ (max - min)

Basics of Cost Management

The law of diminishing returns identifies a situation in which you are putting more and more of something (dollars, people, and so on) into your project, and then getting proportionately less and less out of it.

Variable versus fixed costs: Variable costs rise directly with the size of the project (for example, the costs associated with skilled labor or materials consumed directly by the project). Fixed costs do not change because you decide to produce fifty more units. Fixed costs are non-recurring expenses associated with putting a production line in place.

Direct versus indirect costs: Direct costs are incurred directly by a specific project and usually include such items as salaries of project staff (project manager and full-time functional experts), materials used directly on the project, subcontractor expenses, and so on. Indirect costs are part of the overall organization's cost of doing business and are shared (allocated to) among all the projects that are under way. These costs include such things as security guards, electricity, fringe benefits, insurance, tax, and in general, anything that would be considered part of overhead.

Depreciation of Capital

When money is spent to purchase capital equipment, there are several ways to write off these expenses from taxable income. The straight-line method takes an equal credit during each year of the useful life of the equipment. There are two methods of accelerated depreciation that are used for writing off the expense even faster than the straight-line approach: double declining balance and sum-of-the-year's digits. You do not need to know the formulas, just their names.

Value Analysis

Value analysis is a cost reduction tool that involves careful analysis of a design or item to identify all the functions as well as the cost of each function. The approach then considers whether the function is really necessary and whether it can be provided at a lower cost without degrading performance or quality. It is also a technique used in product analysis.

Cost Risk and Contract Type

This subject is covered more thoroughly in the section titled Project Risk Management. However, you might see several questions on the exam about which party to a contract bears the cost risk. The idea is simple and you can answer any question on this subject if you know the following:

- With a **fixed-price contract**, the seller is legally obligated to deliver the product or service described in the contract. This requirement holds true even if the contractor spends more money than expected in fulfilling the contract. Therefore, with a fixed-price contract, the seller bears the cost risk.
- Conversely, with a **cost-reimbursement contract**, the cost risk is borne by the customer. This is true because in such a contract the buyer agrees to cover the contractor's costs plus an agreed-upon amount of profit. Also, in such contractual arrangements, the contractor is legally required to provide only its "best effort" in fulfilling the contract deliverables.

For this section know that the seller has the biggest risk in a fixed-price contract. Likewise, in a cost-reimbursement or cost-plus contract, the big risk is going to be borne by the customer.

Cost Budgeting (7.2)

Cost budgeting is the process of allocating cost to the individual work items in the project. Project performance will be determined based on the budget allocated to the various parts of the project. The result of the cost budgeting process is the cost baseline of the project. The cost baseline for the project is the expected actual cost of the project.

The cost baseline is the output of cost budgeting. It is a time-phased budget that is used to measure and monitor cost performance. Be aware that many projects may have multiple cost baselines that are used to measure different aspects of cost performance. An example is a spending plan or cash-flow forecast that can be used for measuring disbursements.

Cost Baseline

The cost baseline is the basis for the earned value reporting system. It is the budget for the estimated cost of the project spread over the time periods of the project. When managing a project we are concerned about three baselines: the schedule baseline, the cost baseline, and the scope baseline.

The cost baseline is the part of the project concerned with the amount of money that the project is predicted to cost and when that money will be used. The three baselines are closely related, and changes to one of them will result in changes to the others. If a change is made in the project scope baseline, either by adding or removing some of the work that is required, the schedule baseline and the cost baseline will probably have to be changed as well.

Cost Management Plan

A cost management plan is developed to provide guidelines for the project manager to follow when dealing with cost variances. The amount of detail included in a cost management plan is dependent on the needs of the project stakeholder. The plan should outline steps that need to be taken if the actual project costs are higher or lower than the approved project budget.

To make a cost management plan useful, the accumulated costs of the project must always be available by looking at the cost baseline, which is displayed as an S-curve. The project stakeholders can then compare the approved budget to the cost baseline to determine if the project costs are on target.

Quality Planning (8.1)

Quality planning involves defining the quality standards for a project and deciding how to achieve those standards. The scope statement is used as a point of reference during quality planning because it outlines not only the end results of a project, but also the project objectives, which should be in-line with the stakeholder expectations.

An important part of quality planning involves making sure quality is part of a product's design from the beginning of a project, since quality cannot be infused into a product through inspection. Remember that the result of the quality planning process is the quality plan. Also remember a fundamental principle from Deming is that "quality should be planned in, not inspected in."

Therefore, although inspection is certainly part of project quality management, increased inspection is not generally considered the best path to improved quality. So hiring more inspectors would not be the correct answer to the question, "What is the best way to improve quality?"

Quality Policy

PMI® stresses the importance of having a quality policy for the project. Quality policy is a company's statement of how it will produce quality products and what it will do if products are defective. Most often, upper management dictates a quality policy to be implemented by project managers and team members. Not all quality polices are formal documents. If a company does not have a formal quality policy, then the project managers and team members should draft one before starting a new project. It is important that a project's stakeholders know the terms of the quality policy before a project begins.

Quality Planning Tools and Techniques, PMI® discusses four quality planning tools and techniques:

1. **Cost Benefit Analysis** - Cost benefit analysis must be considered in the quality planning process. Cost benefit analysis weighs the benefits versus cost to make sure a project meets quality requirements without going over the project's budget. The project manager must consider cost benefit tradeoffs during quality planning. The primary benefit of meeting quality requirements is less rework which translates to higher productivity, lower costs, and increased stakeholder satisfaction. The primary cost of meeting quality requirements is the expense associated with project quality management activities. The benefits of the quality management discipline outweigh the costs.
2. **Benchmarking** - Involves comparing actual or planned project practices to those of other projects (either within the performing organization or external) to generate ideas for improvement and to provide a standard by which to measure performance.
3. **Design of Experiments** - Design of experiments is a statistical method that helps identify which factors might influence specific variables and is applied most often to the product of the project (for example, automotive designers may wish to determine which combination of suspension and tires will produce the most desirable ride characteristics at a reasonable cost.) It can also be applied to project management issues such as cost and schedule trade-offs. Example: senior engineers will cost more than junior engineers but will usually complete the assignment in less time. An appropriately designed experiment which computes project costs and duration for various combinations of senior and junior engineers will often yield an optimal solution from a relatively limited number of cases.
4. **Cost of Quality** (COQ) - One major area of emphasis on the exam is cost of quality. Cost of quality refers to the total amount of money and resources that are necessary to make sure a project's quality standards are met. It is defined as the cost of conformance (the cost of proactive quality processes) and the cost of nonconformance (the cost of a quality failure). In either form, cost of quality is a results-oriented approach to measuring and assessing the effectiveness or benefit of an organization's project quality management process. It is a useful means of bringing management's attention to the need for quality, but it provides little meaningful capability to manage quality proactively. Three types of incurred costs: prevention, appraisal, and failure. Failure costs are broken down into internal and external costs and may also be referred to as the cost of poor quality.

Additional quality planning tools - Other quality planning tools are also often used to help better define the situation and help plan effective quality management activities. These include:

Brainstorming - is simply listing all ideas put forth by a group in response to a given problem or question. Creativity is encouraged by not allowing ideas to be evaluated or discussed until everyone has run dry. Any and all ideas are considered legitimate and often the most far-fetched are the most fertile. Structured brainstorming produces numerous creative ideas about any given "central question". Done right, it taps the human brain's capacity for lateral thinking and free association.

Brainstorms help answer specific questions such as:
- What opportunities face us this year?
- What factors are constraining performance in Department X?
- What could be causing problem Y?
- What can we do to solve problem Z?

However, a brainstorm cannot help you positively identify causes of problems, rank ideas in a meaningful order, select important ideas, or check solutions. To conduct a successful brainstorm:

- Make sure everyone understands and is satisfied with the central question.
- You may want to give everyone a few seconds to jot down a few ideas before getting started.
- Begin by going around the table or room, giving everyone a chance to voice their ideas or pass. After a few rounds, open the floor.
- More ideas are better. Encourage radical ideas and piggybacking.
- Suspend judgment of all ideas.
- Record exactly what is said. Clarify only after everyone is out of ideas.
- Don't stop until ideas become sparse. Allow for late-coming ideas.
- Eliminate duplicates and ideas that aren't relevant to the topic.

A brainstorm starts with a clear question, and ends with a raw list of ideas.

Affinity Diagrams - the affinity diagram wasn't originally intended for quality management. Nonetheless, it has become one of the most widely used of the Japanese management and planning tools. The affinity diagram was developed to discovering meaningful groups of ideas within a raw list. In doing so, it is important to let the groupings emerge naturally, using the right side of the brain, rather than according to preordained categories.

Usually, an affinity diagram is used to refine a brainstorm into something that makes sense and can be dealt with more easily. It is recommended using the affinity diagram when facts or thoughts are uncertain and need to be organized, when preexisting ideas or paradigms need to be overcome, when ideas need to be clarified, and when unity within a team needs to be created.

To create an affinity diagram, you sort the brainstormed list, moving ideas from the brainstorm into affinity sets, and creating groups of related ideas. As you sort ideas:

- Rapidly group ideas that seem to belong together.
- It isn't important to define why they belong together.
- Copy an idea into in more than one affinity set if appropriate.
- Look for small sets. Should they belong in a larger group?
- Do large sets need to be broken down more precisely?

- When most of the ideas have been sorted, you can start to enter titles for each affinity set.

Force Field Analysis - is a useful technique for looking at all the forces for and against a decision. In effect, it is a specialized method of weighing pros and cons. By carrying out the analysis you can plan to strengthen the forces supporting a decision, and reduce the impact of opposition to it. To carry out a force field analysis, follow these steps:

- List all forces for change in one column, and all forces against change in another column
- Assign a score to each force, from 1 (weak) to 5 (strong)
- Draw a diagram showing the forces for and against change. Show the size of each force as a number next to it

Once you have carried out an analysis, you can decide whether your project is viable. In the example above, you might initially question whether it is worth going ahead with the plan. Where you have already decided to carry out a project, Force Field Analysis can help you to work out how to improve its probability of success. Here you have two choices:

- To reduce the strength of the forces opposing a project, or
- To increase the forces pushing a project

Nominal Group Techniques - in the nominal group technique, participants are brought together for a discussion session led by a moderator. After the topic has been presented to session participants and they have had an opportunity to ask questions or briefly discuss the scope of the topic, they are asked to take a few minutes to think about and write down their responses. The session moderator will then ask each participant to read, and elaborate on, one of their responses. These are noted on a flipchart. Once everyone has given a response, participants will be asked for a second or third response, until all of their answers have been noted on flipcharts sheets posted around the room.

Once duplications are eliminated, each response is assigned a letter or number. Session participants are then asked to choose up to 10 responses that they feel are the most important and rank them according to their relative importance. These rankings are collected from all participants, and aggregated.

Sometimes these results are given back to the participants in order to stimulate further discussion, and perhaps a readjustment in the overall rankings assigned to the various responses. This is done only when group consensus regarding the prioritization of issues is important to the overall research or planning project.

The nominal group technique can be used as an alternative to both the focus group and the Delphi techniques. It presents more structure than the focus group, but still takes advantage of the synergy created by group participants. As its name suggests, the nominal group technique is only "nominally" a group, since the rankings are provided on an individual basis.

Matrix Diagrams - permit organization of knowledge so that relationships between factors, causes, objectives, (or any thing that one wants to show) can be shown. Matrices, of course, provide rows and columns with intersecting cells that can be filled with information that describes the relation between the items located in the rows and columns.

Flowcharts - are maps or graphical representations of a process. Steps in a process are shown with symbolic shapes, and the flow of the process is indicated with arrows connecting the symbols. Computer programmers popularized flowcharts in the 1960's, using them to map the logic of programs. In quality improvement work, flowcharts are particularly useful for displaying how a process currently functions or could ideally function. Flowcharts can help you see whether the steps of a process are logical, uncover problems or miscommunications, define the boundaries of a process, and develop a common base of knowledge about a process. Flowcharting a process often brings to light redundancies, delays, dead ends, and indirect paths that would otherwise remain unnoticed or ignored.

Prioritization Matrices - is a useful technique you can use with your team members or with your users to achieve consensus about an issue. The Matrix helps you rank problems or issues (usually generated through brainstorming) by a particular criterion that is important to your organization. Then you can more clearly see which problems are the most important to work on solving first. This tool should be used when:

- Key root causes have been identified and the most critical causes must be narrowed down
- When the issues are complex and they have strong interrelationships
- There are limited resources for improvement activities so you must concentrate on the critical few.

Quality Management Plan

The quality management plan describes how the project management team will implement its quality policy. The quality management plan should describe the project quality system: the organizational structure, responsibilities, procedures, processes, and resources needed to implement quality management. It also provides input to the overall project plan and must address quality control, quality assurance, and quality improvement for the project. The quality management plan may be formal or informal, highly detailed or broadly framed, depending on the requirements of the project.

Quality Metrics

A metric describes, in precise terms, what something is and how the quality control process measures it. A measurement is an actual value. Quality metrics should be used in all quality processes. Some examples of quality metrics would be system reliability, system availability and mean time to failure.

Quality Checklists

A quality checklist is a list of check-off items that permit data to be collected quickly and easily in a simple standardized format that lends itself to quantitative analysis. A quality checklist frequently contains a graphic representation of an object and is used to record such information as where specific damage was located. A quality checklist is intended to make data collection fast and easy and it should be carefully designed so that the data are useful and have a clear purpose. Checklists are frequently used to collect data on numbers of defective items, defect locations, and defect causes.

Types of Costs

There are two types of costs incurred in quality management. Be able to recognize examples of each: prevention costs and appraisal costs, which are the cost of conformance; and failure costs, which are the cost of nonconformance.

Cost of Conformance

Prevention costs: Up-front costs are oriented toward the satisfaction of customer requirements:

- Design reviews
- Training and indoctrination
- Planning
- Vendor, supplier, and subcontractor surveys
- Process studies

Appraisal costs: Costs associated with the evaluation of the product or the process to see whether customer requirements were met:

- Product inspections
- Lab tests
- Vendor controls
- In-process testing
- Internal/external design reviews

Cost of Nonconformance (Failure Costs)

Internal failure costs: Costs associated with the failure of the processes to make the products acceptable to the customer before the products leave the control of the organization:

- Scrap / Rework
- Repair
- Downtime
- Defect evaluation
- Corrective actions

External failure costs: Costs associated with the determination by the customer that requirements have not been satisfied:

- Customer returns
- Customer complaints
- Customer inspections
- Customer visits to resolve quality complaints
- Corrective actions

Rework

Rework is the corrective action taken to make a defective product conform to a project's quality standards. Reworking a product takes more time and uses more resources than if the product is made correctly the first time. The use of additional time and resources increases the cost of quality, which is the total amount of money and work used to make quality products.

Key Quality Planning Outputs

The quality management plan describes the quality management system: the organizational structure, responsibilities, procedures, processes, and resources needed to implement quality management.

Operational definitions describe what something is and how the quality control process measures it. They may also be called metrics.

Checklists are outputs of quality planning that are used to verify that a set of required steps has been performed. Completed checklists (an output of quality control) should be part of the project's records.

Human Resource Planning (9.1)

The first of the process groups in project human resource management is human resource planning. According to PMBOK®, this determines "roles, responsibilities, and reporting relationships, and creates the staff management plan." The roles and responsibilities can be for either a group of people or an individual. The groups may be internal, or they may be a contracted project management firm. In the case of the latter, it is absolutely necessary that the roles of the people as well as their responsibilities be documented before beginning the project.

With internal groups, the overall organizational policies and structures apply. So too do the roles and responsibilities and the reporting relationships that the team members have within the organization. The structure of reporting lines is extremely important for the project manager to consider because this will determine how the project manager handles the team.

For the most part, an internal project manager does not have complete control over the project team. The various team members with their variety of skill sets usually report to managers in the functional area they represent. As we discuss types of power later in this chapter, you will see how important this issue is for the project manager to consider and manage. Often the external or contracted project manager, if he or she is running his or her own contracted project team, will have control over the entire function of the team. This is one of the major differences in a project manager's span of control.

Communications planning and organizational planning interact as planning processes. The project's final structure will determine the communication requirements of the project, and the communication planning will follow the organizational planning.

The inputs to organizational planning are enterprise environmental factors, organizational process assets, and the project management plan that includes the activity resource requirements (PMBOK®). Organizational culture and structure are the major topics within the input of enterprise environmental factors. Some of the factors involving organizational culture and structure are organizational, technical, interpersonal, logistical, and political.

The organizational factor includes information about the departments that will be involved in the project, the current working relationships between the various departments, and the relationships, formal and informal, that exist between the departments that will be used to execute the project.

There will be many relationships and reporting lines within an organization, and as a project manager, you will be expected to know these in order to better manage the project. The issue of current working relationships is also a major one for a project manager. If there is a history of either good or bad relationships between departments, you should be aware of it. Although past relationships between departments do not always indicate future behavior with respect to your project, they can be used as guidelines and can give you a "heads up" on potential issues.

The second type of relationship deals with the formality of the relationship. The formal relationships will be shown in organizational charts and are easy to ascertain. The informal relationships are ones that will determine the overall dynamics of the project team and as such are something that the project manager must monitor constantly.

The technical interfaces will be between various technical disciplines or functions. The interpersonal interfaces will be between various individuals working on the project and may be formal, as in the case of a reporting line to a manager, or informal, as in the relationship between two people who are on the project team and need to communicate to complete their tasks. In addition, you need to know the job descriptions of the various team members, which will help determine choices of personnel. Finally, the trust levels between the various project team members are very important dynamics for the project manager to manage. At least it would be good to know whether there are any questions about trust between potential team members so that issues may be brought forward and handled early in the project.

The logistical part of the enterprise environmental factors consists of the working spaces and the distances between people on the team. If your team is multinational, and several members of the team are working in other countries, you must work to make sure that you can accommodate issues such as time changes, lack of interpersonal communication, and various local customs that will impact the work of the project team. Collocation is usually recommended for making the best project team. Collocation means having the entire project team in the same building, either with adjoining facilities or housed in one large room.

Finally, the political aspects of the organizational culture will have an impact on how the project team works. Not political in terms of national parties, but rather in terms of smaller groups. The only time national parties may enter into project management might be when the politics of a certain country factor into the completion of the project. Permits and licenses may be a part of this issue. Project team politics may include informal power that some department has within a given organization. For instance, in many IT organizations, the development department has the greatest organizational power because that department is the one that actually creates the product or service.

The second input into human resources planning is organizational process assets, which are sets of processes in an organization that are useful for performing the project. Two of the major process assets listed in PMBOK® are templates and checklists. These two give guidelines to the project manager and, if in fact they already exist, will make it easier to reduce the amount of planning time because processes are already in place for certain tasks in the organization. Even though the current project will not exactly mirror a past project, the templates and checklists used before may be extremely helpful. Be sure to monitor these two assets to make sure that your current project's checklist content is taken care of, and do not assume that the past checklists or templates are carbon copies of what you need currently.

The project plan is the last of the inputs to human resource planning. The project plan has a variety of information useful to the new project manager. First, the activity resource requirements have been detailed so that planning flows from available information. Second, there are a variety of project management activities such as risk management and procurement that are listed in the overall project plan that can help the project manager assess and assign people to various tasks that are needed in the project.

Three tools and techniques for human resource planning are found in the 3rd edition of the PMBOK®. They are organization charts and position descriptions, networking, and organizational theory. There are a variety of formats used to document the team members' roles, responsibilities, and relationships. According to the PMBOK®, most of the formats fall into three types: hierarchical, matrix, and text-oriented.

The Work Breakdown Structure is an example of a hierarchical chart. It shows relationships of the various tasks and people in a top-down, graphic format. The WBS looks like a family tree and is common in organizational control.

In addition to the WBS, PMBOK® lists two other types of breakdown structures. The first is the Organization Breakdown Structure, or OBS. The difference between the WBS and the OBS is that the OBS shows departments or units of the organization and is not organized along the lines of deliverables.

The next breakdown structure type is the Resource Breakdown Structure, or RBS. This type of hierarchical chart breaks down the project by resource types so that the project manager can see quickly which resources can be grouped together. For instance, quality testers may be listed together, although they may be used at different times during the project for different areas of quality testing. The RBS does not have to be only for human resources and may include materials, communication technologies, and other types of resources needed to execute the project.

The outputs to the human resource planning are roles and responsibilities, project organization charts, and the staffing management plan. PMBOK® suggests that four items should be considered when listing the roles and responsibilities of a person on the project. In addition to roles and responsibilities themselves, the other items are authority and competency.

Authority is defined as "the right to apply project resources, make decisions, and sign approvals." Authority is generally assigned in the organizational structure, although there may be projects where there will be matrixed authority. It is best when the responsibilities of the individual are matched with the authority to get tasks done. It is extremely frustrating to be given the responsibility for a task without the necessary authority to see it through.

The competency item in roles and responsibilities deals with the skills of the project member to complete project tasks and responsibilities. People are occasionally assigned to a project who do not have the requisite skills to get particular tasks done or who are not sufficiently trained to do the tasks in a timely manner. Knowing the skill levels of project team members is important when planning human resources for any type of project.

The project organization chart is a graphic display of the various members of the project team and the managers to whom they report. This chart can help the project manager to gain an understanding of the communication lines needed to run the project.

The staffing management plan is a subset of the project management plan. This plan details the resources needed for the project. Depending on the size and complexity of the project, this plan will be formal or informal, detailed or broadly stated. The more complex the project, the more detail is included. In a large DoD project, this type of plan will almost always be formal. On a project with a smaller scope, the plan may be informal. The detail and formality of the staffing management plan depends on the needs of the project.

A variety of information can be captured in the staffing management plan. Some items are optional. These include staff acquisition, a timetable, release criteria, training needs, recognition and rewards, compliance, and safety. Each of these items can be detailed or even left out if the project warrants it.

Staff acquisition includes several questions that must be answered in order to have good human resource planning. Among these questions are whether to keep your HR search in-house or go to outsourcing for resources. Team logistics is another topic that may be included in the staff acquisition plan, although this topic might be found in other places in planning. The logistics issues include the various locations of team members and the ways the team may work from off-site offices.

Costs are another issue in staff acquisition. After you have determined the level of skills needed to complete the project, you will have to compute the costs associated with the necessary skills. This type of management decision is often a tradeoff between time and cost, although in the best of all possible projects, you will not have to worry about skimping at all.

The timetable for the project can be part of the staffing management plan. You can depict the necessary resource usage using a variety of illustrations. If you look in the PMBOK® Guide Figure 9-6, you will see a resource histogram that is useful in determining how much time is expected from the various team members and/or functions. Many types of charts are available to show the information. You choose the one with which you are the most comfortable and that gives you manageable information.

The release criteria include both the timing of the release of team members and the method in which you will release them. The cost involved with retaining people who are not needed to continue the project can be a major one. This and the fact that orderly transitions to new projects are desirable make the use of release criteria important.

Yet another item to be considered in the staffing management plan is the need for training. In some projects, training is needed because the people assigned to the project do not have complete information on the tasks that are required of them. A training plan can be a great help in shoring up the skill levels needed on the project.

Although not listed by PMBOK® at this point, training for end users is important to consider early in the project. If you are installing a new AR system and want end users to understand and use the new software quickly and effectively, it is a good idea to detail the planning that will make this happen. End-user training can make or break the final outcome of the project, so it should be a part of the overall staffing plan because you will need to assign a person or people to actually conduct the training.

Recognition and rewards are major parts of the motivation of a project team. In order to make sure that everyone is on the same page, there must be clear criteria for team member rewards and a system to obtain these rewards. In order to be effective, the rewards should be linked directly to something under the project member's control. Frustration can occur if the team member has no control over his or her own rewards. The key to all of this is to make the reasons for rewards clear and to get agreement from various team members concerning what they will be rewarded for during the execution of their particular set of required project tasks.

The compliance part of the staffing management plan deals with tactics for complying with contracts, government regulations, and any other applicable policies that the organization has put in place. Usually, these policies will be available through the human resources department, and it is a good idea to check for any compliance issues before beginning the project.

Another area of compliance is that of legal requirements. Legal requirements may constrain how you choose projects and how projects are executed. An example of this would be a project to shut down support for a previous version of software and to migrate all users to a new version. You should check first with the legal department to make sure that no contracts have been written that would stop you from discontinuing help desk service. This is not an unusual issue, and you should examine it at the beginning of the project.

Finally, safety can be a major issue within a staffing management plan. The organization should set policies and procedures concerning the safety of all people involved in the project, which can be included in the staffing management plan. Many construction companies consider safety to be the major issue on a project. It is a good idea to make sure that the policies are in place and then to carry them out.

Communications Planning (10.1)

The process of determining the information and communications needs of the project stakeholders:

- Who needs what information?
- When will they need it?
- How will it be given to them?
- Who will give it to them?

While all projects share the need to communicate project information, the needs and methods of distribution can vary. Identifying the informational needs of the stakeholders and determining a suitable means of meeting those needs is an important factor for project success. Communications planning is often tightly linked with organizational planning since the organizational structure will have a major effect on the project's communications requirements. The majority of communications planning is usually done in the early phases of the project; however, the process results should be regularly reviewed and revised as appropriate.

The project communications variable is broken down into the following components: communications planning, information distribution, performance reporting and managing stakeholders. Project communication is a project variable that consists of orchestrating timely, accurate, and concise distribution of project data and updates to the appropriate people. The goal of project communication is to make sure everyone involved in a project has the information they need to fulfill their responsibilities.

A project's success or failure depends largely on the quality of communication within the project team, within the project's parent organization, and outside the project, with contractors and vendors. The smallest breakdown in communication can result in project failure. Therefore, project communication should be a priority during project planning and throughout project execution.

Communications Requirements

Once you have identified a project's stakeholders, the next step is to determine what their information requirements are. When determining information requirements, it is helpful to answer the following questions:

- Who is responsible for which project activities?
- Where are the stakeholders located?
- When do stakeholders want information?
- How often do stakeholders want information?
- What kinds of information do stakeholders want?

Communications Technology

Once you have determined what information the project's stakeholders need, you must decide how to get them the necessary information. The means of communication depends on such things as proximity of stakeholders, their level of involvement in a project, and the type of information they both need and want. Factors that may affect the project include: frequency need of the information, available technology, expected project staffing, and length of the project.

For example, if project team members work in close proximity to each other, then hardcopy reports, e-mail messages, meetings and telephone calls are appropriate. If stakeholders want to see progress reports but are thousands of miles from the project site, then reports can be faxed or e-mailed to them.

Stakeholder Analysis

Conducting a stakeholder analysis enables you to identify all project stakeholders. It should consider methods and technologies suited to the project that will provide the information needed to ensure that resources are not wasted on unnecessary information or inappropriate technology. You must also consider information distribution when considering or defining stakeholders.

Communications Management Plan

The communications management plan outlines the roles and responsibilities of project participants in the review, approval and dissemination of information about key project processes, events, documents and milestones. The communications management plan is the output of the communications planning process and is a subsidiary component of the project plan.

The communications management plan should contain and provide the following information:

- What methods will be used for gathering and storing various information
- Who should receive the information and how will it be sent
- A description of the information to be distributed including formats and content
- Schedules showing when each type of communication will be produced
- A method for updating the communications plan

The Communications Management Plan is a subsidiary element of the overall project plan. It may be formal/informal, highly detailed or broadly framed depending on project needs.

A preliminary Communications Plan should be developed early in the project. The basic steps are as follows:

1. Identify the project audience(s) - include internal and external stakeholder groups.
2. Assess information needs - determine what groups need to know, want to know, and expect, taking into consideration frequency and length of involvement of each audience and organizational standards of practice. NOTE: Project resources should be expended only on communicating information that contributes to success or where a lack of communication can lead to failure.
3. Identify information sources and assign responsibility for collecting information to be communicated.
4. Identify the best media and methods available for use on the project, e.g. meetings, presentations, e-mail - remember people absorb information in different ways.
5. Identify key messages, announcements, and/or marketing that needs to be delivered and can or should be included with routine or recurring communications.
6. Define when and how communications will be provided.
7. Document the approval process needed for any of the communications.
8. Assign responsibilities for creating and delivering the various types of communications.
9. Identify all triggers, such as key events/milestones/deliverable dates that will initiate communications.
10. Define a process for handling ad hoc inquiries the project is likely to encounter.
11. Develop a library of project information and assign responsibilities for its maintenance.
12. Create internal and external feedback loops to help evaluate the effectiveness of communications as well as other project management processes.
13. Schedule the work of communications and related triggers into the project schedule to ensure they are part of the overall plan.
14. Define a process for updating/changing the Communications Plan.

Every project should go through all 14 steps at least one time. The steps should be revisited as a project progresses. Projects with long implementation timeframes should go through the steps multiple times, revising and updating the Communication Plan each time. Any significant change in a project should prompt a review of the Communications Plan. Communication is a key success factor for almost all projects.

Like other project management artifacts, the Communications Plan is scaleable. The plan for a very large or high risk project may be quite complex. More stakeholders will mean more information needs and that may mean more delivery mechanisms. There may be several individuals with responsibilities for the different types of communications required by a project.

There may be many steps involved in the process of developing and approving communications on a large project in order to ensure communication is accurate, effective, and sensitive to the needs of the project. Highly visible projects may require separate public information or communications expertise.

Most projects will require some form of both internal and external communication on a regular basis to sustain momentum on the project and to fulfill organizational reporting requirements. For small projects that have only a handful of stakeholders who are intimately familiar with all project details, it may be sufficient to provide a standard status report to all stakeholders on a regular basis. Be sure to include an open invitation for feedback on even such small projects.

Communication Channels

As the scope of a project grows, it is also natural in most cases for the size of the project team to grow. In fact, it is known that the number of possible communication channels among project team members is determined by the following formula: $(n^2 - n) \div 2$ where "n" represents the number of people on the team. Know this formula!

Using the formula above—$(n^2 - n) \div 2$—we could calculate the communication channel for the picture above. Based on the formula and information given $(5^2 - 5) \div 2 = (25 - 5) \div 2 = 20 \div 2 = 10$ different communication channels.

A sample exam question may be similar to this: If you have a communication team with five members and you add four more people to the team, how many additional communication channels were added?

Such a mathematical relationship is known as a geometric series. In ordinary language this simply means that as team size grows, the number of potential communication channels grows at greater than a linear rate. Although not everyone on the team needs to communicate with everyone else on each type of communication, the potential exists to overwhelm the team with communication requirements. Accordingly, the larger a team grows the more important it is for the project manager to reorganize the team structure to enhance formal communications.

There is an easy way to handle this on the exam if you do not want to memorize the mathematical formula. When it comes to communications channels, think of it as a game of connecting the dots. All you need to do is draw a circle to represent each participant in the communications loop. Let's say there are four members in the communications loop. You draw the line from the first circle over to the other three, then from the second to the remaining two, and from the third to the remaining one. What you wind up with is a series of lines connecting them. That series of lines represents the number of communications channels that must exist, and is the same as the formula $(n^2 - n) \div 2$.

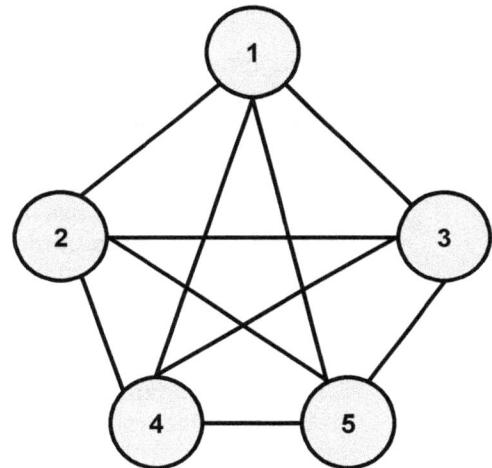

Figure 14 - Communication Channel

Risk Management Planning (11.1)

Risk management planning must be done during the whole life of the project. In the beginning of the conceptual stage of the project, risks are identified almost without effort as the different aspects of the project. It is important that when these risks are thought of, they are recorded and placed in a risk management file or folder so that they can be dealt with later in the project.

As time goes by and progress is made on the project, the risks need to be reviewed, and the identification process must be repeated for the discovery of new risks. This must be an ongoing, continuous process. Risks that are identified early in the project may change as time goes by. As the project advances, some risks will disappear and other risks that were not thought of earlier will be discovered. As the possibility of the risk approaches, the risk needs to be reevaluated to be sure that the assessment of the risk made earlier is still valid.

The output of this process is the project's risk management plan, which is prepared with the assistance of the project manager, project team leaders, and other key stakeholders as needed.

The risk management plans includes:

- **Risk Management Methodology** - defines the approaches, tools, and data sources used to perform risk management on this project. Different types of assessments may be appropriate, depending upon the project stage, amount of information available, and flexibility remaining in risk management.
- **Roles and Responsibilities of Team Members** - Defines the lead, support, and risk management team membership for each type of action in the Risk Management Plan. Risk management teams organized outside of the project office may be able to perform more independent, unbiased risk analyses of project than those from the sponsoring project team.
- **Detailed Qualitative and Quantitative Analyses** - This area includes identified project risk probabilities and impacts. The process of assessing the impact and likelihood of identified risks. This includes results from qualitative and quantitative analyses.
- **Schedule of Risk Management Activities** - Defines the frequency and duration of the risk management process, and when it will be performed throughout the project life cycle. Results should be developed early enough to affect decisions. The decisions should be revisited periodically during project execution.
- **Risk Threshold Criteria** - the threshold criteria for risks that will be acted upon, by whom, and in what manner. The project manager, customer, and sponsor may have a different risk threshold.
- **Risk Documentation Procedures** - Documents how all facets of risk activities will be recorded for the benefit of the current project, future needs, and lessons learned. Documents if and how risk processes will be audited.
- **Risk Ranking/Scoring Techniques** - The ranking/scoring methods appropriate for the type and timing of the qualitative and quantitative risk analysis being performed. Methods and scoring of the various risk components must be determined in advance to ensure consistency.

Risk Identification (11.2)

Risk identification is the responsibility of all members of the project team. The project manager is responsible for tracking risks and for developing contingency plans that address the risks identified by the team. Sometimes a risk identification brainstorming session can help in the initial identification process. Such meetings help team members understand various perspectives and can help the team better understand the big picture.

Risk identification involves determining which risks might affect the project and documenting their characteristics. Participants in risk identification generally include as many of the following as possible: project team, risk management team, subject matter experts from other parts of the organization, customers, end users, other project managers, stakeholders, and outside experts. Risk identification is an iterative process. The first iteration may be performed by a part of the project team, or by the risk management team.

The entire project team and primary stakeholders may make a second iteration. To achieve an unbiased analysis, persons who are not involved in the project may perform the final iteration. Often, simple and effective risk responses can be developed and even implemented as soon as the risk is identified.

Risk identification is a recurring event; it is not performed once and then set aside. The risk identification process begins in the Project Initiation Phase, when initial risk areas are identified. During the Planning Phase, risks and mitigation measures are identified and documented. During the resource allocation, scheduling, and budgeting processes, associated risk planning is also documented.

Risk identification, management, and mitigation continues after the Project Initiation Phase throughout the life of the project. New risks develop as the project matures and external and internal situations change. When the probability of a risk event increases or when a risk becomes a reality and the project manager must deal with a real problem, re-planning occurs. At this point, the project manager and project team develop strategies that assess the impact of the risk event. This re-planning results in budget, schedule, or resource changes for completion of the project.

Risk identification involves recognizing and classifying all of the areas of potential risk related to a project. The attention to detail used when performing risk identification determines how effectively project risks can be managed. This process involves identifying three related factors:

1. Potential sources of risk
2. Possible risk events
3. Risk symptoms.

The timing of risk identification is also important. PMI® advocated that risk identification should first be accomplished at the outset of the project and then updated regularly throughout the project life cycle. It is an iterative process.

Information Gathering Techniques

- **Brainstorming** - This is probably the most used technique in the risk identification process. Its goal is to obtain a comprehensive list of potential risks that can be addressed later in the risk process. Brainstorming is useful in generating any kind of list by pulling out the ideas and thoughts of the participants. After the brainstorming process, risks are categorized by type, and their definitions are sharpened.

- **Delphi Technique** - This method relies on gathering expert opinions through the following process. A group of experts are asked to provide answers to a list of questions. The experts work individually and are often not even physically present in the same location. The answers from all the experts are combined and summarized, and the information is provided to everyone. The process is repeated until some reasonable consensus emerges from the group. Historical experience has shown that some degree of consensus usually emerges after about three rounds.
- **Interviewing** - The person responsible for risk identification identifies the appropriate individuals, briefs them on the project, and provides background information such as the WBS and any assumptions. Interviewees then identify risks based on their experience, project information, and other sources they may find useful.
- **Root Cause Identification** - Helps identify what, how and why something happened, thus preventing recurrence. Root causes are underlying, are reasonably identifiable and can be controlled by management.
- **Strengths, Weaknesses, Opportunities, and Threats (SWOT) Analysis** - A strengths, weaknesses, opportunities, and threats (SWOT) analysis also may be conducted to increase the breadth of risks considered. SWOT analysis is a simple framework for generating strategic alternatives from a situation analysis. It accomplishes this by assessing an organizations strengths (what an organization can do) and weaknesses (what an organization cannot do) in addition to opportunities (potential favorable conditions for an organization) and threats (potential unfavorable conditions for an organization). SWOT analysis is an important step in planning and its value is often underestimated despite the simplicity in creation. The role of SWOT analysis is to take the information from the environmental analysis and separate it into internal issues (strengths and weaknesses) and external issues (opportunities and threats). Once this is completed, SWOT analysis determines if the information indicates something that will assist the firm in accomplishing its objectives (a strength or opportunity), or if it indicates an obstacle that must be overcome or minimized to achieve desired results (weakness or threat).

Other Risk Identification Tools and Techniques

- **Checklists** - These can be developed based on historical information and knowledge from previous projects. Be aware of the advantages of checklists (quick and simple) and disadvantages (it is impossible to ensure all risks are covered in the checklist and it may limit its users). Take care to explore items on the checklist before using it to make sure the checklist is relevant for the specific project. Also note that if checklists are used, they should be reviewed and updated as appropriate during the closing stages of the project.
- **Assumption Analysis** - Explores the validity of the assumptions on which the project is based.
- **Diagramming Techniques** - Cause-and-effect or fishbone diagrams and system or process flowcharts are discussed in Chapter 6. Influence diagrams that show graphically causal influences, time ordering of events, or other relationships among variables and outcomes also can be used.

Risk Identification Output

The risk register is the output of this process. The assessment and management of risk are (respectively) recorded and monitored using a risk register. The Risk Register records identified risks according to probability of risk, likely impact. The Risk Register should contain the following information as a minimum:

- Risk Reference - this should be a unique reference code for the risk. This will be essential to ensure that no risks are missed and will act as a key where risks are escalated
- Description - should describe the nature of the risk and how the risk will impact on the project. When identifying and describing risk you should think in terms of the following, or similar phrases to express the risk in terms of threat and impact (or cause and effect) - i.e.
    - 'There is a risk of/that........ which may result in ......'; or,
    - 'There is a threat of .... which may result in ....';
- Owner - This is the person who carries the responsibility for ensuring that the risk is monitored and, where appropriate, effectively managed. They might not be the person who has to do the necessary tasks, but they must be continuously aware of the risk status;
- Proximity - Timing of the threat of the risk. Is the threat strongest at a particular point in time? (i.e. certain period, date etc?) Does the threat disappear sometime in the future? Or does the probability or impact change over time?
- Risk Responses - Risk response measures should be represented on the relevant project plan as they require activity and consume resource – as above risk should be re-assessed to see if either probability or impact has been reduced by the identified/deployed counter-measure and assessed residual risk should be recorded/shown on the risk register;
- Target Date or Trigger - Timing by which risk responses needs to be started (or completed) based on what it is and how it will address the risk - e.g. contingency actions will identify the trigger that would warrant the plan being invoked. Other actions may need to be undertaken at a specific point in time.

Here is a trick that may help you. PMI® argues that risk identification should first be accomplished at the outset of the project. So you may run into a question that asks, when should we first do risk identification? The answer is, throughout the entire project. Good project managers do risk identification constantly. However if the question is phrased as, when should we first do risk identification? The answer is, at the concept phase, at the very beginning of the project.

Qualitative Risk Analysis (11.3)

The qualitative risk analysis process prioritizes risks according to their potential effect on project objectives. Qualitative risk analysis is one way to determine the importance of addressing specific risks and guiding risk responses. The time criticality of risk-related actions may magnify the importance of a risk.

Qualitative risk analysis requires that the probability and consequences of the risks be evaluated using established qualitative analysis methods and tools. Qualitative risk analysis should be revisited during the project's life cycle to stay current with changes in the project risks. This process can lead to further analysis in quantitative risk analysis or directly to the risk response planning step.

Inputs to qualitative risk analysis include the risk management planning information developed in step 1, which includes project complexity and technology maturity, data precision techniques, measurement scales, organizational risk factors, and risk assumptions. The potential project risks identified in step 2 and any other pertinent information that would help in the qualitative risk analysis process are also inputs.

Tools and techniques for performing qualitative risk analysis include a probability/impact matrix – which is a matrix that assigns risk ratings (very low, low, moderate, high, and very high) to risks or conditions based on combining probability and impact scales. Risks with high probability and high impact are likely to require further analysis, including quantification, and aggressive risk management. The risk rating is accomplished using a matrix and risk scales for each risk.

PMI® suggests that a probability and impact matrix be constructed to assign a risk rating such as very low, low, moderate, high, and very high to risks and risk conditions based on combining probability and impact scales. A risk's probability scale falls between 0.0 or no probability to 1.0 or certainty. The impact scale reflects the impact of the risk on the project objectives. The intent is to assign a relative value to the impact on the project objectives if the risk occurs. The probability and impact matrix is a common way to combine two dimensions to determine whether a risk is considered very low, low, moderate, or high. The risk score or risk exposure helps put the risk into a category that will guide risk response actions.

Figure 15 - Risk Probability Scale

Risk probability assessment may be difficult because of dependence on expert judgment. It should be noted that risk impact assessment can be done using ordinal scales (very high to very low) or cardinal scales (either linear or non-linear). Risk rating matrix can be prepared by combining the probability and impact scales. Risks with high probability and high impact require either further analysis by quantification or aggressive risk management.

Qualitative risk analysis can produce the following results:

- An overall risk ranking for the project. Risk ranking may indicate the overall risk position of a project relative to other projects by comparing the risk scores. This rating can be used to assign personnel or other resources to projects with different risk rankings, to make a cost-benefit analysis decision about the project, or to support a recommendation for project initiation, continuation, or cancellation.
- Prioritized risks. Risks and conditions can be prioritized by a number of criteria. These include rank (very low, low, moderate, high, and very high) or work breakdown structure level, such as Phase, Activity, and Task. Risks may also be grouped by those risks that require immediate attention and those that can be handled in a later part of the project.

Quantitative Risk Analysis (11.4)

The quantitative risk analysis process aims to analyze numerically the probability of each risk and its consequence on project objectives. Quantitative risk analysis should be performed after qualitative risk analysis. Quantitative risk analysis should be performed for identified risks that require precise probability and impact measures; risks where the quantitative data is readily available; risks associated with large scale projects requiring such data, or for risks identified on projects that are predetermined to be of high risk.

Quantitative risk analysis uses techniques such as Monte Carlo simulation and decision analysis to:

- Determine the probability of achieving a specific project objective
- Quantify the risk exposure for the project, and determine the size of cost and schedule contingency reserves that may be needed
- Identify risks requiring the most attention by quantifying their relative contribution to project risk, via a risk rating
- Identify realistic and achievable cost, schedule, or scope targets

In order to quantify risks, a quantitative value must be assigned to each weighting factor. One such scale may use the following:

- Very low = 10 percent (.1)
- Low = 30 percent (.3)
- Moderate = 50 percent (.5)
- High = 70 percent (.7)
- Very high = 90 percent (.9)

Examples of software development risk factors

Project Size:

- Low = less than 10,000 lines of source code
- Medium = 10,000 to 100,000 lines of source code
- High = more than 100,000 lines of source code

Project Effort:

- Low = less than 1 person year
- Medium = 1 to 10 person years
- High = more than 10 person years

Project Cost:

- Low = less than $100,000
- Medium = $100,000 to $1,000,000
- High = more than $1,000,000

You will be heavily tested on the common tools used for quantifying risk. You do not have to perform any complex calculations; however, you must be familiar with the concepts as presented in the PMBOK® Guide and in the following review.

Interviewing

Interviewing techniques are used to help quantify the probability and consequences of risks on project objectives. An interview with project stakeholders and subject matter experts may be the first step in quantifying risks. The information needed depends upon the type of probability distributions that will be used.

Documenting the justification of the risk ranges is an important component of the risk analysis because it can lead to effective strategies for risk response in the risk response planning process.

Sensitivity Analysis

Sensitivity analysis helps to determine which risks have the most potential impact on the project. Sensitivity analysis examines the extent to which the uncertainty of each project element affects the objective being examined when all other uncertain elements are held at their baseline values.

Statistical Independence

The concept of statistical independence is a necessary condition for the use of tools such as expected value and decision-tree analysis. A practical definition of statistical independence is that two events are said to be independent if the occurrence of one is not related to the occurrence of the other.

If events are occurring at random, they are independent; if events are not occurring at random, they are not independent. A set or group of possible events are said to be mutually exclusive and collectively exhaustive if they are all independent, and the sum of their probabilities of occurrence is 1.0. This is the basic notion behind expected value.

Expected Monetary Value (EMV)

Expected monetary value (EMV) is a mathematical formula that can help make comparisons between a range of uncertain outcomes.

$EMV = P \times O$

P = Probability and O = Outcome

For example a risk has a 75% chance of occurring and may cost $1,000

The EMV of the risk is: $0.75 \times \$1,000$ so EMV = $750

Decision-Tree Analysis

A decision analysis is usually represented in the form of a decision tree. The decision tree is a diagram that describes a decision under consideration and the implications of choosing one of the available alternatives. It incorporates probabilities of risks and the costs or rewards of each logical path of events and future decisions. Solving the decision tree indicates which decision yields the greatest expected value to the decision maker when all the uncertain implications, costs, rewards, and subsequent decisions are quantified.

The following image depicts a decision tree. In order to make this decision correctly, one must determine whether it is more important to arrive on time or to travel economically. In this example, the decision to fly results in an expected value of $410 (-$300 + (.85 X $800) + (.15 X $200), while the decision to drive results in an expected value of $500 (-$150 + (.75 X $800) + (.25 X $200). In this case, the decision to drive would be made, baring other factors.

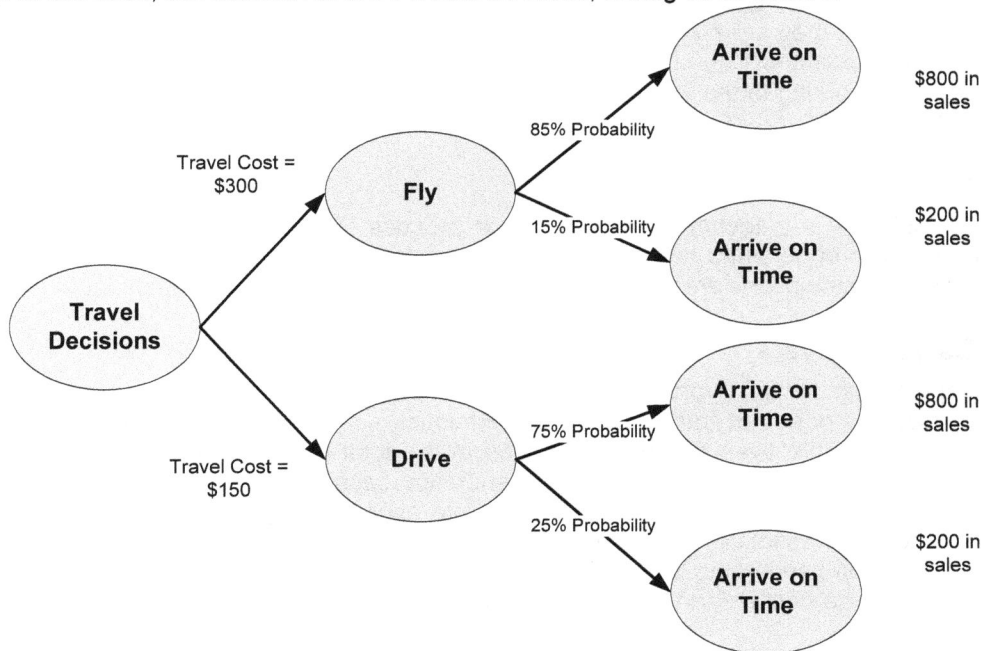

Figure 16 - Decision-Tree Analysis

Decision-Tree Analysis Guidelines

- A box represents a decision; circles represent events with multiple possible outcomes.
- The primary decision (root decision) you are evaluating is placed at the left side of the decision tree, and the tree is drawn from that root.
- Find the most advantageous path at each decision node (box). What makes a path advantageous—lowest cost, greatest return, and so on depends on the specific situation.
- Draw all possible paths for the scenario.
- Place dollar values on each path segment if appropriate.
- Place probabilities on the path segments leading from events. Decision nodes have no probabilities associated with their alternatives.
- Determine the risk values for each path segment by multiplying all probabilities to the left of the segment (including any probability for the segment itself) by each other and then by the dollar value of the segment (if any).
- For each decision node, determine the most advantageous path by adding the risk values for the alternatives. You must work from right to left. Determine the paths for the rightmost decision nodes, and then work
- Your way to the left. The reason for choosing one path is that the paths are mutually exclusive; you can only choose one path.
- For event nodes, consider each path and add the results. The reason for including all paths is that they are mutually inclusive; that is, together they form the entire universe of possible outcomes.
- Continue working to the left until you can determine the most advantageous path for your root decision.

Simulation

A project simulation is a technique to emulate a process. Simulation is usually conducted a number of times to understand the process better and to measure its outcomes under different situations. Project simulations are typically performed using the Monte Carlo technique.

Monte Carlo Analysis

The concept of simulation, typically using Monte Carlo analysis, is also tested. A project simulation uses a model that translates the uncertainties specified at a detailed level into their potential impact on objectives that are expressed at the total project level. One crucial point is that Monte Carlo analysis is considered a superior approach to analyzing the schedule when compared to CPM. This is true because CPM fails to account for path convergence and, as a result, tends to underestimate project durations. Another important point is that the choice of statistical distribution used in the Monte Carlo routine can have important effects on the results of the simulation. For a cost risk analysis, a simulation may use the traditional project WBS as its model.

When it comes to risk quantification, you are going to deal with the idea of statistical independence. That is, what risks do not relate to each other? Their probabilities do not change based on the occurrence of other risks. With statistical dependence one risk leads to another. That is when risks are statistically dependent.

For expected value understand that it is the probability multiplied by the impact. That is the basics of expected value. For example, there is a 10 percent probability that your car will be in an accident costing $10,000. Ten percent of $10,000 is $1,000. That is the expected monetary value of that accident.

Monte Carlo analysis and path convergence: Path convergence goes back to the issue of statistical dependence and independence. You have all three paths. All three paths in the network are critical. Draw three lines going into a single point. It could be the finish node of your project. You have three lines. The first line is a first path, and it has a probability of on-time completion of 40 percent. The second has path has probability of on-time completion of 40 percent. The third has a probability of on-time completion of 20 percent. What are the odds that you are going to complete those three paths, which are all critical, in time to bring in the project on time?

To do that you need to recognize that they are statistically dependent. All three have to be done on time for the project to be done on time. Thus, you multiply the probabilities: 40 percent times 40 percent is 16 percent and 20 percent of 16 percent is 0.032 or 3.2 percent. That means there is only a 3.2 percent probability that all three paths are going to get completed on time. That is the idea of path convergence, and it is generally applied when you do multiple simulations of a project.

Utility Theory

Utility theory is an attempt to infer subjective value, or utility, from choices. Utility theory can be used in both decision making under risk (where the probabilities are explicitly given) and in decision making under uncertainty (where the probabilities are not explicitly given). Extensions of utility theory include subjective probability as well as distortions of probability. There are three traditions in utility theory. One attempts to describe people's utility functions and is called the descriptive approach. Another attempts to use utility in the construction of a rational model of decision making and is called the normative approach. The third attempts to bridge the descriptive and normative approaches by considering the limitations people have with the normative goal they would like to reach; this is called the prescriptive approach.

Risk Response Planning (11.5)

Risk response planning is the process of developing options and determining actions to reduce threats to the project's objectives. Risk Response Planning includes the further identification and assignment of individuals or teams to take responsibility for each agreed upon risk response.

Risk response planning must be appropriate to the severity of the risk, cost effective in meeting the challenge, timely, realistic within the project context, agreed upon by all parties involved, and owned by a responsible person. Selecting the best risk response from several options is often required.

Strategies for dealing with negative risks or threats:

- Risk Avoidance - is changing the project plan to eliminate the threat of a specific risk event. Although the project team can never eliminate all risk events, some specific risks may be avoided. Creativity is often required in order to come up with proper risk avoidance strategies.

- Risk Transference/Deflection - is seeking to shift the consequence of a risk to a third party via a contract provision with a third party, through an insurance policy, or a vendor warranty. This third party also takes ownership of the risk response. It is important to note that transferring the risk to another party does not eliminate it.
- Risk Mitigation - is reducing the probability and/or the consequences of an adverse risk event to an acceptable threshold. It is commonly known that taking early action to reduce the probability of a risk occurring or its impact on the project is more effective than trying to repair the consequences after it has occurred. Mitigation costs should be appropriate, given the likely probability of the risk and its potential consequences.
- Risk Acceptance - this is a risk response strategy that prepares for, and deals with, the consequences of a risk event – either actively (developing a contingency plan) or passively (accepting the consequences). There is no plan on the part of the team to take action on this risk.

Contingency Planning

Contingency plans are developed as a result of a risk being identified. Contingency plans are predefined action plans that can be implemented if identified risks actually occur. If a risk event actually occurs, the contingency plan may need to be implemented and contingency reserves allocated, depending on the risk's impact.

As a guideline, contingency plans may initially be developed for the top five risks associated with a project, but don't forget to monitor the remaining identified risks further into the project. For large projects, the top five risks of each major subsystem may be actively tracked. To properly implement a contingency plan, a contingency reserve is usually required where dollars and/or time are held by the project manager to apply to the execution of a contingency plan. Without maintaining a contingency reserve, the project manager is forced to go back for additional time or dollars for every risk as it becomes a problem. It is far more desirable to maintain a level of contingency reserve where problems can be dealt with from within the original budget and schedule of the project.

There are some situations where nothing can realistically be done to prevent or deal with a risk. In this case, the project must be managed in such a way that the probability of the event occurring is minimized. If the event does occur, the project manager must re-plan the project and include the effect of the risk event.

Strategies for Positive Risks or Opportunities

The following options are intended to deal with potentially positive impacts on project objectives:

- Exploit - This type of strategy may be selected for risks with positive impacts where the organization wishes to ensure the opportunity is realized. This strategy seeks to remove the confusion associated with a particular upside risk by making the opportunity definitely happen.
- Share - Sharing a positive risk involves allocating ownership to a third party who is best able to capture the opportunity for the benefit of the project.
- Enhance - This strategy changes the "size" of an opportunity by increasing probability and/or positive impacts, and by identifying and maximizing key drivers of these positive-impact risks.

Plan Purchases and Acquisitions (12.1)

Plan purchases and acquisitions is a process of identifying what goods or services you are going to purchase from outside of the organization. Part of what you will accomplish in this process is determining whether you should purchase the goods or services at all, and if so, how much and when.

During this step, the project manager is responsible for describing the subcontract procurement need in terms of specification. Specification is a precise description of a physical item, procedure, service, or result for the purpose of purchase and/or implementation of an item or service.

In addition to remembering the above definition of project procurement, you should also know who on the project team is primarily responsible for creating the project specification. The project manager is responsible for ensuring that the job gets done but must rely on the technical people to do the work. In identifying the need, the project manager also determines whether it is more advantageous to make or buy the needed item or service.

Contract Categories and Risks

PMI® places a great deal of emphasis on types of contracts and the assignment of risk between buyer and seller. Contract type selection is a tool and technique in plan purchases and acquisitions. The buyer's objective is to place maximum performance risk on the seller while maintaining incentive for economical and efficient performance. The seller's objective is to minimize risk while maximizing profit potential.

PMI® recognizes three broad categories of contracts: fixed-price or lump-sum contracts, costs-reimbursement contracts, and time-and-materials (T&M) contracts. They are defined as follows:

- Fixed-price or Lump-sum - These contracts set a specific, firm price for the goods and/or services rendered. The buyer and seller agree on a well-defined deliverable for a set price. In this kind of contract, the biggest risk is borne by the seller. Fixed price contracts are usually used for projects that will take a long time to complete and have a high value to the company. This is the most common contract type, because it is best suited for situations with reasonably definite specifications and relatively certain costs.
- Cost-reimbursement - These types of contracts are as the name implies. The costs associated with producing the goods or services are charged to the buyer. All of the costs the seller takes on during the project are charged back to the buyer, thus the seller is reimbursed. Cost reimbursable contracts carry the highest risk to the buyer, as the total costs are uncertain. Three common types of cost-reimbursable contracts are cost-plus-percentage of cost (CPPC) also known as a cost-plus-fee (CPF) contract, cost-plus-fixed Fee (CPFF), and cost-plus-incentive Fee (CPIF).
- Cost-plus-percentage-of-cost (CPPC) - A CPPC contract provides for the reimbursement of allowable costs of services performed plus an agreed-upon percentage of the estimated cost as profit. The seller is only obligated to make its best effort to fulfill the contract within the estimated amount; the buyer funds all overruns. This contract type is prohibited in U.S. federal contracting and is only rarely used in the commercial sector.
- Cost-plus-fixed Fee (CPFF) - A CPFF contract provides for the reimbursement of allowable costs plus a fixed fee paid proportionately as the contract progresses. Although there is a ceiling on the seller's profit, there is no motivation to control costs. Therefore, most risk remains with the buyer. This contract type is used predominantly for research

and development projects in which the effort required remains uncertain until the project is well under way.

- Cost-plus-incentive Fee (CPIF) - A CPIF contract provides for the reimbursement of allowable costs plus a predetermined fee as a bonus for superior performance. If the actual cost is less than the expected cost, the buyer and seller share the savings, based on a predetermined formula. This contract type is used predominantly for projects with long performance periods and substantial hardware development and test requirements.
- Time-and-materials (T&M) - Time and materials contracts are a cross between the fixed price and cost reimbursable contract. The full amount of the material costs is not known at the time the contract is awarded. This resembles a cost reimbursable contract, as the cost will continue to grow during the contract's life. The buyer assumes most of the risk in time and material contracts.

Contract Examples
CPPC:
Estimated cost: $1,000K   Percentage: 10% ($100K)
Estimated total price: $1,100K (Estimated cost + 10%*Estimated cost)
If cost increases to $1,100K the total price would be $1,100K plus 10% of the actual costs = $1,210K.

CPFF:
Estimated cost: $1,000K   Percentage: 10% ($100K)
Estimated total price: $1,100K (Estimated cost + 10%*Estimated cost)
If cost increases to $1,100K the total price would be $1,100K plus 10% of the original estimated costs = $1,200K.

CPIF:
Estimated cost: $1,000K   predetermined fee: $100K
Sharing formula: 85/15 (buyer absorbs 85% of the uncertainty and the seller absorbs 15% of the risk)
Actual cost: $800K Savings: $200K
Seller gets: $800K + $100K + $30K = $930K (Actual cost + Fee + 15%*Savings)
Buyer saves: $170K

FFP: (Lump Sum)
Price: $1,000K
Example A: Actual cost: $700K
Seller makes a profit of $300K (Price - Actual Cost)
Example B: Final cost $1,100K
Seller loses $100K on contract

For the test know the following:
CPPC, CPFF, CPIF, FPI, FFP --- seller's risk moves from low to high
FFP, FPI, CPIF, CPFF, CPPC --- buyer's risk moves from low to high

Contract Origination

To determine the type of procurement documents to develop, the contracting specialists survey potential sellers and originate either a unilateral or a bilateral contract. A contract, as defined by

PMI®, is a mutually binding agreement that obligates the seller to provide a specific product and obligates the buyer to pay for it. A contract is a legal relationship subject to remedy in the courts.

A unilateral contract takes the form of a purchase order—a standardized form listing routine items at standard (for example, vendor catalog) prices. The seller usually accepts the purchase order automatically. Unilateral contracts issued in this way normally do not involve any negotiation and contain relatively low monetary amounts.

A bilateral contract is initiated through a request for quotations, request for proposals, or an invitation for bid. The choice of which bilateral method to use is guided by the following factors:

- An invitation for bid is usually appropriate for routine items when the primary objective is to find the best price. You must be able to clearly and accurately describe the items to be purchased. There are normally no negotiations and, although not an absolute requirement, the lowest bid usually wins.
- A request for quotations is used for relatively low monetary purchases of commodity items.
- A request for proposals is used for complex or nonstandard items of relatively high monetary value.

Contract Incentives

Incentives in a contract provide a "carrot" for the contractor in an attempt to bring the objectives and interests of the contractor in line with those of the buyer. Experience has shown that contract incentives are indeed usually cost effective. Incentives can be structured in a variety of ways and are flexible in that they can be used in conjunction with any of the types of contracts identified by PMI®.

As you read through this information, make sure you recognize what role the project manager has in the process. When it comes to procurement planning, the project manager has a very large role. They are responsible for creating the project specification with our project team. Also be familiar with the make-or-buy analysis—should we actually do this ourselves or should we subcontract the work out?

Another key component of this is trying to determine what the appropriate contract type is for any given project. There are different weights on who is responsible and who is taking the risk associated with each type of contract. The seller takes the greatest risk in firm-fixed-price contracts. By contrast, the buyer is taking the lowest risk in a firm-fixed-price contract.

At the high end of the spectrum, the buyer takes the greatest risk in a cost-plus-percentage-of-cost contract. The lowest risk to the seller occurs in a cost-plus-percentage-of-cost contract. Those contracts are so advantageous to the seller that they are illegal in certain environments, including the United States Federal Government.

You should know the range of risk that goes between the contract types. It goes firm-fixed-price at the lowest; fixed-price-incentive fee is next, then cost-plus-incentive fee, cost-plus-fixed fee, and then finally, cost-plus-percentage-of-cost. That is the range from low risk to high risk for the buyer. By contrast that is the range from high risk to low risk for the seller, and you need to be aware of that dichotomy.

Make-or-Buy Analysis

This is a simple method to determine the cost-effectiveness of creating a product in-house as compared to the cost of buying the product or having it produced outside the organization. All costs, both direct and indirect, should be considered when performing a make or buy analysis. The costs should then be compared with each other with consideration given to any compelling argument on either side by the project team. Consideration should also be given to the potential of leasing versus purchasing items. This could save money for the organization if cost is applied correctly against the useful life of the product or service supplied. Many of the decisions will be based on the length of need for the item or service as well as the overall cost.

Make-or-buy analysis is accomplished during the plan purchases and acquisitions phase (the first phase) in PMI's six-phase approach to procurement management. The purpose is to determine what to procure from outside the project team and when the procurement should occur. You should also be aware of the following key points:

- Make-or-buy analysis should consider both the direct as well as the indirect costs of a prospective procurement. In this context, PMI® considers the indirect costs of buying an item from the outside to include the cost of managing and monitoring the purchasing process. Direct costs such as salaries of full-time project staff are incurred for the exclusive benefit of the project, whereas indirect costs or overhead costs such as executive salaries, insurance, and benefits are allocated to the project by the performing organization as a cost of doing business.
- Make-or-buy analysis should reflect the perspective of the performing organization as well as the project's immediate needs. For example, purchasing a capital item rather than renting or leasing it may not be cost effective. But if the performing organization has an ongoing need for the item, then the portion of the purchase cost allocated to the project may be less than the cost of the rental.

There are several possible decisions that might result from the make-or-buy analysis:

- Procure all or virtually all of the goods and services from a single supplier or from multiple suppliers
- Procure a significant portion of the goods and services from a single supplier or from multiple suppliers
- Procure a relatively minor portion of the goods and services from outside sources (single or multiple suppliers)
- Make everything in house; procure nothing from the outside

Expert Judgment

This process uses the expertise of people from within and outside the organization that have knowledge or training in the area in question to determine what steps should be taken. These people review the needs and the costs and deliver their opinion for consideration in the procurement decision.

Key deliverables (outputs) produced include a procurement management plan and the contract statement of work (SOW). The procurement management plan is a subsidiary element of the project plan and includes such information as follows:

- The type of contract to be used
- The need for independent estimates
- The roles and responsibilities of the organization's procurement department and the project management team
- Where standardized procurement documents are located
- Multiple-vendor management techniques
- How procurement will be integrated into the project life cycle

The SOW describes the procurement item in sufficient detail so that prospective sellers can determine whether they are capable of providing the item. It is a narrative description of the products or services to be supplied under contract.

If the procurement item is presented as a problem to be solved, the SOW may be called a statement of objectives (SOO). Although the SOW is prepared during procurement planning, it may be revised and refined as it moves through the procurement process. Each individual procurement item requires a separate statement of work, but multiple products or services may be grouped as one procurement item in a single SOW. It is important that the SOW be as clear, complete, and concise as possible.

Plan Contracting (12.2)

Plan contracting begins once a project manager has gone through the plan purchases and acquisitions process and decided that resources are needed from outside the project's parent company.

A list of prospective contractors is a good starting point when deciding from which companies you want to procure project resources. Some companies keep lists of contractors they have used in the past. This list generally includes information about the contractors, such as what resources they provide, which contracts they have used and how successfully they fulfilled those contracts. This documentation is collectively called the "procurement documents," which are used to seek proposals from prospective sellers. Procurement documents should be structured to facilitate accurate and complete responses from prospective sellers.

The following should always be included with your procurement documents:

- Statement of Work
- A description of the desired form of response
- Required contractual provisions such as a copy of a model contract or nondisclosure provisions

Procurement Management Plan

The procurement management plan identifies what products and/or services to purchase in support of the statement of work. The plan will define how the relationship between the contracting organization and the contracted vendor will be managed; outline the types of contracts to be used; the evaluation criteria, and the timeframe in which to procure the goods and/or services; ensure that a valid, approved contract is in place before work begins; and defines the acceptance criteria of the goods and/or services to be rendered.

Contract Statement of Work

The statement of work (SOW) is the document which describes in clear understandable term what products and services are to be delivered or services to be performed by the contractor. Preparation of an effective SOW requires an understanding of both the products and services that are needed to satisfy a particular requirement. A SOW prepared in explicit terms will facilitate effective contractor evaluation after contract award. The SOW becomes the standard for measuring contractor performance. Therefore, the SOW must clearly define the work to be performed. In preparing the SOW for a system acquisition, the use of a standardized work breakdown structure as a template for constructing the SOW will help streamline the process. Use of the work breakdown structure will also provide the framework and facilitate a logical arrangement of the SOW elements, provide a convenient checklist to ensure all necessary elements of the program are addressed, and direct the contractor to meet specific contract reporting needs.

Evaluation Criteria

An evaluation criterion refers to the method your organization will use to choose a vendor from the proposals you receive from the solicitation process. Scoring models might be used along with a rating model or system. Sometimes, the evaluation criteria are made public in the procurement process so that vendors know exactly what you are looking for. They may be objective, such as "a supplier needs to be ISO certified," or subjective, such as "the proposed supplier must have documented previous experience with similar projects." When price is not the primary determinant of award, sellers may be evaluated by the following evaluation criteria:

- Understanding of product/project needs
- Technical proficiency

Review Questions

1. The calculated duration for a project is 28.166. The standard deviation is 5.5. What technique would you use to compute the probability of completing a project on a specific day?

   (A) Probability analysis
   (B) Variance analysis
   (C) Error calculation formula
   (D) Monte Carlo simulation

2. Based on historical data, the amount of overtime associated with the design effort of a project is estimated at 100 hours with 0.40 probability, 200 hours with 0.40 probability, and 300 hours with 0.20 probability. What is the expected value of the amount of overtime?

   (A) 160 hours
   (B) 100 hours
   (C) 260 hours
   (D) 180 hours

3. The project team is arguing about the prospective sellers who have submitted proposals. One team member argues for a certain seller while another team member wants the project to be awarded to a different seller. The project manager should remind the team to focus on what item in order to make a selection?

   (A) Procurement audits
   (B) Procurement management plan
   (C) Evaluation criteria
   (D) Procurement documents

4. Which of the following statements are true regarding the scope definition process?

   (A) Scope definition involves identifying specific activities that must be performed to produce the project deliverables.
   (B) Scope definition involves formalizing acceptance of the project scope.
   (C) Scope definition involves subdividing the major project deliverables into smaller, more manageable components.
   (D) Scope definition involves controlling changes to the project scope.

5. All of the following are needed to develop a project estimate except?

   (A) Network diagram
   (B) Work breakdown structure
   (C) Change control procedure
   (D) Risks

6. A project manager has been instructed to use the project charter to help identify risks on the project. This does not make sense to him. If you were asked to explain the reason the project charter is used in this way, what is the BEST explanation?

   (A) The project charter describes the business needs of the project.
   (B) Reviewing what is said and not said in the charter will help determine risks.
   (C) The project charter is issued by management.
   (D) Reviewing the charter will help determine a description of the product of the project.

7. The project manager has completed determining risk response strategies with the team. The team's manager has asked for the amount of risk reserves needed for the project. What is the first thing the project manager should do?

   (A) Prioritize the list of risks.
   (B) Create the risk reserves.
   (C) Determine secondary risks.
   (D) Create the overall risk rating for the project.

8. When should a schedule baseline be created?

   (A) At the end of the project and then ignored because management does not care.
   (B) At the beginning of the project and used to compare schedule performance on status reports.
   (C) At the beginning of the project and used during the project to gauge performance.
   (D) At the end of the project and included in the archive.

9. Which of the following best describes when the team and stakeholders identify risks?

   (A) After the charter is received and before the work breakdown structure is created.
   (B) During scope verification.
   (C) Before the project charter is created.
   (D) Whenever there is a change to the project.

10. A project manager for a large manufacturing concern is working on a project that calls for a new building to be constructed to house a new clean system manufacturing process that is critical to the success of the project. Construction is not a core competency of his company. His team has the ability to create a detailed SOW with penalties if specific statements of work deliverables are not meet. He is in procurement planning evaluating which contract would work the best. Which of the following is best type of contract for this situation?

   (A) FP (Fixed price)
   (B) CPFF (Cost plus fixed fee)
   (C) CPIF (Cost plus incentive fee)
   (D) T&M (Time and materials)

11. A project manager is taking over a project from another project manager while the project is in planning. If the new project manager wants to see what the previous project manager's plans for managing changes to the schedule were, she would look at the:

    (A) communication plan.
    (B) project plan.
    (C) time management plan.
    (D) schedule management plan.

12. All the following are true except?

    (A) The stakeholders do not have a role in determining the project plan unless they are part of the project team.
    (B) Stakeholder management is part of the project plan.
    (C) The project manager needs to determine the skills of the stakeholders.
    (D) The stakeholders' impact on the project must be assessed.

13. A project manager knows that she can delay the start of certain activities within the project schedule to coincide with the mitigation of a known risk. She knows exactly the mitigating task & duration needed, should the risk event occur. She is confident that the finish date will not be impacted by the time delay. Which of the following aspects of schedule development has the project manager used in this situation?

    (A) Her CPM float calculations have revealed those activities that allow sufficient time for the inserted task.
    (B) The project manager's risk management plan was to build in task buffer time to all the project tasks during schedule development in order to cover any risk event occurrence.
    (C) The reliance on her certainty that, for risk planning purposes, assumptions are considered to be true, real, or certain.
    (D) That her CPM probability factors provide her with certainty that there will be activities in the current schedule that will not be performed at all.

14. During activity definition, the team discovers that they do not know enough to define the activities for a work package. What would be the best course of action?

    (A) Define the work package activities at a later date.
    (B) Make a decision based on the information available at the appropriate time.
    (C) Ask the end-user.
    (D) Ask the sponsor.

15. Barriers can influence communication when sending or receiving information. Which of the following is not a barrier?

    (A) Attitudes and emotions
    (B) Feedback
    (C) Personalities and interests
    (D) Prejudices

16. You are a project manager on a US $5,000,000 software development project. While working with your project team to develop a network diagram, you notice a series of activities that can be worked in parallel but must finish in a specific sequence. What type of activity sequencing method is required for these activities?

    (A) Arrow diagramming method
    (B) Precedence diagramming method
    (C) Conditional diagramming method
    (D) Critical path method

17. In a projectized organization the project team:

    (A) has no loyalty to the project.
    (B) will be less interested in the project.
    (C) will not always have a home.
    (D) reports to many bosses.

18. An Activity-On-Node (AON) project diagram shows the following activities on two critical paths, D-E-J-L and D-E-G-I-L. Each activity is at least three days in duration, except for the activity L that is one day in duration. If you are directed to reduce the project by one day, which activities are MOST likely to change?"

    (A) L
    (B) E or J
    (C) G or I
    (D) D or E

19. A project has three critical paths. How does this affect the project?

    (A) It makes it easier to manage.
    (B) It increases the project risk.
    (C) It requires more people.
    (D) It makes it more expensive.

20. You have been recently hired to be a project manager at a bio-tech company to develop a new drug to treat pancreatic cancer. The drug has been under development and clinical testing for the past 5 years. The FDA is currently reviewing the clinical data in order to determine whether the drug has any serious side effects. If the FDA does not approve the drug, the project will be in trouble. This is an example of which of the following types of risks?

    (A) project management risk
    (B) internal risk
    (C) organizational risk
    (D) external risk

21. A resource histogram shows resources by:

    (A) unit of time.
    (B) task.
    (C) area of expertise.
    (D) phase.

22. Your project team identified six related projects with major dependencies on your deliverables. Some of these projects have a very similar scope and may overlap with your deliverables. In light of this, which of the following should you be most concerned about?

    (A) Scope verification
    (B) Communications planning
    (C) Risk response planning
    (D) Scope change control

23. The requirement to complete the project in three months using only four resources is an example of:

    (A) constraints.
    (B) earned value analysis components.
    (C) benefit cost ratios.
    (D) law of diminishing returns.

24. You are the project manager at the Booke Shoppe, a rapidly growing retail bookstore selling hard-to-find books and periodicals. Currently, your company is planning on opening additional stores throughout the United States. Your primary market includes densely-populated, major metropolitan cities. Your company is deciding among New York and Los Angeles. Based on the following data, which project should be recommended using the discounted cash flow technique?

    - Project New York - Make $100,000 in 2 years
    - Project Los Angeles - Make $110,000 in 3 years
    - Assume that the cost of capital is 12%.

    (A) Project Los Angeles since it yields the highest total cash flow.
    (B) Both projects yield the same present value.
    (C) Project Los Angeles since it yields the highest present value.
    (D) Project New York since it yields the highest present value.

25. A project manager for a large manufacturing concern is working on a project that calls for a new building to be constructed to house a new clean system manufacturing process that is critical to the success of the project. Construction is not a core competency of his company. His team has the ability to create a detailed SOW with penalties if specific statements of work deliverables are not meet. He is in procurement planning evaluating which contract would work the best. Which of the following is best type of contract for this situation?

    (A) FP (Fixed price)
    (B) CPFF (Cost plus fixed fee)
    (C) CPIF (Cost plus incentive fee)
    (D) T&M (Time and materials)

26. Barriers can influence communication when sending or receiving information. Which of the following is not a barrier?

    (A) Prejudices
    (B) Attitudes and emotions
    (C) Personalities and interests
    (D) Feedback

27. Which of the following statements is false regarding analogous estimating techniques?

    (A) Analogous estimating uses the duration of a similar activity to determine duration of current activity.
    (B) Analogous estimating is a tool and technique of the activity definition process.
    (C) Analogous estimating is also called top-down estimating.
    (D) Analogous estimating is a form of expert judgment.

28. To manage a project effectively, work should be broken into small pieces. Which of the following does not describe how far to decompose the work?

    (A) Until it cannot be logically subdivided further.
    (B) Until it has a meaningful conclusion.
    (C) Until it can be realistically estimated.
    (D) Until it can be done by one person.

29. The project team is arguing about the perspective sellers who have submitted proposals. One team member is arguing in support of one seller while another team member wants the project awarded to a different seller. What step of the procurement process is the team in?

    (A) Plan Contracting
    (B) Select Sellers
    (C) Request Seller Responses
    (D) Plan Purchases and Acquisitions

30. What is another name for the waiting time between two tasks?

    (A) Float
    (B) Slack
    (C) Lead
    (D) Lag

31. The stakeholders' role and when they will be involved on the project is included in the:

    (A) resource histogram.
    (B) communication plan.
    (C) stakeholder management plan.
    (D) quality plan.

32. The calculated duration for a project is 28.166. The standard deviation is 5.5. What technique would you use to compute the probability of completing a project on a specific day?

    (A) Error calculation formula
    (B) Monte Carlo simulation
    (C) Probability analysis
    (D) Variance analysis

33. While planning the project, you discover that an expert resource might be available to work on your project. However, the resource manager will not commit to the resource being on your team at the present time. Which of the following is the best option to estimate the task:

    (A) as though you had an average resource doing the task.
    (B) as if the expert resource were available.
    (C) using the Delphi technique.
    (D) as if you had an inexperienced resource.

34. Which of the following best describes what lag means?

    (A) The amount of time a task can be delayed without delaying the project.
    (B) The amount of time a task can be delayed without delaying the early start date of its successor.
    (C) Waiting time.
    (D) The product of a forward and backward pass.

35. What does a benefit cost ratio of 2.6 indicate?

    (A) Payback is 2.6 times the cost of the project.
    (B) Profit is 2.6 times the cost of the project.
    (C) Cost is 2.6 times the payback.
    (D) Cost is 2.6 times the profit.

Answers

1. D
2. D
3. C
4. C
5. C
6. B
7. C
8. C
9. D
10. A
11. D
12. A
13. A
14. A
15. B
16. B
17. C
18. D
19. B
20. D
21. A
22. C
23. A
24. D
25. A
26. D
27. B
28. D
29. B
30. D
31. C
32. B
33. C
34. C
35. A

Chapter 6
Executing Process Group

Once a project moves into the Executing Process Group, the Project Team and all necessary resources to carry out the project should be in place and ready to perform project activities. The Project Management Plan is completed and baselined by this time as well. The Project Team's and specifically the Project Manager's focus now shifts from planning the project efforts to participating in, observing, and analyzing the work being done.

The Executing Process Group is where the work activities of the Project Management Plan are executed, resulting in the completion of the project deliverables and achievement of the project objective(s). This Process Group brings together all of the project management disciplines, resulting in a product or service that will meet the project deliverable requirements and the customers need. In this Process Group, elements completed in the Planning Process Group are implemented, time is expended, and money is spent.

This Process Group requires the Project Manager and Project Team to:

- Conduct, coordinate and manage the ongoing work activities
- Perform quality assurance activities continuously to ensure project objectives are achieved
- Monitor identified risks for triggering events and implement containment or contingency strategies as necessary
- Distribute information to project stakeholders

In short, it means coordinating and managing the project resources while executing the Project Management Plan, performing the planned project activities, and ensuring they are completed efficiently.

The Executing Process Group allows the project's deliverables to be produced and the objectives to be met. This Process Group facilitates the completion of the work activities, the expenditure of resources, and the application of the quality assurance processes to ensure that the end product(s) is viable and meets customer requirements.

Several processes are part of this Process Group. They may include:
- Develop Team
- Select Sellers
- Perform Quality Assurance
- Information collection and distribution

The figure below shows how these processes fit into the Executing Process Group.

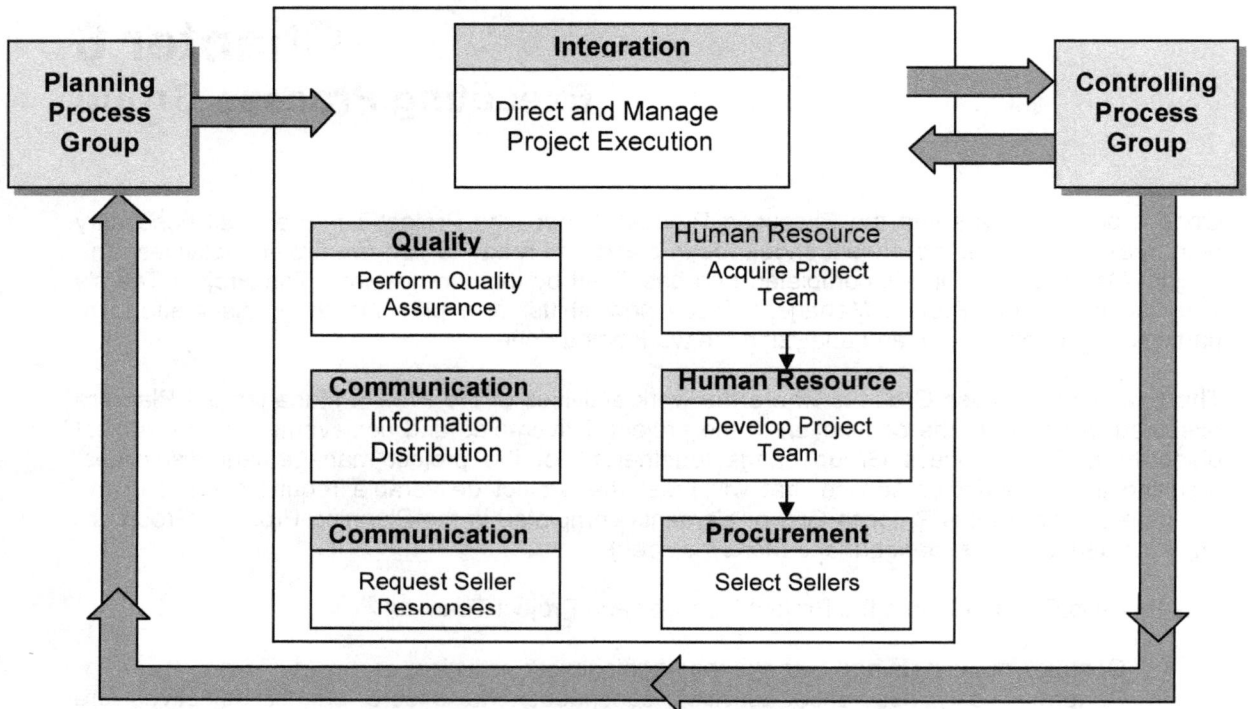

Figure 17 - Executing Process Group Processes

The Execution Process Group involves coordinating and managing project activities and the subsequent output. The focus of the Project Manager and the Project Team is on the day-to-day management of the overall effort. In addition to the processes and activities defined above, the subsidiary management plans are implemented and project performance is monitored and managed accordingly.

Project Plan Execution (4.4)

The inputs to project plan execution are the project plan itself, corrective action, preventive action, change requests, defect repair, and administrative closing procedure. The first three topics have been discussed already, but it is important to note the difference between preventive action and corrective action.

According to the PMBOK®, preventive action is "anything that reduces the probability of potential consequences of risk events." This is a proactive type of management where the project manager considers the risk events that might occur that will in some way hinder the completion of the project. He or she then takes management actions that reduce or mitigate the risks on the project.

Corrective action is "anything done to bring expected future project performance in line with the project plan." Corrective action comes from the various control processes you will have on the project. It is reactive and comes after an event occurs. For the exam, it is a good idea to know the definitions of these two types of actions. They are close in definition, but they are not the same.

A project manager has a specialized set of skills that he or she brings to a project. Areas such as scope management, risk management, quality management, and all of the knowledge areas are specific to project management.

At the same time, the project manager must also have a standard set of skills that you would find with a general manager. It is possible that you will not have training in these particular management skills because many people come to project management from other areas. Some of these skills as finance, sales/marketing, research and development, and various planning types such as strategic and tactical. In addition, the motivational skills and all other HR skills such as team building, communication, leadership, conflict resolution, negotiating, and problem solving are also important to the project manager.

The project manager needs general management skills on almost every project. One of the ongoing problems for project management as an overall profession is that often project managers are elevated to the project manager position because of competency in a technical area. This does not help much in understanding the different skill sets found in general management, but there are certainly a great many resources to read about general management, which is highly recommended for anyone who wants to be as professional as possible.

Product skills and knowledge are also part of the tools and techniques used in project plan execution. Subject matter experts help round out a project by providing specific technical knowledge. The project manager is not necessarily the person with the most knowledge about the technical areas of the project. This is a common mistake that general managers make when choosing a project manager. The job of the project manager is to bring the project to a successful conclusion, not to be a technical expert on all of the aspects of the project.

When putting together a project team, the project manager should always consider what information he or she lacks on the technical side and make sure that the staffing of the project includes one or more people who are technically proficient. But knowing how to project manage is not the same as being able to explain how something on the project works technically. This is an ongoing issue for all project managers. As project management itself is recognized as a profession, more and more organizations will choose project managers based on project management skill sets rather than technical skill sets. That is the reason why PMP® is an important designation. It indicates that you have studied and understand project management as a topic by itself.

Another extremely important tool in project plan execution is the status review meeting. Status review meetings will be discussed at some length in the communication knowledge area, but here are some of the ways you can make a status meeting more productive and useful.

The most important thing you can bring to a status meeting is a prepared agenda. The first step is to send out an email asking all the people scheduled to be at the meeting if they have specific topics that should be on the agenda. After you have gathered that information, you blend it with the topics that you were planning to discuss and send out an agenda a few days before the meeting.

The second step in preparing an agenda is to time every item on it. Give a finite time that will be allowed for discussion of a single topic. The first time you do this, you will get some pushback from people who are used to rambling and taking time to "explore" topics. So your job at the first timed agenda meeting is to cut off discussion after the allotted time has passed. The best way to do this is to give a five-minute warning before the topic is supposed to end. That way, everyone on the team knows that you are watching the time. The first time you do this is often problematic for people not used to time control and the discipline it takes to make meetings effective. But I guarantee that after the people in the status review meetings realize that they will be saving large amounts of time, they will like the control factor.

Not every stakeholder needs to be at every meeting. You may have weekly status meetings for the project core team and bring in other stakeholders only once a month. This helps speed up meetings and makes them effective at the same time.

According to PMBOK®, the outputs from the project plan execution are work results and change requests. Work results are the "outcomes of the activities performed to accomplish the project." You hold your status meetings to discuss work results, and as usual, the work results are measured against the plan baseline. As the project manager, you will manage against the variances seen from the original plan.

Change requests happen during the execution of the project. The changes can be requested on many different parts of the project plan, such as scope, costs, and schedule times. Change requests are natural, and your job as a project manager is to make sure that change requests are kept   under   control.

Perform Quality Assurance (8.2)

Perform quality assurance is a managerial function that addresses all the planned and systematic activities implemented within the quality system to provide confidence that the project will satisfy the relevant quality standards.

Quality assurance refers to project activities that are planned and executed to ensure quality products and services. The goal of quality assurance is the improved quality of a project's processes and improved quality of end products. Any problems encountered during the execution of quality assurance activities must be corrected. Correcting problems can lead to greater efficiency, decreased cost of production, and a higher-quality product.

Quality assurance is important not only because it leads to the correction of problems, but also because it gives customers and project stakeholder's confidence that the finished product will be free of defects.

The following issues and concepts fall under quality assurance:

- **Quality Audits** - This is a process of reviewing specific data at key points of the project's life cycle. The quality audit is a quality assurance tool and technique that serves as a structured review of quality management activities. Its objective is to identify lessons learned that can be used to improve performance on this project or on other projects in the organization.

- **Requested Changes** - Quality improvement includes taking actions to increase the effectiveness and efficiency of the project to provide an added benefit to the project stakeholders. This may require the use of change requests or corrective action.
- **Perform Quality Control** - Quality control is a technical function that involves establishing the technical baseline for the project and then collecting specific data by which to measure conformance to that baseline. Quality control measures are used throughout a project's life cycle to make sure work is done properly and that actual project results match the expectations outlined in the project's quality management plan. During quality control, both the processes used to complete the project, as well as the end product, are examined to make sure they meet quality standards.

The purpose of quality control is to ensure that a finished product has certain quality characteristics and that unacceptable product traits are corrected.

It is important to understand that quality control is not only a component of the quality management variable, but that it is also part of the fourth step of the project management process—project control.

The difference between quality control and quality assurance is that quality assurance focuses on developing and implementing quality-related activities, whereas quality control focuses on ensuring that the quality-related activities achieve their desired effect.

Acquire Project Team (9.2)

The acquire project team process involves obtaining and assigning personnel to perform project activities. The project manager's goal during staff acquisition is to obtain personnel who have the skills that are outlined in the project's staff management plan.

It is important to understand that acquiring staff is a component of the human resource management variable and is also part of the planning step of the project management process. A key input to this process is the staffing pool description.

Before acquiring staff for a project, it is helpful to answer the following questions:
- What type of organizational structure will be used for the project?
- Who should be on the project team?
- What skills would each team member bring to the project?
- Will team members work well together?
- What can result when the project loses a key team member?

Because staff assignments must be negotiated on most projects, negotiating is a principal tool and technique. Negotiation is defined as the art of achieving what you want from a transaction, leaving all other parties involved content that the relationship has gone well. Negotiating for project personnel is not an easy task. The most critical element of successful negotiating is preparation. **NEVER GO INTO A NEGOTIATION PROCESS UNLESS YOU ARE PREPARED**.

Negotiating also relates to the project manager's ability to influence the organization to "get things done," so again, review the definitions for power and politics. PMI® explains that the team's influencing competencies and politics play an important role in negotiating staff assignments. For example, a functional manager may be rewarded based on staff utilization. This in turn creates an incentive for this manager to assign available staff who may not meet all the project's requirements.

Virtual Teams

A team is a small number of people with complementary skills who are committed to a common purpose, performance goals, and approach for which they hold themselves mutually accountable. Generally, teams have from two to twenty-five people. Teams need complementary skills or the right mix of skills to do the job assigned. A team's purpose and performance goals go together. Both must be clear or confusion will likely result. It is important that the team own and commit to the purpose and shape it if necessary. In addition, teams need to develop a common approach or method on how they will work together to accomplish their purpose. Finally, groups become teams when they hold themselves accountable for the outcome.

A virtual team is a group of people who primarily interact electronically and who may meet face-to-face occasionally. Examples of virtual teams include a team of people working at different geographic sites and a project team whose members telecommute.

Strategies for Virtual Teams

- Hold an initial face-to-face startup
- Have periodic face-to-face meetings, especially to resolve conflict and maintain team cohesiveness
- Establish a clear code of conduct or set of norms and protocols for behavior
- Recognize and reward performance
- Use visuals in communications
- Recognize that most communications will be non-verbal -- use caution in tone and language

Benefits of Virtual Teams

- People can work from anywhere at anytime.
- People can be recruited for their competencies, not just physical location.
- Many physical handicaps are not a problem.
- Expenses associated with travel, lodging, parking, and leasing or owning a building may be reduced and sometimes eliminated.

Functions of the Project Manager

- Planning, scheduling, and estimating
- Performance, cost, and trend analysis
- Progress reporting
- Maintaining client/consultant relations
- Logistics management
- Cost control
- Procedure writing and administration
- Interface management (identifying; documenting; scheduling; communicating; and monitoring personnel, organizational, and system interfaces relating to the project)
- Integration of the efforts of project subsystems

- PMI® considers planning, organizing, leading, and controlling the four most important functions of the project manager. Effective management of the dual reporting relationship—a situation in which team members are accountable to both a project manager and a functional manager—generally is the project manager's responsibility.

Roles of the Project Manager

- Integrator
- Communicator
- Team leader
- Decision maker
- Climate creator/builder

Qualifications of the Project Manager

- Works well with others
- Experienced in his or her area of expertise
- Supervisory experience
- Familiar with contract administration
- Able to accurately present the company's position
- A qualified negotiator
- Experience and Education Requirements of the Project Manager
- Formal college education desirable
- Continuing education in topics such as negotiation, conflict management, group dynamics, and leadership
- Experience as a functional manager, or preferably, a project management assistant

Types of Power

According to PMI®, the project manager can exert the following types of power:

- **Legitimate Power** - Legitimate power is derived from the person's formal position within the organization. The project manager's ability to use this power derives from his or her position in the organizational hierarchy and his or her degree of control over the project, as modified by the organizational climate. Use of this power should be in conjunction with expert and reward power whenever possible.
- **Coercive Power** - Coercive power is predicated on fear (for example, a subordinate fears being deprived of something for failing to do what the supervisor asks). The ability to use this power derives from the project manager's control over the project and project personnel.
- **Reward Power** - Reward power involves positive reinforcement and the ability to award people something of value in exchange for their cooperation. The project manager's ability to use this power derives from his or her position in the organizational hierarchy and degree of control over the project.
- **Expert Power** - Expert power can only be exercised by individuals who are held in particular esteem because of their special knowledge or skill. The project manager's ability to use this power derives from reputation, knowledge, and experience.
- **Referent Power** - Referent power is based on citing the authority of a more powerful person (for example, one's supervisor or someone's spouse is the CEO) as the basis for

one's own authority. The project manager's ability to use this power derives from his or her position in the organizational hierarchy.

PMI® recommends that project managers rely on reward and expert power to the greatest extent possible, and that they avoid use of coercive power. Please be aware that in addition to the above list, other project management luminaries have also coined terms to describe forms of power or influence. These terms include:

- **Purse-string Power** - Denotes budget or spending authority held by the project manager
- **Bureaucratic Power** - The ability of the project manager to use the rules and procedures of the organization to maximize personal effectiveness.
- **Charismatic Power** - Power and influence derived from the project manager's personality and persona to encourage people to accomplish things they may not be inclined to do.
- **Penalty Power** - Involves negative reinforcement and the ability to withhold something of value as a response to lack of cooperation or poor performance.

What types of power do we have as a project manager? Legitimate, coercive, reward, expert and referent. The thing that is critical here is to recognize that reward and expert power are the best kinds of power that a project manager can exert. The worst kind, from PMI's perspective, is coercive power—power by virtue of threat.

Developing the Project Team (9.3)

The definition of developing a project team is that it "improves the competencies and interaction of team members to enhance project performance" (PMBOK®). The objectives include improving the skill sets of project team members so that future work will be done more effectively and efficiently and building trust between members of the team so that teamwork is improved. The first objective, improving skill sets, should be done systematically. The skills that need to be improved should be defined so that progress can be seen. It is particularly helpful to write down various milestones in skill development because this will be a part of the recognition of the professional growth of the team member.

The second of these objectives, building trust and cohesiveness, does not have a standard way of operating. There are so many issues involved in getting trust between project team members that the topics could have a separate chapter or even a separate book. It must be said that simply doing a few team exercises will not make the project team better. Building trust and cohesiveness is a lengthy process that does not happen on each project.

For some reason, general management skills are styled "soft skills" in section 9.3.2 of the PMBOK®. I am not certain what makes these skills (discussed at length earlier) "soft." These are usually the skill sets that determine the success of the project. The so-called "hard" skills often concern mathematical or statistical skills. I have yet to meet a person who can look me in the eye and say that getting a person to perform over a period of time is easier than getting a machine to do the same thing. Time to get rid of the pejorative term "soft skills" and start using "people skills" as the alternative.

Training includes activities used to make the project team members better at their project tasks. This can include online training, classroom work, computer-based training, and on-the-job training. The training may be formal, as when an instructor or teacher leads the training, or it may be informal, as when a colleague or mentor does it. In order to see the outcomes of the training, you should first measure the skills you are about to train and then measure them again at the end of the training to be sure that the people have gained something from the training.

Team-building activities are often very difficult to relate to the current project. Being able to do exercises together is not the same as being a good team. It is usually advisable to have professional facilitation.

Ground rules are the baseline rules by which the project will be run. Some of these will be formal, backed by the organization. Others may be informal but may have been put in place by the project team over a period of time or over several different projects. Usually the important ground rules about how to treat each other are not written down but instead are passed down from project to project. The project manager must set an example to make the ground rules work.

Collocation is advisable if at all possible. Having your people in the same place gives face-to-face communication opportunities that are not possible with project team members in different geographical locations. The place where collocated people meet is sometimes call the war room, although recent events in our country make these words a little insignificant compared to the dangers and perils facing our armed services.

The output from developing a project team is the team performance assessment. The project manager and the project management team should do assessments of the project team's performance and focus on the team as a whole. Although it is important to do individual reviews, it is just as important to reward and recognize the team as a whole. Dwight Eisenhower once said, "It does not matter who gets the credit, as long as the team wins."

Information Distribution (10.2)

The information distribution process is clearly intertwined with communication planning. The same quartet of questions applies for distribution as it did in the communication planning processwho, what, when, and how are the questions that need to be answered. Focus on these when determining information distribution needs.

The input to information distribution is the communication management plan. This was described earlier in this chapter.

According to the PMBOK®, the tools and techniques used in information distribution are communication skills, information gathering retrieval systems, information distribution methods, and the lessons learned process. The term "communication skills" has many meanings and dimensions, all of them depending on the context of the communication. In the PMBOK®, the dimensions that are listed are the ability to write and communicate orally, formal and informal reports, and internal and external communication. Another listed dimension is the direction of the communication. This is described as including upward and downward communication as well as horizontal communication. (Horizontal, or lateral, communication occurs between people of equivalent level, such as equal-ranking members of the project team.) Massive amounts of information are available concerning the best ways in which to handle these topics. This is not the place to deliver that information.

The information gathering and retrieval systems may be paper systems, such as filing systems, which are done manually. In this day and age, it is likely that you will have electronic systems available, which will give access to both non-technical information, such as the status of the project, and technical information, such as design specifications and test plans. It is important that all people who should have access to information can actually get to it.

The distribution methods will include any type of channel that will help the project team successfully complete the project. Status meetings are one of the most important means of distributing information. You can determine in advance what needs to be distributed, and having the whole team at the meeting, or at least everyone represented, will give you a way to communicate with all stakeholders at once. You can have paper copies of information to send as well as electronic copies. In addition, you can have databases that can be accessed by appropriate team members that contain information necessary to execute the project. Voice mail may be used, but if it is, be sure not to assume that just because you have left a voice mail, the other party has received and understood it. If you are working with an international team, you may have videoconferencing. This technology does not take the place of having people in the same room, but it can be very helpful if you have information to pass, want to do it in real time, and do not want to spend time traveling. All of the distribution methods should be related to the best way to get information to the project team members so that they can successfully work on the project.

The outputs from information distribution are updates to organizational process assets and requested changes. The changes cited here are changes to the information distribution process. The two outputs have been discussed at length elsewhere in this book.

Request Seller Responses (12.3)

This is the process where bids and proposals are obtained from the prospective sellers. The sellers are responsible for these responses and are the ones putting forth the time and effort to respond.

Inputs to requesting seller responses include organizational process assets, the procurement management plan, and procurement documents. The organizational assets may include information on past performance of sellers that will be relevant to the choosing of a seller for the new project. Some organizations keep this information, and it often helps to pre-select qualified sellers.

The tools and techniques of requesting bidder responses are bidder conferences, advertising, and developing a qualified sellers list. Bidder conferences are meetings with prospective sellers to ensure that they have a clear understanding of the procurement requirements. During these bidder conferences, which are also called vendor or contractor conferences, all potential sellers are invited to bring questions about procurement requirements and discuss them. In some projects, any questions asked in these meetings must be posted to an Internet site so that any vendors not present at the conference will have the same information as those who were at the conference.

Advertising can build the number of potential sellers by getting information out to a large number of vendors. In some government jurisdictions, certain types of procurement items must be advertised publicly. Some government jurisdictions require that any pending government contracts be made public, usually through newspapers, but more and more through websites on which sellers may search for all current open projects.

A qualified sellers list can be developed in many ways. If the organization has lists of current qualified sellers, this list will be the basis for new projects. One thing to remember is that new companies may be offering solutions to your procurement requirements but may not be on your qualified sellers list. In many cases, it is hard to get on this type of list, which can discourage some companies that are highly qualified. Other places to get names for a qualified sellers list can be the Internet, associations, trade catalogues, and directories available in libraries. It is always a good idea to keep these lists updated both by looking at new potential sellers and by weeding out old lists. This will give you a good chance to get the best possible procurement for your organization.

The outputs from requesting seller responses are the qualified sellers list, the procurement document package, and proposals. The proposals are done by the seller and give information that describes the way in which the seller will be able to supply items requested. The seller's proposal is a formal legal offer in response to the buyer's request. There may also be a round of oral explanation. The information given orally is also binding.

The procurement document package is the entire package of materials sent to the sellers by the buyer. The procurement document package is the document set that guides the seller in responding to the buyer's needs.

Select Sellers (12.4)

Selecting sellers is the process where sellers are chosen based on the responses that have been made to requests by the buyer. The sellers' responses are filtered through evaluation criteria that are selected by the buyer, and the final award, which may go to one or several sellers, is made based on these criteria. Often the criteria are weighted so that certain criteria are more important than others. Price is always a criterion unless the project is in response to a massive emergency. In certain types of projects, the technical solutions offered as well as the skill sets of the vendors may be a major factor in determining who will get the contract.

Inputs to selecting sellers include organizational process assets, the procurement management plan, evaluation criteria, procurement document package, proposals, qualified sellers list, and the project management plan. All of these were discussed earlier in the chapter.

The tools and techniques for selecting sellers may include a weighting system, independent estimates, a screening system, contract negotiation, seller rating systems, expert judgment, and proposal evaluation techniques. The weighting system usually assigns a value to each of the evaluation criteria. By summing all of the criteria ratings, you will have a number that gives you one of the major tools for determining who will be the vendor of choice.

Independent estimates are done either by the buyer or by another independent organization. The independent estimates can be compared to the sellers' estimates when responding to the buyer's proposal.

A screening system is tied to the weighting system. In the screening system, go/no-go criteria are established so that a minimum standard is set for the seller. This screens out the sellers that do not have the prerequisites necessary to bid for the project.

Contract negotiation occurs before the final contract is approved and signed. During contract negotiation, various aspects of the contract may be negotiated. When agreement is reached, the final contract is the output of the process.

Rating systems for sellers are tied to both weighting systems and screening systems. The organization puts together its requirements and performance criteria and makes this into a rating system. All the sellers should be rated using the same metrics.

Expert judgment may be used when looking at proposals that contain specialized information. The subject matter expert looks at the portions of the contract that are within his or her specialty area and gives an opinion on the seller's proposal.

Proposal evaluation techniques are a blend of evaluation criteria, screening systems, rating systems, weighting systems, and possibly expert judgment. Various inputs can be used from reviewers of the proposal to build a proposal evaluation system that can be used for multiple projects.

The outputs from selecting sellers are the actual selected sellers, the contract, a contract management plan, issues of resource availability, updates to the procurement management plan, and requested changes. All of these have been discussed previously.

Review Questions

1. Which motivational theorist said that people cannot ascend to the next level until the levels below are fulfilled?

    (A) Deming
    (B) Maslow
    (C) Herzberg
    (D) McGregor

2. Senior management regularly evaluates project performance to maintain confidence in quality product standards. Which of the following best describes this?

    (A) Quality management
    (B) Quality planning
    (C) Quality assurance
    (D) Quality control

3. Employees who believe their efforts will lead to effective performance and expect to be rewarded for their accomplishments remain productive as rewards meet their expectations. This is called:

    (A) a halo effect.
    (B) a motivational theory.
    (C) the expectancy theory.
    (D) a perquisite.

4. A project manager had a complex problem to solve and made a decision about what needed to be done. A few months later, the problem resurfaced. Most likely what did the project manager not do?

    (A) Confirm that the decision solved the problem
    (B) Proper risk analysis
    (C) Use an Ishikawa diagram
    (D) Have the project sponsor validate the decision

5. To accommodate a new project in your department, you need to move resources from one project to another. Because your department is currently working at capacity, moving resources will inevitably delay the project from which you move the resources. You

    (A) Internationalization
    (B) Communication
    (C) Lack of competent programmers
    (D) Cultural influences

6. What theory proposes that efforts will lead to effective performance and will be rewarded for accomplishments?

    (A) Conditional reinforcement
    (B) Maslow's hierarchy
    (C) McGregor's
    (D) Expectancy

7. The management theory that all people can direct their own efforts is:

    (A) Theory Y
    (B) Herzberg's theory
    (C) Maslow's hierarchy
    (D) Theory X

8. At a critical design review meeting for a large project, several important issues surfaced. After hearing about a major technical problem, one of the subcontractor's engineers mentions that he experienced a similar situation on another project; he has some ideas on how to solve the current problem. What type of power is the engineer using?

    (A) Expert
    (B) Referent
    (C) Manipulative
    (D) Experience

9. A project team is worried that the integration of the components of the project will result in uncovering flaws. Instead of continuing their work, they are constantly looking for flaws to try to prevent their system from being the only one found to have flaws during integration. It might be best for the project manager to:

    (A) compromise the situation.
    (B) let management know of the concern.
    (C) tell the team to create quality testing plans.
    (D) smooth the situation.

10. The most appropriate reason to focus on team development is to enhance the ability of the _____ to contribute.

    (A) Team
    (B) Stakeholders
    (C) Project manager
    (D) Management

11. A project team is having difficulty communicating over long distances. There are 13 team members from two countries when five people from India are added. This is of concern to the project manager because:

    (A) it will be harder to use reward power.
    (B) communications grow exponentially.
    (C) conflict can be increased with an increase in project priorities.
    (D) communication blockers grow linearly.

12. A project manager has just been hired and is trying to gain the cooperation of others. What is the best form of power for gaining cooperation under these circumstances?

    (A) Penalty
    (B) Expert
    (C) Legitimate
    (D) Referent

13. Which motivational theory defines the hierarchy of needs?

    (A) McGregor
    (B) Herzberg
    (C) Maslow
    (D) Deming

14. A project team member comes to the project manager during project execution to tell him that they feel the project cannot meet its quality standards. The project manager calls a meeting of the affected stakeholders to work through the problem. Which step of the quality management process is the project manager in?

    (A) Quality assurance
    (B) Quality analysis
    (C) Quality control
    (D) Quality planning

15. All of the following are examples of a benefit from a risk management plan except?

    (A) By managing the plan, you are able to avoid some risks while mitigating the effects of others.
    (B) You are in control of the project as it progresses with few surprises.
    (C) The need for contingency reserves is minimized.
    (D) The need for workarounds is minimized.

16. During project execution, a project manager from the information systems department is trying to complete the project, yet is constantly faced with interference from the manager of the engineering department. The engineering department keeps changing the resources assigned to the project team and its availability. What type of matrix does this represent?

    (A) Strong matrix
    (B) Weak matrix
    (C) Functional matrix
    (D) Tight matrix

17. Emotions are running high during negotiations to purchase major equipment for your project when the seller starts to pack up his things. This an example of which negotiation strategy?

    (A) Fair and reasonable
    (B) Missing man
    (C) Deadline
    (D) Withdrawal

18. You are asked to select tools and techniques to implement a quality assurance program to supplement existing quality control activities. Which of the following would you choose?

    (A) Quality audits
    (B) Statistical sampling
    (C) Pareto diagrams
    (D) Trend analysis

19. When should scope verification be done?

    (A) At the end of the project
    (B) At the beginning of the project
    (C) During each phase of the project
    (D) During planning

20. In which motivation theory do hygiene factors play a part?

    (A) Herzberg's
    (B) McGregor's
    (C) Theory Y
    (D) Maslow's hierarchy

21. You are the seller to develop the software needed for your client's new product. The project is in execution when you discover that the client is going to make a major change. This change will dramatically change the software requirements. What is the BEST thing to do?

    (A) Inform the client of the impact to the project of making such a change
    (B) Stop work on parts of the project that will not change
    (C) Ask the client when the change will be finalized and manage the project accordingly
    (D) Stop work on the software and await instructions

22. You are the project manager for an information technology division of a large financial services firm in the United States. Your company offers a web-based trading platform that provides options and futures trading for the U.S. commodities markets. Due to the rise in popularity of futures and options trading, your company has grown rapidly. To keep up with the demands, you have been assigned the responsibility of upgrading the company's network and computing infrastructure. You were currently in the process of purchasing the necessary network equipment, when a potential problem was identified. Specifically, a network engineer has reported some significant hardware compatibilities problems. To make matters worst, you are experience difficulty coordinating with the various organizational and technical interfaces within the organization and integrating all the various project elements. Which of the following statements are true?

    (A) You are in the integrated change control process.
    (B) You are in the project plan execution process.
    (C) You are in the resource planning process.
    (D) You are in the risk planning process.

23. Your project is behind target for time and budget. Deliverables are passed on as required, but they often come back with problems. This rework is becoming a big problem. What should you do?

    (A) Estimate the costs of the rework and a revised project completion date. Get the stakeholders to sign off on the new timeline and revised budget.
    (B) Try to determine who is failing you and the team.
    (C) Initiate a quality audit.
    (D) Revise the quality management plan.

24. During a team meeting, the team adds a specific area of extra work to the project because they have determined it would benefit the customer. What is wrong in this situation?

    (A) The team is gold plating.
    (B) These efforts shouldn't be done in meetings.
    (C) Nothing. This is how to meet or exceed customer expectations.
    (D) Nothing. The project manager is in control of the situation.

25. The Java development of a project is outsourced to India. The project schedule is starting to slip. What is the least likely cause of the slippage?

    (A) Lack of competent programmers
    (B) Cultural influences
    (C) Internationalization
    (D) Communication

26. You are a project manager for a large electrical system implementation. One of your key resources has started to miss deadlines and work quality is beginning to suffer as well. You are confident that this person is well aware of the work deadlines and required quality specifications. What action should you take?

    (A) Report the problem to HR for corrective action
    (B) Reassign some work to other team members until performance starts to improve
    (C) Meet with the employee in private and try to determine the factors impacting performance
    (D) Escalate the situation to the employee's functional manager and ask for assistance

27. Your project team is composed of six chemists and two administrative assistants. One component of your scientific research project involves the development of a complex, real-time programming system that uses commercial-off-the-shelf products. You are outsourcing this portion of the work. No team members have contract administration experience, and no contracts department staff can be assigned to the project. To ensure that you create a successful relationship with the prospective seller, you must provide two team members with project procurement management training. Direct and indirect training costs should be:

    (A) paid for by your organization.
    (B) charged directly to the project budget.
    (C) paid for by the procurement department.
    (D) considered an input to cost budgeting.

Answers

1. B
2. D
3. C
4. A
5. C
6. D
7. A
8. A
9. D
10. B
11. B
12. C
13. C
14. A
15. C
16. B
17. D
18. A
19. C
20. A
21. A
22. B
23. C
24. A
25. A
26. D
27. A

Chapter 7
Monitoring and Controlling Process Group

Control is a formal process in project management. The PMBOK® defines Project Control as a project management function that involves comparing actual performance with planned performance and taking corrective action to yield the desired outcome when significant differences exists. By monitoring and measuring progress regularly, identifying variances from plan, and taking corrective action when necessary, project control ensures that project objectives are met.

Project control involves the regular review of metrics and report status to identify variances from the planned baseline. The variances are determined by comparing the actual performance metrics from the execution phase against the baseline metrics assigned during the planning phase. If significant variances are observed, adjustments to the plan are made by repeating and adjusting the appropriate Project Management Planning processes.

A significant variance from the plan does not explicitly require a change, but should be reviewed to determine whether preventive action is warranted. For example, a missed activity finish date may require adjustments to the current staffing plan, reliance on overtime, or trade-off between budget and schedule objectives. Controlling also includes taking preventive action in anticipation of possible problems.

While the Monitoring & Controlling Process Group relationship to other Process Groups is relatively concise and clear, control is often difficult to implement as a formalized system. Project control is still important however, because a project is unlikely to be considered successful by stakeholders if it is not monitored and controlled effectively. Success in this context translates to metrics (project, cost, completion dates, etc.) and customer's expectations (features, functionality, performance, etc.).

The control processes implemented during this Process Group are the Performance Reporting and Integrated Change Control, with several constituent processes interacting with these processes as depicted in the image on the following page.

Only by monitoring and controlling a project can project progress and stakeholder's expectations be achieved in unison. Projects rarely fail because of one issue. Rather, failure is usually a collection of minor items that individually have negative impact in a specific project area. However, when looked at over the life of a project, these minor items can cause significant impact to cost, schedule, risk, and functionality and can manifest themselves as deviations from the original Project Management Plan.

As discussed in the Planning Process Group section, the Project Management Plan will include the initially agreed upon baseline project schedule and budget. These become the primary tools for evaluating project performance.

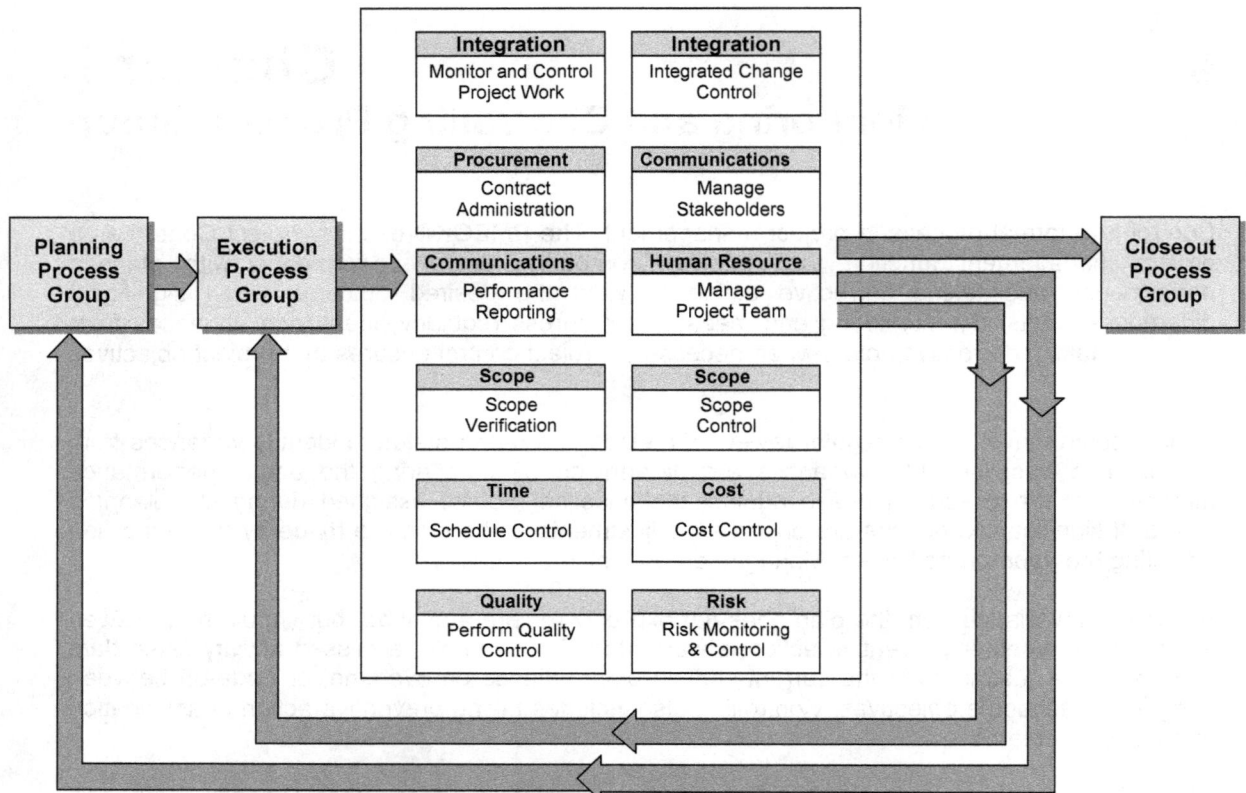

Figure 18 - Monitoring and Controlling Process Group Processes

Monitor and Control Project Work (4.5)

Monitoring and controlling project work involves the regular review of metrics and report status in order to identify variances from the planned project baseline. The variances are determined by comparing the actual performance metrics from the Execution Phase against the baseline metrics assigned during the Planning Phase. These variances are fed into a control processes to evaluate their meaning. If significant variances are observed (i.e., variances that jeopardize the completion of the project objectives), adjustments to the plan are made by repeating and adjusting the appropriate project planning processes. A significant variance from the plan does not explicitly require a change, but should be reviewed to see if preventive action is warranted. For example, a missed activity finish date may require adjustments to the current staffing plan, reliance on overtime, or trade-off between budget and schedule objectives. Controlling also includes taking preventative action in anticipation of possible problems.

While the Project Control Phase's relationship to other project phases is relatively concise and clear, control is often difficult to implement as a formalized project control system in an organization. Project control is still important, however, because a project is unlikely to be considered successful by stakeholders if it is not controlled effectively. Success in this context translates to raw metrics (project cost, completion date, etc.) and customers' expectations (features, functionality, performance, etc.).

Only by controlling a project can project progress and stakeholder's expectations be satisfied in unison. Projects rarely fail because of one issue. Rather, failure is usually a collection of minor items that individually have negative impact in a specific project area. However, when looked at over the life span of a project, these minor items can cause significant impacts to cost, schedule, risk, and functionality and can manifest themselves as deviations from the original Project Plan.

Corrective and Preventive Action

Corrective action appears throughout the PMBOK® Guide. Corrective action is defined as anything done to bring expected future performance in line with the plan. In short, corrective action is the day-to-day responses to all the obstacles and problems a project may encounter. Preventive action is anything that reduces the probability of potential consequences of potential risk events.

The description of corrective action: it is what is important about it when it comes to integration management. Specifically, this is the one and only spot that it is an input into the process. Throughout the rest of the PMBOK® Guide, it is an output.

Earned Value Technique

Earned value is mentioned throughout the PMBOK® Guide but its first mention is as a tool and technique for Monitor and Control Project Work. Earned value is used to integrate the project's scope, schedule, and resources and to measure and report project performance, from initiation to closeout.

Integrated Change Control (4.6)

The purpose of integrated change control is to influence factors that create change so that the change is beneficial, determine when a change has occurred, and manage actual changes if and when they do occur. This process is concerned with coordinating changes across the entire project.

The change control system is the principal tool used for integrated change control. As described in PMBOK® Guide, it consists of formal, documented procedures that define the steps used to change formal documents. A well-developed and documented change control process is crucial to the project management process success. The basic objectives of a change control system are to:

- Continually identify changes, actual or proposed, as they occur.
- Reveal the consequences of the proposed changes in terms of cost and schedule impacts.
- Permit managerial analysis, investigation of alternatives, and an acceptance or rejection checkpoint.
- Communicate changes to all stakeholders.
- Insure that approved changes are implemented.
- Update the development process.

Some organizations assign the project manager a level of authority for accepting change requests. This does not mean that the project manager can arbitrarily make the changes. It means the he can make recommendations for changes to the customer without first consulting management, provided the request is for a change that does not affect the budget or schedule more than a preset amount. Otherwise, the change requests are passed through the project manager to a change control board (CCB) for review.

Change Control Board (CCB)

The CCB may be part of a change control system and be responsible for approving or rejecting change requests. Although some projects may have multiple CCBs, there are circumstances under which the project manager may be able to handle certain types of changes without the need for a formal CCB review.

A change control system consists of a formal, documented procedure for handling change. However, you do need to be aware that a change control board, or a CCB, is what is responsible for authorizing the change that goes through this system.

Configuration Management

The purpose of the configuration management approach is to establish a contractual orientation. Make sure you do exactly what you said you would do and comply with the end user's stated desires. Configuration management protects the end user from unauthorized changes by project staff and protects the project staff from shifts in the end user's desires.

The basic thrust of configuration management is to do the following:

- Carefully define a system deliverable.
- Rigorously control changes to the deliverable.
- Ensure that the ultimate deliverable is consistent with the defined system as modified by approved changes.

Basic Steps in Configuration Management

1. Develop the specifications - Develop the specifications for a complete program configuration item (CPCI). Have the end user sign off on these specifications.
2. Develop a general design - Develop the general design of a CPCI directly from the specifications describing the deliverable and nothing else. Thus the specifications serve as the baseline for the general design. There should be a one-to-one relationship between specification items and items in the general design. Inspect the specifications and general design to ensure that they are compatible.
3. Develop a detailed design - Repeat the process above, except this time use the general design as the baseline for the detailed design. Inspect the detailed design for compatibility with the general design.
4. Implement and test the system - Use the detailed design as the guide to carrying out the project. Rigorously control changes to the design. In testing the system, compare system performance against the original specifications (as modified through a controlled approval process). Remember that the original specification is the only document in which the user agreed upon a description of what the system is supposed to do.
5. Audit the items and system to verify conformance to requirements - An audit should be conducted to ensure that what has been designed conforms to the specific requirements.

These audits may be called functional configuration audits or physical configuration audits.

Change Control in Configuration Management

The three basic objectives of a change control are:

1. Screen the user requests. Use a request for change form. Assess the consequences of the requested changes. If the request has no effect on the project it objectives, it can be accepted by the project manager. Otherwise, it should be approved by a higher level of management.
2. Keep track of accepted changes. Keep a file of accepted changes and always update specifications based on changes.
3. Update the development process. Update all baselines and inform project staff of changes.

The basic steps are outlines here, and what you need to understand is that these steps lead you to a notion called traceability. You can trace the general design, to the detailed design, back to the general design, and back to the specifications. Also understand that in configuration management change control, there is ardent screening going on. All changes must be screened, tracked, accepted, approved, and the development process updated.

Scope Verification (5.4)

Scope verification is the project management responsibility that focuses on ensuring that the products created during the Project Execution Phase are correct and meet agreed upon requirements. This may sound similar to quality control, but according to the Project Management Body of Knowledge, "Scope verification differs from quality control in that it is primarily concerned with the acceptance of the work results while quality control is primarily concerned with the correctness of the work."

The baseline for the creation of any deliverable is the baseline scope plus or minus any agreed upon changes (see the Project Scope Control subsection). Falling short of or going beyond the agreed upon scope will jeopardize the acceptability of the deliverable. Scope verification is achieved through inspection or formal reviews of the deliverables. Once a project deliverable is accepted by the customer, a formal acceptance document should be drafted and signed stating such.

It is important to understand that scope verification is a component of the project scope variable and that it is also part of the third step in the project management process–executing.

Inspection is the tool and technique used for scope verification and involves activities, such as measuring, examining, and testing that are undertaken to determine whether results conform to requirements. You should be familiar with terms that could be used for inspections, including reviews, product reviews, audits, and walkthroughs.

Accepted deliverables is the output from scope verification. It is documentation that the client or the sponsor has accepted the product of the project, phase, or major deliverable. Recognize that this acceptance may be conditional, especially at the end of a phase.

PMI® wants you to know who verifies the scope and the answer is all the critical stakeholders should verify the scope. All the key stakeholders need to have a voice in determining what the scope is, and what is going to be delivered by the project team.

Scope Control (5.5)

Scope control is a straightforward concept. The intent of implementing a scope control process is to identify and manage all elements (e.g., people and requirements) inside and outside of the project that increase or decrease the project scope beyond the required or defined need of the original, agreed upon Project Scope Statement. Attributes of Scope Control include:

- Influencing the factors that create scope changes to ensure that the changes are beneficial
- Determining that a scope change has occurred
- Managing the actual changes when and if they occur. Scope changes will come from the perceived need for a change in a project deliverable that may affect its functionality and in most cases the amount of work needed to perform the project. A scope control change is a very crucial occurrence.

Scope Creep

Scope creep is a common project affliction that results from slowly adding more work over the life of the project. These changes are a problem if scope creep is so great that all of the original cost and schedule estimates become unachievable. A clear scope statement enables the project team to realize immediately that extra work is being added. Therefore, a clear scope statement is a beneficial tool to control scope creep.

When combating scope creep, it is important to realize that changes will occur during all projects. The project manager must be aware of these scope changes and compensate for them so they do not have a negative effect on the project's objectives.

Change Control System

A scope change most likely will require additional project funds, resources, and time. Therefore, a committee that consists of stakeholders from all areas of the project should be willing to convene and discuss the potential change and its anticipated impact on the project and the organization. This group of stakeholders should be a predefined cross section of people that will have the ability to commit their interests at a strategic management level. Once a decision is made to increase or reduce scope, the change must be authorized by all members of the committee. Any changes that are agreed upon must be documented and signed as a matter of formal scope control.

In addition, the impact of the scope change will be felt throughout the Planning Phase processes and documents. Documents such as the WBS and Project Schedule will have to be re-evaluated and updated to include the scope change impacts. Scope changes need to be communicated clearly and effectively to the project team by the project manager. Team members will want, and need, to understand how the scope change affects their roles in the project.

The inputs to baseline project scope include documenting the requirements and objective of the project. Sources of this documentation are customer requirements, business case materials, and other documents developed in the planning processes and utilized during Project Execution. They include the following:

- Work breakdown structure
- Performance reports
- Change requests
- Project Scope Statement

A work breakdown structure, as described in the Planning Phase, will organize and help clearly define the total scope of the project. With the successive decomposition of deliverables into smaller work packages, it should serve to develop and clarify a common understanding of the project goals and objectives between stakeholders.

Performance reports, created as part of the Execution Phase, will provide information on scope performance measured against the plan. The resulting variances are reviewed and interpreted to determine if there is a need for corrective action. These reports will also provide information on the progress of interim products and deliverable completion.

Change requests may occur in many forms—oral or written, clear or subtle, internally or externally driven, operation or regulatory requirements, or driven by technology limitations. The problem, as stated earlier, is not that changes occur, but that changes go unmanaged. Changes in scope may be an expansion or reduction in scope of the project. Most change requests in scope are the result of the following:

- An external event
- An error or omission in the original definition of scope of the product (e.g., failure to include electronic funds transfer as a payment option)
- An error or omission in the defining of the scope of the project (e.g., failure to include training in the project implementation)
- A value-adding change (e.g., use of Internet access versus dial-up telecommunications)

The Project Scope Statement includes a section that describes how changes in project scope are to be handled. The Project Scope Statement is normally included as part of the Project Plan. While agencies may have general guidelines, the basic needs of the "Approach" section of the Project Scope Statement should address the following:

- How scope changes will be identified and documented
- How scope changes will be approved and by whom
- How often scope changes will be made and accepted
- The point at which the approval of scope changes must be approved at higher levels

Schedule Control (6.6)

From a time management point of view, time control or project control is about the schedule baseline and any changes that might occur. The schedule baseline is the original, approved project schedule and becomes the standard used to measure schedule performance. The baseline should never be changed without proper review and approval.

Change requests may occur in numerous ways but any approved change should be documented in writing. Changes may either extend or accelerate the schedule. Changes almost always increase the project cost!

Control is a big issue with PMI®, and when it comes to project schedule control, it is the same issue as with project cost control and project scope control. Control is governed by the baseline. You use a schedule baseline, you establish that baseline, and that is the original approved project schedule. Any variance to the schedule is going to be reflected against that schedule. Any change requests are going to be evaluated against that original baseline.

Variance Analysis

Variance analysis is a key tool and technique for schedule control. The general formula for any kind of variance is Plan-Actual. Therefore, if a task was planned to take four days and it actually takes five days, the schedule variance (SV) would be equal to -1 day. If the SV is a positive number, then more work was completed than originally planned up to that point. If the SV is a negative number, then less work was completed than originally planned up to that point. The earned value formula for schedule variance follows:

- SV = EV-PV or
- SV = BCWP - BCWS
- Where EV is the earned value or the budgeted cost of work performed
- And PV is the planned value or budgeted cost of work scheduled

Comparing target dates with the actual and forecast start and finish dates provides useful information for the detection of deviations and for the implementation of corrective solutions in case of delays. Pay attention to the float variance and to critical and subcritical activities (for example, analyzing the ten subcritical paths in order of ascending float).

Schedule Updates

Sometimes schedules need to be changed or updated to reflect such things as changes in activity sequence or resource redistribution. It is important to keep a project's schedule up-to-date so team members can verify their activity completion times and resource constraints.

A revision is a type of schedule update. Revisions are alterations of a project's original start and completion dates. Most often, revisions are made based on changes to the project's scope. Rebaselining may be required if schedule delays are severe. Use rebaselining only as a last resort for schedule control; new target schedules should be the normal mode of schedule revision.

Corrective Action

Corrective action may be needed as a result of schedule control. This often involves expediting special actions to ensure completion of an activity on time or with the least possible delay. Root cause analysis may be needed to identify the causes of the variation.

Cost Control (7.3)

Cost control involves identifying when changes have been made to the cost baseline and managing those changes. In addition, cost control includes monitoring factors that cause changes to the cost baseline, as well as influencing those changes so that they are beneficial to the project.

Cost control is heavily related to other project variables and should be considered in conjunction with other control components, such as schedule control. For example, making changes based on cost variances can result in changes to the project schedule. Inappropriate responses to cost variances can cause quality or schedule problems or produce an unacceptable level of risk later in the project. An important part of cost control is to determine what is causing the variance and to decide whether the variance requires corrective action.

Cost Change Control System

Defines the procedures by which the cost baseline may be changed and is maintained in the cost management plan. It includes the forms and any necessary documentation necessary for authorizing changes.

Earned Value Management (EVM)

Comparing planned cash flow with actual cash flow has its uses, but it does not tell you whether the project will be over or under budget. To get the true picture of cost performance, the planned and actual costs for all completed tasks need to be compared. This is accomplished with a technique called earned value management. Earned value management uses cost data to give more accurate cost and schedule reports. It does this by combining cost and schedule status to provide a complete picture of the project. For example, projects can be ahead of schedule (good) but over budget (bad). Alternatively, they can be ahead of schedule (good) and under budget (good).

All EVM control account plans must continuously measure project performance by relating three independent values: the planned value, the earned value, and the actual costs incurred.

Planned Value (PV) = portion of approved cost estimate planned to be spent on the activity in a given period.

Question	Answer	Acronym
How much should be done?	Planned Value	PV
How much work is done? This is the actual earned value of the project, because it is the value of the work that has been completed.	Earned Value	EV
How much work did the "is done" work cost?	Actual Cost	AC
What was the total job supposed to cost?	Budget at Completion	BAC
What do we now expect the total job to cost? This is a re-estimate of the total project budget. It's a way of saying that if current cost performance trends continue, the final cost can be predicted.	Estimate at completion	EAC

Planned Value (PV) = portion of approved cost estimate planned to be spent on the activity in a given period.

Actual Cost (AC) = total of costs incurred in accomplishing work on the activity during a given period.

Earned Value (EV) = value of work actually completed. Interpretation of EV: "Task A, which I was supposed to complete today, is scheduled to cost $1,000. I have completed only 85 percent of this task. Thus, I have completed $850 worth of work, which is my earned value (EV)."

Cost Variance (CV)

Recalculating the estimated cost at completion using earned value implies that current trends will continue. Nevertheless, be careful not to assume that just because you are over budget now, you will be granted more money for your budget. Instead, the cost variance (CV) should be used as a warning flag to help you identify problems early, when there is still time to get back on track.

Interpretation of CV: "I have done $850 worth of work (EV), but it actually cost me $900 to do this (AC). It has cost me $50 more to do what I have done than I originally thought (CV)."

Cost Variance (CV) = EV - AC
CV = BCWP - ACWP

Schedule Variance (SV)

Is the project on schedule? This is a question that all stakeholders want answered. However, it can be difficult to measure the degree to which a project is ahead or behind schedule. What if the majority of tasks are on schedule, but a few are ahead of schedule and others are behind? What is the accurate description of this project's schedule status? In this kind of situation, earned calculations can help measure schedule variances (SV) just as they help measure cost variances (CV). Interpretation of SV: "As of today, I was supposed to have done $1,000 worth of work on Task A (PV). I have actually done $850 worth of work (EV). Thus, I am behind in my schedule by $150 worth of work (SV)."

Using the cost figures as the basis for schedule measurement is useful because it takes into account the number and size of tasks that are behind schedule. In other words, if ten concurrent tasks, each worth $25,000, are all one week behind schedule, the scheduled variances will be larger than if only one of those tasks is one week behind schedule.
Schedule variance (SV) = EV - PV

The formulas for cost variance (CV) and schedule variance (SV) will yield either a positive or negative numeric value. If the value is positive, then the project is under budget and ahead of schedule; if negative, then the project is over budget and behind schedule. It is common to have a negative cost variance (i.e., to be over budget) and to have a positive schedule variance. This means that although you have overspent at that point, you are ahead of schedule. So the project is not necessarily in trouble. It may mean that you were able to begin some tasks sooner than planned.

Cost Performance Index (CPI)

CPI is the relationship between actual costs expended and the value of the physical work performed and is widely used as a forecasting tool because it is very accurate. Once a project is roughly 20 percent complete, the total CPI for a project generally does not change by more than 10 percent. Therefore, CPI gives the project team and stakeholders a quick and reliable estimate of final project costs.

Interpretation of CPI: "I have done $850 worth of work (EV). It has cost me $900 to do so (AC). Each dollar I actually spent generated 94.4 cents worth of work (cost performance factor)."

$$CPI = EV \div AC \quad / \quad CPI = BCWP \div ACWP$$

Schedule Performance Index (SPI)

SPI is the relationship between the value of the initial planned schedule and the value of the physical work to be performed. Interpretation of SPI: "I have done $1,500 worth of work (EV). The value of work scheduled is $1,000. Each dollar of scheduled work generated $1.50 worth of work (schedule performance factor).

$$SPI = EV \div PV \quad / \quad SPI = BCWP \div BCWS$$

To interpret CPI and SPI: if they are equal to 1, then the project is on budget and schedule; if the equation equals less than 1, then the project is over budget and behind schedule; if the equation is greater than 1, then the project is under budget and ahead of schedule.

CPI and SPI provide the same information as CV and SV whether the project is on budget and schedule – but in a decimal format. For instance a CPI of 0.85 means that for every dollar spent, you have generated 85 cents of worth or work. This is a much more meaningful measure and is very good for use in status reports.

Estimate to Complete (ETC)

The estimate to complete (ETC) is the amount of money needed to fund the project to completion. The estimate to complete (ETC) is a useful calculation because it tells the project manager how much money will be needed to complete the project. It is especially useful within small companies because it provides an estimate of cash-flow requirements for the project's remaining life.

$$ETC = EAC - AC \quad / \quad ETC = EAC - ACWP$$

Estimate at Completion (EAC)

What do we now expect the total job to cost? The EAC is a forecast of most likely total project costs based on project performance and quantitative risk analysis.

The PMBOK® Guide provides three formulas for computing EAC:

Formula	When Used
EAC = AC + (Remaining PV ÷ CPI)	Use when current variances are seen as typical of future variances
EAC = AC + ETC	Use when past performance shows original estimates were fundamentally flawed or are no longer relevant because of a change in conditions
EAC = AC + Remaining AC	Use when current variances are seen as a typical

Another formula that may appear on the exam, and is not included in the PMBOK® Guide, is:
EAC = BAC ÷ CPI

Variance at Completion (VAC)

Compares what the total job is supposed to cost - Budget at Completion (BAC) to what the total job is expected to cost - Estimate at Completion (EAC). Variance at Completion (VAC) is calculated as: BAC - EAC = VAC

BAC and VAC

Budget at completion, or BAC, is the estimated total cost of the project finished, which is generally calculated before a project begins. The BAC is calculated by assigning together all individual BCWS calculations for each portion of a project. Another name for BAC is the "baseline."

Variance at completion, or VAC, indicates a deviation from the budget at completion, which was projected before the project began. When finding the estimate at completion, or the total estimated cost for a project once the project is partially complete, you should determine the VAC using the following equation: VAC = BAC − EAC

Determining the VAC helps indicate any significant cost variances that should be reported to project stakeholders. If the variance is great enough, the project manager should consult the team's cost management plan in order to take the correct cost control measures.

The 50-50 Rule of Progress Reporting

The 50-50 rule was established to overcome the problem of making subjective estimates (for example, estimating how far along we are on a task).

When beginning a task, charge 50 percent of its PV to its account. When the task is finally completed, charge the remaining 50 percent to its account. Variations of the 50-50 Rule include:

- 20 - 80 rule: More conservative
- 0 - 100 rule: Most conservative. The assumption here is that a task does not have value until it is completed.

Revised Cost Estimates

These are adjustment and/or updates to the cost information portion of the project. They differ from budget updates, which are a special category of revised cost estimates. Budget updates are changes to an approved cost baseline and generally are revised only in response to scope changes. In some cases, cost variances may be so severe that rebaselining is required to provide a realistic measure of performance.

Specifically with this section you need to be comfortable with the following three components:

- Budget cost of work performed (BCWP): How much is the work that has been worth? How much money was planned to spend on the work that has been done so far?
- Budgeted cost of work scheduled (BCWS): What is the budget that was set aside as of today or up to this point in time – the budgeted cost for the work scheduled as of today?
- Actual cost of work performed (ACWP): What is the actual cost of the work performed? How much has been spent for the work that has been accomplished.

Perform Quality Assurance (8.3)

Quality control and quality assurance are similar in that both components use a project's quality management plan and operational definitions to evaluate whether or not a project and product are achieving the desired levels of quality. The quality control and quality assurance components are also similar in that both result in quality improvement.

Included below are some important terms and concepts associated with quality control:

- **Variable** - A quality characteristic that is measurable in increments. Examples are diameter measured in inches, cooking time measured in minutes, and weight measured in pounds.
- **Attribute** - A quality characteristic that is classified as either conforming or nonconforming to specifications or requirements. It results in a go or no-go decision. Attributes are easily segregated into a "yes-no" outcome. As an example in flipping a coin there is a 50-percent probability of getting "heads" on any single flip
- **Probability** - An important concept in quality control is that of probability. In its simplest form, probability refers to the chance that something will happen.

For variables, probability is a more complicated concept. We measure the occurrences of an event or characteristic, and distribute them over the entire range of the characteristic. Such a distribution is formally called a probability distribution. The most common probability distribution has a bell shape and is symmetric about its mean; it is known as a normal distribution or a bell curve.

A population is the entire group of items or occurrences that we might wish to measure. Because populations can be very large, however, we often sample the population, using a smaller group to get a picture of the larger group.

Standard Deviation

In measuring samples and comparing them to their overall population, one important concept is that of standard deviation. Simply defined, the standard deviation is the amount on either side of the mean of a normal distribution that will contain approximately 68.3 percent of the total population. The amount within two standard deviations will include 95.5 percent, and within three standard deviations will include 99.7 percent of the population.

Calculating standard deviation is complex. Most automated quality control packages include the provision to calculate standard deviation and other statistically important values. In fact, most pocket calculators available today can also provide this value for a series of discrete observations of a variable characteristic. The following is provided to show manually how to calculate standard deviation:

The "Standard Deviation" for data can be calculated in the following steps:

1. all the deviations (differences) from the mean of the set of numbers are squared
2. the mean of these squares is then calculated
3. the square root of the mean is the standard deviation

Given the set of numbers {20, 23, 25, 26}, the "Standard Deviation" can be calculated as follows:

Step 1:
The mean of these numbers is found to be 23.5 [eg. mean = (20+23+25+26)/4 = 23.5]. The deviations from the mean are respectively:

23.5 - 20 = 3.5
23.5 - 23 = 0.5
25 - 23.5 = 1.5
26 - 23.5 = 2.5

The squares of these deviations are:
$3.5^2 = 12.25$
$0.5^2 = 0.25$
$1.5^2 = 2.25$
$2.5^2 = 6.25$

Step 2:
The sum of these squares is 12.25 + 0.25 + 2.25 + 6.25 = 21. This is now divided by (n-1), which is 3, to get 7.

Step 3:
Finally, the square root of 7 is approximately 2.6457513

Answer:
In summary, the Standard Deviation of the set of numbers {20, 23, 25, 26} is 2.6457513

Process Control

Building on the statistical concepts we have just discussed, the PMBOK® Guide emphasizes process control as an important means of managing quality. Key to this concept is the idea of statistical process control (SPC) and its main tool—control charts—commonly called SPC charts.

A SPC chart will show you the current capability of the process—what is called voice of the process in some courses and recent publications. The important point to remember about SPC charts is that there are many different types you may use, depending on the characteristic you are measuring and its variability.

Sampling

Sampling is a useful means of assessing the value of a characteristic when examining an entire population is not feasible. There are two main types of sampling:

- Attribute sampling is the examination of one or more attributes in a lot. A limit of acceptability is established for the entire lot. For example, we may consider a "lot" of 10,000 parts. A random sample of 150 parts is selected for examination. For that sample, the acceptance number is 3, meaning that if more than 3 parts are found to be defective; the entire lot of 10,000 will be rejected. You can conduct single-attribute sampling, double-attribute sampling, multiple-attribute sampling, or sequential attribute sampling (single-attribute sampling performed sequentially on the same lot for different attributes).
- Variable sampling provides a more dynamic approach to sampling. This is the basis for creating control charts, where a process variable is measured and charted to determine process capability. Variable sampling may also be used to estimate the fraction of a lot that is nonconforming, and thus to make decisions about further inspection or use of the lot.

Both attribute sampling and variation sampling tell whether a product does or does not conform to quality standards. However, variation sampling also accounts for the degree to which a product does or does not conform.

Prevention and Inspection

Prevention and inspection have different purposes. Prevention requires careful planning to avoid errors before a project begins. Inspection occurs during project execution or after a project is completed. When defects are found during inspection, rework is required to correct the defects before products are distributed to customers.

Special Causes and Random Causes

Special causes of variation, which are often caused by human error, are generally unexpected or unanticipated. Random causes, also called common causes, of variation are normal difficulties associated with a certain process, such as equipment failure or faulty product design. Project team members who contribute to special causes of variation should be able to correct the causes on their own, whereas project managers are responsible for solving random causes of variation since the causes are part of the project's process.

Tolerance and Control Limits

Tolerance refers to the amount off acceptable variations from product quality standards. Control limits apply to a project's process rather than to a product. A project is considered "in control" if its processes are within specified control limits.

Statistical Quality Control

Statistical quality control is used to evaluate the extent of product variation and to identify what changes, if any, must be made to production processes in order to decrease product variation. Data points on a graph represent incidents of product variations, and a normal distribution curve indicates whether or not the variations are of a degree acceptable for quality standards.

Quality monitoring involves the use of statistics. Therefore, it is important to know the following basic statistical terms:

- Population – refers to the total number of product units produced during a project.

- Sample size – refers to the number of product units taken from the population for evaluation during a project's quality monitoring process. This number varies depending on the product, the time of the inspection, and a company's needs.
- Mean – this refers to the sum of the sample divided by the number of units in the sample. For example, in the sample {2, 4, 6, 8}, the mean is (2 + 4 + 6 + 8) ÷ 4. The mean is 5.
- Median – When an odd—numbered set of data is arranged sequentially, the middle number in the set is the median. For example, in the set {3, 6, 9}, the median is 6. When an even-numbered set of data is arranged sequentially, the median is the average of the middle two numbers. For example, in the set {2, 4, 8, 9}, the median is (4 + 8) ÷ 2, the median is 6.
- Mode – In a sample of data, the number that occurs most frequently represents the mode. For example, in the set {2, 3, 4, 3, 5, 3, 4}, the mode is 3.

Quality Control Tools

There are seven main quality control tools (often called the basic seven tools), which are illustrated and discussed below.

Flowcharts

Flowcharts permit you to examine and understand relationships in a process or project. They show how various elements of a system interrelate. They provide a step-by-step schematic, or picture, that serves to create a common language, ensure common understanding about sequence, and focus collective attention on shared concerns. Flowcharts are used in all three of the quality management processes. Several different types of flowcharts are particularly useful in the continuous improvement process. Three frequently used charts are known as the top-down flowchart, the detailed flowchart, and the work-flow diagram.

The top-down flowchart presents only the major or most fundamental steps in a process or project. It helps you or your team to easily visualize the process in a single, simple flow diagram. Key value-added actions associated with each major activity are listed below their respective flow diagram steps. You can construct a top-down flowchart fairly quickly and easily. You generally do so before attempting to produce detailed flowcharts for a process. By limiting the top-down flowchart to a value-added activity, the likelihood of becoming bogged down in detail is significantly reduced.

EVALUATE	SCHEDULE	COMMUNICATION	EVALUATE	FEEDBACK
Dialogue with users	Oversee activities	Communicate with personnel	Check punctuality	Inform personnel and users
Dialogue with personnel	Create schedule	Create billboards	Personnel satisfaction	Incentives to personnel
		Dissemination	User's satisfaction	

Figure 19 - Top-Down Flowchart

The detailed flowchart provides very specific information about process flow. At its most detailed level, every decision point, feedback loop, and process step is represented. Detailed flowcharts should be used only when the level of detail provided by the top-down or other simpler flowcharts is insufficient to support understanding, analysis, and improvement activity. The detailed flowchart may also be useful and appropriate for critical processes where precisely following a specific procedure is essential.

The work-flow diagram is a graphic representation of how work actually flows through a physical space or facility. It is very useful for analyzing flow processes, illustrating flow inefficiency, and planning process flow improvement.

Scatter Diagrams

Scatter diagrams are used to investigate the possible relationship between two variables that both relate to the same "event." A straight line of best fit (using the least squares method) is often included. Things to look for:

- If the points cluster in a band running from lower left to upper right, there is a positive correlation (if x increases, y increases).
- If the points cluster in a band from upper left to lower right, there is a negative correlation (if x increases, y decreases).
- Imagine drawing a straight line or curve through the data so that it "fits" as well as possible. The more the points cluster closely around the imaginary line of best fit, the stronger the relationship that exists between the two variables.
- If it is hard to see where you would draw a line, and if the points show no significant clustering, there is probably no correlation.

There is a maxim in statistics that says, "Correlation does not imply causality." In other words, your scatter plot may show that a relationship exists, but it does not and cannot prove that one variable is causing the other. There could be a third factor involved that is causing both, some other systemic cause, or the apparent relationship could just be a fluke. Nevertheless, the scatter plot can give you a clue that two things might be related, and if so, how they move together.

Figure 20 - Scatter Diagram

Histograms

A histogram is a specialized type of bar chart. Individual data points are grouped together in classes, so that you can get an idea of how frequently data in each class occur in the data set. High bars indicate more points in a class, and low bars indicate less points.

In the histogram shown below, the peak is in the 40-49 class, where there are four points. The strength of a histogram is that it provides an easy-to-read picture of the location and variation in a data set. There are, however, two weaknesses of histograms that you should bear in mind; the first is that histograms can be manipulated to show different pictures. If too few or too many bars are used, the histogram can be misleading. This is an area which requires some judgment, and perhaps some experimentation, based on the analyst's experience.

Figure 21 - Sample Histogram

Histograms can also obscure the time differences among data sets. For example, if you looked at data for number of births on a particular day in the United States in 2005, you would miss any seasonal variations, e.g. peaks around the times of full moons. Likewise, in quality control, a histogram of a process run tells only one part of a long story. There is a need to keep reviewing the histograms and control charts for consecutive process runs over an extended time to gain useful knowledge about a process.

Run Charts

Run charts (often known as line graphs outside the quality management field) display process performance over time. Upward and downward trends, cycles, and large aberrations may be spotted and investigated further. In a run chart, events, shown on the y axis, are graphed against a time period on the x axis. For example, a run chart in a hospital might plot the number of patient transfer delays against the time of day or day of the week. The results might show that there are more delays at noon than at 3 p.m. Investigating this phenomenon could unearth potential for improvement. Run charts can also be used to track improvements that have been put into place, checking to determine their success. Also, an average line can be added to a run chart to clarify movement of the data away from the average.

Figure 22 - Sample Run Chart

Questions to ask about a run chart:

1. Is the average line where it should be to meet customer requirements?
2. Is there a significant trend or pattern that should be investigated?

Two ways to misinterpret run charts:

1. You conclude that some trend or cycle exists, when in fact you are just seeing normal process variation (and every process will show some variation).
2. You do not recognize a trend or cycle when it does exist.

Both of these mistakes are common, but people are generally less aware that they are making the first type, and are tampering with a process which is really behaving normally. To avoid mistakes, use the following rules of thumb for run chart interpretation:

- Look at data for a long enough period of time, so that a "usual" range of variation is evident.
- Is the recent data within the usual range of variation?
- Is there a daily pattern? Weekly? Monthly? Yearly?

Pareto Charts

In the late 1800s, Vilfredo Pareto, an Italian economist, found that typically 80 percent of the wealth in a region was concentrated in less than 20 percent of the population. Later, Dr. Joseph Juran formulated what he called the Pareto Principle of Problems: only a "vital few" elements (20 percent) account for the majority (80 percent) of the problems. For example, in a manufacturing facility, 20 percent of the equipment problems account for 80 percent of the downtime. Because the Pareto Principle has proven to be valid in numerous situations, it is useful to examine data carefully to identify the vital few items that most deserve attention.

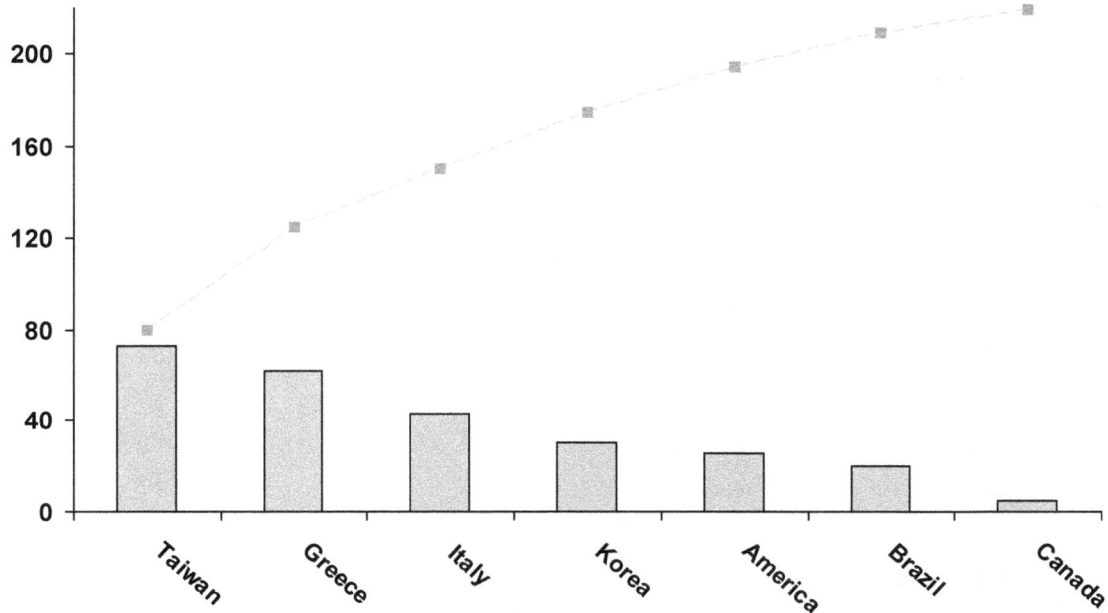

Figure 23 - Paredo Diagram

A Pareto Chart is a bar chart in which the data are arranged in descending order of their importance, generally by magnitude of frequency, cost, time, or a similar parameter. The chart presents the information being examined in its order of priority and focuses attention on the most critical issues. The chart aids the decision-making process because it puts issues into an easily understood framework in which relationships and relative contributions are clearly evident.

Cause and Effect Diagram

Cause and effect diagrams are the brainchild of Kaoru Ishikawa, who pioneered quality management processes in the Kawasaki shipyards, in Japan, and in the process became one of the founding fathers of modern management. The cause and effect diagram is used to explore all the potential or real causes (or inputs) that result in a single effect (or output). Causes are arranged according to their level of importance or detail, resulting in a depiction of relationships and hierarchy of events. This can help you search for root causes, identify areas where there may be problems, and compare the relative importance of different causes.

Cause and effect diagrams are frequently arranged into four major categories. While these categories can be anything, you will often see: manpower, methods, materials, and machinery (recommended for manufacturing) equipment, policies, procedures, and people (recommended for administration and service). These guidelines can be helpful but should not be used if they limit the diagram or are inappropriate. The categories you use should suit your needs.

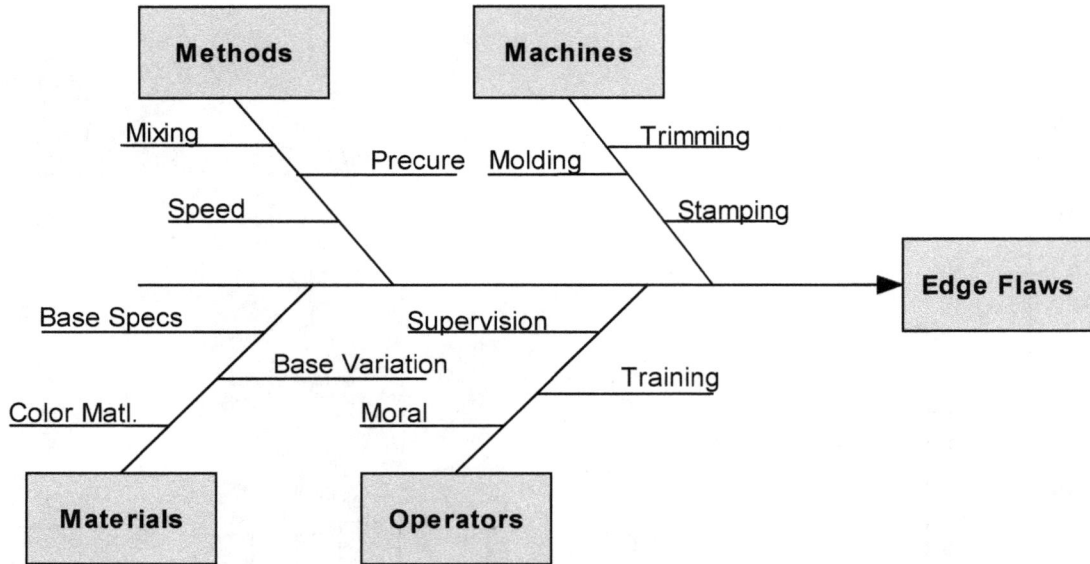

Figure 24 - Cause and Effect Diagram

The cause and effect diagram is also known as the fishbone diagram because it was drawn to resemble the skeleton of a fish, with the main causal categories drawn as "bones" attached to the spine of the fish, as shown above.

Cause and effect diagrams can also be drawn as tree diagrams, resembling a tree turned on its side. From a single outcome or trunk, branches extend that represent major categories of inputs or causes that create that single outcome. These large branches then lead to smaller and smaller branches of causes all the way down to twigs at the ends. The tree structure has an advantage over the fishbone-style diagram. As a fishbone diagram becomes more and more complex, it becomes difficult to find and compare items that are the same distance from the effect because they are dispersed over the diagram. With the tree structure, all items on the same causal level are aligned vertically.

Control Charts

A control chart is a graph that displays data taken over time and computed variations of those data. Control charts are used to show the variation on a variety of variables including average (X) and range (R) and also the number of defects (PN), percent defective (P), defects per variable unit (U), and defects per fixed unit (C). The control chart allows you to distinguish between measurements that are predictably within the inherent capability of the process (normal causes of variation that are to be expected) and measurements that are unpredictable and produced by special causes.

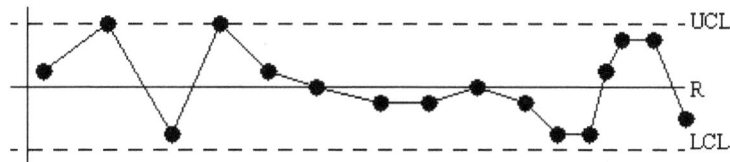

Figure 25 - Control Chart

The upper and lower control limits (UCL and LCL) must not be confused with specification limits. Control limits describe the natural variation of the process such that points within the limits are generally indicative of normal and expected variation. Points outside the limits signal that something has occurred that requires special attention because it is outside of the built-in systemic causes of variation in the process. Note that the circled point on the X-bar chart means that the process is out of control and should be investigated. These points outside the control limits are referred to as special events having either assignable causes or random causes.

The occurrence of assignable causes may be the result of unwanted, external effects such as the following:

- An equipment problem
- An employee problem (poor training, understaffed, and so on)
- Defective materials

There is another important guideline, known as the Rule of Seven, which should be observed whenever interpreting control charts. This rule of thumb (heuristic) states that if seven or more observations in a row occur on the same side of the mean (or if they trend in the same direction), even though they may be within the control limit, they should be investigated as if they had an assignable cause. It is extremely unlikely that seven observations in a row would be on the same side of the mean if the process is operating normally.

Why is this so? If a process is operating normally, the observations will follow a random pattern with some of the points falling above the line and some below the line. In fact, the probability that any single point will fall above or below the line is 50-50 (like a coin toss). Further, the probability that seven points in a row would be on the same side of the line would be calculated as 0.5 to the 7seventh power, which is equal to 0.0078 (or less than 1 percent). Again, this rule provides a guideline that alerts you that something unlikely is happening and you should check it out.

These charts will help you understand the following:

- The inherent capability of your processes
- Bring your processes under control by eliminating the special causes of variation
- Reduce tampering with processes that are under statistical control
- Monitor the effects of process changes aimed at improvement

Two additional concepts are important in the use of control charts. Both concepts involve the idea of standard deviation, often referred to as "sigma." For the exam, you need to understand only the concepts (no formulas or complex calculations are required).

The first concept involves the use by some companies of what is known as the Six Sigma Rule for setting control limits. You are already aware that three standard deviations (sigma) either side of the mean accounts for approximately 99.7 percent of the possible outcomes. Historically, many companies have used plus or minus three sigma's as their standard for setting control limits. In recent years, some companies have chosen to use plus or minus six sigmas as a guide for setting control limits. The use of this more stringent rule means that even fewer actual outcomes might fall outside the control limits.

The second concept involves the effect of sample size on the control limits. Again, you do not need to memorize any formulas, but it helps to know the following information about how the formula for setting control limits works. First, the standard deviation is part of the formula for establishing control limits. The larger the standard deviation, the wider the control limits will be. That much is fairly intuitive. In other words, the greater the natural variations in the process, the wider the control limits need to be. Now, how does sample size affect the control limits? Sample size affects control limits by its effect on the standard deviation. Sample size is in the denominator of the formula for variance from which standard deviation is computed; so whenever sample size is increased, the standard deviation will be smaller. Conversely, if the sample size is decreased, the standard deviation will be larger. Therefore, larger sample sizes will result in more narrow control limits, and smaller sample sizes will result in wider control limits.

Statistical Sampling

Statistical sampling involves choosing a population of interest for inspection. (e.g., selecting ten engineering drawings at random from a list of seventy-five). Appropriate sampling can often reduce the cost of quality control. In some application areas, the project management team must be familiar with a variety of sampling techniques.

Inspection

Quality cannot be infused into a project or a product by inspection. However, inspection is a useful tool for quality control. End products should always go through a final inspection to make sure that they conform to quality standards. Inspection includes activities such as measuring, examining, and testing undertaken to determine whether results conform to requirements. May be conducted at any level (e.g., the results of a single activity may be inspected or the final project product). May be called reviews, product reviews, audits, and walkthroughs. Note: in some application areas these terms have narrow and specific meanings.

Defect

Any type of undesired result is a defect. A defect is a failure to conform to requirements whether or not those requirements have been articulated or specified. This usually requires the product or service to be either repaired or replaced.

Defect Repair Review

Defect repair review is where the quality control department will explain how they plan to minimize defects for there project. A defect is any occurrence contrary to specifications within a deliverable which has already been quality assured. A plan for efficient removal of defects could include such items as standardized reporting mechanisms, effective and up-to-date system documentation, etc.

Corrective Action

Action to eliminate the cause of a detected nonconformity or other undesirable situation. Note: There can be more than on cause for a non-conformance. Corrective action is taken to prevent recurrence, whereas preventive action is taken to prevent occurrence.

Preventive Action

Action taken to eliminate the causes of a potential non-conformity, defect, or other undesirable situation in order to prevent occurrence.

Continuous Improvement and Kaizen

Kaizen was originally defined in the book Kaizen, the Key to Japan's Competitive Success, by Mr. Masaaki Imai. Kaizen means improvement. Moreover, Kaizen means continuing improvement in personal life, home life, social life, and working life. When applied to the workplace Kaizen means continuing improvement involving everyone—managers and workers alike.

Kaizen is a Japanese word meaning gradual and orderly, continuous improvement. The Kaizen business strategy involves everyone in an organization working together to make improvements "without large capital investments."

Kaizen is a culture of sustained continuous improvement focusing on eliminating waste in all systems and processes of an organization. The Kaizen strategy begins and ends with people. With Kaizen, an involved leadership guides people to continuously improve their ability to meet expectations of high quality, low cost, and on-time delivery. Kaizen transforms companies into "Superior Global Competitors."

There are two elements that construct Kaizen: improvement and change for the better and ongoing/continuity. Lacking one of those elements would not be considered Kaizen. For instance, the expression of "business as usual" contains the element of continuity without improvement. On the other hand, the expression of "breakthrough" contains the element of change or improvement without continuity. Kaizen should contain both elements.

Kaizen, as you could learn from the definition, is a common word and very natural to individual, continuous improvement in personal life, home life, social life, and work life. Everybody deserves to and should be willing to improve himself/herself for the better, continually. "If a man has not been seen for three days, his friends should take a good look at him to see what changes have befallen him," quoted from the old Japanese saying, describes how natural Kaizen is.

In our concepts, three functions should happen simultaneously within any organizations: maintenance, innovation, and Kaizen. By maintenance, we refer to maintaining the current status, the procedures are set, and the standards are implemented. This is generally the role of the people in the lower level of organizations—maintaining the company's standards.

Innovation refers to breakthrough activities initiated by top management: buying new machines, new equipment, developing new markets, directing research and design (R & D), change of strategy, etc....

In the middle, there is Kaizen: small steps, but continuing improvement. The lower/middle management and the workers, with the encouragement and direction of the top, should implement Kaizen. The top management responsibility is to cultivate a Kaizen working climate and culture in the organization.

For the PMP® exam know that Kaizen is small, tiny, incremental improvements—always looking for a way to make things better.

Just-in-Time (JIT)

Just-in-time is an inventory control approach process that continuously stresses waste reduction by optimizing the processes and procedures necessary to maintain an operation. Part of this process is JIT inventory where the materials needed appear just in time for use, thus eliminating costs associated with material handling and storage. The philosophy is that with no safety stock in the system, defective parts or processes will grind the system to a halt. A zero working-process inventory forces a company to find and fix quality problems, or it will constantly miss its schedule commitments.

The company benefits from JIT inventory/purchasing by developing long-term relationships with fewer suppliers, thus lowering subcontractor management costs. The contractor benefits by having long-term contracts.

Numerous companies in Japan have adopted JIT, because they believe JIT and high quality go together naturally, but in the United States it has only been marginally successful.

Just-in-time (JIT) is designed as a process that is going to keep flow coming to you, as a vendor, just in time to prepare it, process it, and get it to your customers. Vendors do not want to keep inventory on hand. They do not want to have material in a warehouse. Classic just-in-time management allows for the flow of materials effectively through an organization or process.

Impact of Motivation on Quality

It is generally believed that increased quality is likely to be associated with projects whose team members display pride, commitment, and an interest in workmanship. It is also believed that one way to harm this culture is by allowing frequent turnover of the people assigned to the project.

Priority of Quality versus Cost and Schedule

Quality use to receive lip service in many companies, but it was, in reality, less important than meeting schedules or containing costs. Such a situation was often tipped off by such signals as the quality manager reporting to the production manager (who often cared more about schedule pressures than quality). Although lip service has probably not been eliminated entirely, modern thinking emphasizes that quality should share equal priority with cost and schedule.

Philip Crosby titled his book Quality is Free on the premise that the cost of doing things twice is far greater than the cost of doing them right in the first time. When performance is cut, costs go up for many reasons, including these:

- Rework (performing the same tasks twice because they were not done right the first time) during the project will drive costs higher and delay completion.

- Rework after the project finishes is even more expensive than rework during the project. Any potential development cost savings are wiped out by the high cost of fixing the product.
- Failure due to poor product performance can also be expensive. Product recalls always bear the expense of contacting the consumers as well as fixing or replacing the product. Product failures such as collapsing bridges and malfunctioning medical equipment can even cost lives.
- Poor product performance causes damage to the reputation of the firm and ultimately reduces the demand for its products or services.

The above paragraphs are very important because they drive home the point that sometimes, in some quality practices, what you are doing in the real world may not really matter. This is one of them. The argument in most quality circles is that quality is of equal importance to cost and schedule. In some circles, it is even said that quality is more important than cost or schedule. Nevertheless, for the PMP® exam, you need to know that quality is of equal importance to cost and schedule. You need to know, if asked, what is more important, quality, cost, or schedule? The answer: they are equally important.

Impact of Poor Quality

The following effects on a project are possible results of poor quality:

- Increased project costs as a result of costs of nonconformance (for example, rework, scrap, product recalls, and so on)
- Decreased productivity
- Increased risk and uncertainty (less predictability in cost, schedule, and technical outcomes)
- Increased costs of monitoring (if conformance to specifications is low, increased monitoring will probably become necessary)

What happens when we do not have good quality? Look at the bullet points and memorize each and every one of them. They are listed as bullets in order to make it easier to remember. Poor quality results in higher costs, poor productivity, increased risk, and increased uncertainty.

Trend Analysis

Trend analysis uses scatter diagrams to monitor the performance of technical operations, project costs, and a project's schedule. During trend analysis, a project manager determines the mathematical equation that best fits the slope of the line on a scatter diagram. The equation is then used to predict how changing one project variable will affect another project variable.

Design and Quality

Quality should be designed into, not inspected into (worth repeating). More specifically, careful design of a product or service is believed to increase reliability and maintainability (two important measures of quality).

The primary responsibility for developing design and test specifications rests with the project engineers (they have the expertise needed to perform this vital task). Rework is any action taken to bring a defective or nonconforming item into compliance with requirements or specifications. The project team should make every effort to minimize rework.

Look at the first sentence. It says "Quality should be designed into, not inspected into." We do not inspect quality into something. You may be asked a few questions that lure you into the idea that going back and inspecting for quality is the right answer. IT IS NOT. We design quality so that it's built in. Remember, responsibility for quality rests with the person who owns that given activity. Quality on the project is the responsibility of the project manager. Quality on a task is the responsibility of the person doing that task.

Managing the Project Team (9.4)

Managing the project team involves "tracking team member performance, providing feedback, resolving issues, and coordinating changes to enhance project performance" (PMBOK®). As a result of managing the project team, the staffing management plan is updated, issues are resolved, change requests are submitted, and lessons learned are added to the organization's database if one is available. This topic is as complex and "hard" as any that the project manager has to face.

The inputs to managing the project team are organizational process assets, project staff assignments, roles and responsibilities, project organization charts, the staffing management plan, team performance assessment, work performance information, and performance reports, according to the PMBOK®. All of these have been discussed earlier.

The tools and techniques for managing the project team are observation and conversation, project performance appraisals, conflict management, and the issue log. As with all types of management, it is important to work directly with project members and to have personal interaction with them instead of just waiting for reports. Observation and conversation are two important parts of managing the project team. In fact, these are a major part of the management style known as MBWA, Management by Walking Around. As your project progresses, interpersonal management will keep you informed of how your team members are feeling and the ways in which you can help them be better at their jobs. No job is more important than this in project management.

How complex or simple the performance appraisals are will depend on the complexity of the project, labor contract requirements, any organizational policies that apply, and the length of the project. Some may be formal. These will generally be structured by the organization itself to get information about your project team. Other appraisals may be informal, particularly if the appraisals are ad hoc as you are doing MBWA.

If your performance appraisals are formal, you should begin with a set of objectives for the appraisal. Written documents are used for the most part in formal appraisals, and these documents should help you reach the objectives you set for the appraisal. During formal appraisals, you should give feedback to the team member. This feedback can be negative or positive, depending on performance. A management technique that works well is to give positive feedback before and after the negative. This is known as the "sandwich" technique, where you put negative feedback in between positive feedback. Do not be worried about negative feedback. Most people know when they have done something that is negative. Just make sure that you have it documented and can deliver the criticism without making it personal. Try to have positive ways to correct the actions when you do a performance report. In fact, this would be a good time to set personal objectives for the team member. Write these down and bring them up again when you have your next formal appraisal meeting.

Conflict management, if successful, can result in a better team performance. The more formal the ground rules and role definition are, the less conflict there may be. At first, it is a good idea to have the team members try to work out their own differences. If this is not possible, you should address the problem early and use a collaborative approach. It is important that you do not compromise when working on a conflict. Compromise is likely to make all parties unhappy and will not solve the conflict; it will merely keep it going until a later date. If you have continuing conflicts, you may have to use disciplinary actions or actions suggested by the organization for conflict resolution.

An issues log has been discussed before. The key to the log is to keep it as a written document and make it a permanent part of the overall project records. This means that you note the conflict, detail actions taken to deal with the conflict, and note the final outcome of the conflict. The more you record, the better off you will be in the future.

The outputs for managing the project team are requested changes, recommended corrective actions, recommended preventive actions, organizational process assets updates, and updated project management plans.

The requested changes listed as an output for managing the project team are changes in personnel. Sometimes you will be forced to make changes because of events out of your control. Other times you will choose to make changes because of something you believe will make the project work more effectively. When making a staffing change request, you should use the same standard change control process that is used for other areas of managing the project.

The recommended corrective actions in this section deal with human resource issues such as staffing changes (reductions or additions), additional training, and disciplinary actions. The disciplinary actions should be done in accordance with organizational policy. Disciplinary actions should be kept in written form in an organizational guide. If they are not, you should question the HR department for guidelines. Do not do your own version of disciplinary actions. The organization decides how to discipline.

Recommended preventive actions are those actions that are taken to avoid problems in the future. If possible, it is a good idea to take preventive action before a problem or conflict occurs. If you see a potential problem or some actions that you are certain will lead to problems in the future, you should try to forestall these problems.

The updates of the organizational process assets center around lessons learned documentation. As far as possible, document knowledge that has been learned during the project so that the information is available for future reference. If you have a historical database in place, lessons learned will go into it. For projects that do not have a complete database, you can save lessons learned as a separate file for future information.

Some of the lessons learned in the HR area are organization charts, positions, descriptions, ground rules, useful recognition events, skills or competencies of the team members that were uncovered during the execution of the project, and issues and solutions as found in the issues log.

Finally, updating the project plan will finish the output for managing the project team. Change requests and approved change requests should both be kept. In addition, you should note corrective actions to see if they result in updates to the staffing management plan.

Performance Reporting (10.3)

Performance reporting is the process of collecting and disseminating performance information to provide stakeholders with knowledge of how resources are being used to achieve project objectives. When reporting periods do not coincide with project phases, it might be helpful to team members if the project manager includes dates for reporting periods on the project's schedule. Including reporting periods on the schedule helps team members know when they need to write performance reports.

Types of performance reporting include:

- Status reporting - where the project currently stands
- Progress reporting - what has been accomplished versus what is in process
- Forecasting - where the project is going.

It is important to understand that performance reporting is not only a component of the communications variable, but also part of the fourth step of the project management process: controlling.

Performance reporting can affect project costs when time for writing the reports is not allocated in a project's schedule. The time spent writing the reports should be included as part of a project's costs. If the time is not recorded, then the project's total cost will be inaccurate. The time between one performance report and the next is called a reporting period. A reporting period might coincide with the beginning and end of a project phase.

A variety of techniques are used for performance reporting. Earned value analysis is important to performance reporting because it can give the project manager and team members the most accurate measure of whether or not a project's activities are being completed as planned. The most commonly used measures are the cost variance and the schedule variance. These two values can be converted to efficiency factors to reflect the project's cost and schedule performance. The cost performance index is the most commonly used cost-efficiency indicator, and the cumulative CPI is widely used to forecast project costs at completion.

Status Review Meeting

A status review meeting is held regularly to determine progress against the project plan, from a cost, schedule, and quality perspective. It is preferable to collect status prior to the meeting so people can discuss issues intelligently.

Performance Reports

Performance reports provide the information as documented in the communications management plan. The performance reports present the analysis of information in organized, summarized, and leveled format. It is essential to arrange for some report to be made regularly on each feature of the performance standards so that the requirements will be measured. Regular and prompt reports should be made by the project manager for all stakeholders of items for which a performance standard has been established, measurable or not. Some of the reports will be by-products of other data processing functions; most of the information will come from the project team. Typical performance report format include:

- Bar chart
- S-curves
- Tables
- Earned value analysis

Earned value analysis is the most commonly used method of performance measurement in its various forms. It integrates scope, cost (or resource), and schedule to help the project management team assess project performance. Earned value (EV) involves calculating three key values for each activity:

- The Planned Value (PV) is that portion of the approved cost estimate planned to be spent on the activity during a given period.
- The Actual Cost (AC) is the total of costs incurred in accomplishing work on the activity during a given period.
- The Earned Value (EV) is the value of the work actually completed.
- The above three values are used in combination to provide measures of whether or not work is being accomplished as planned. These include the Cost Variance (CV=EV-AC) and the Schedule Variance (SV=EV-PV).
- The cost and schedule variances (CV and SV, respectively) can be converted to efficiency indicators to reflect the cost and schedule performance of any project.
- The most commonly used cost-efficiency indicator is the Cost Performance Index
- (CPI = EV/AC). The cumulative CPI (the sum of all individual EV budgets divided by the sum of all individual AC's) is widely used to forecast project costs at completion.
- The Schedule Performance Index (SPI = EV/PV) is sometimes used in conjunction with the CPI to forecast the project completion estimates.

The following are common classifications of performance reports:

- Routine – Routine or regular, performance reports are not necessarily scheduled, but might be distributed at intervals that coincide with project phases or milestones. The frequency of performance reports depends on how smoothly the project is functioning.
- Exception – Exception performance reports provide project team members with information they need to make decisions or notify them of a change that affects their work. Exception performance reports are also distributed to stakeholders to inform them that a decision has been made.
- Special Analysis – Special analysis performance reports contain information about the results of a special study. Special studies might be conducted as part of a project or to determine a solution to a problem encountered during a project. Special analysis reports are useful not only to a current project, but are valuable documentation of lessons learned for future projects.

Documentation

Good documentation is usually associated with successful projects. This is true regardless of the project's size. It is not acceptable to ignore documentation just because "the project is too small" to bother with it. Further, good documentation coupled with a disciplined change control process will go a long way toward reducing unauthorized changes in the scope of a project. PMI® states that all documentation is produced to record and analyze project performance, including documents that describe the project's product, must be available for review during administrative closure.

There are two types of project documentation that PMI® considers especially important in fostering good project communication:

- Progress Reports - One of the most important ongoing components of effective project communication
- Project Management Plan - The careful analysis required to document the project plan tends to reduce uncertainty on the project, and the distribution of the plan does a lot to keep appropriate people informed

Manage Stakeholders (10.4)

Stakeholder management refers to managing project communications to satisfy the needs and wants of the project stakeholders. Managing stakeholder's increases the likelihood the project will not veer off schedule because of unanswered stakeholder questions or concerns, increases the ability of persons to work together as a team, and limits disruptions during the project. The project manager is usually the one who maintains and monitors stakeholder management.

Communications Management Plan

As stated previously the communications management plan outlines the roles and responsibilities of project participants in the review, approval and distribution of information about key project processes, events, documents and milestones. Stakeholder needs and wants and project expectations provide an understanding of stakeholder goals, objectives, and level of communication needed during the project. The needs, wants and expectations are identified, analyzed, and documented in the communications management plan.

Importance of Communication

By using communication skills, project managers help to plan, direct, control, and coordinate their operations throughout the project life cycle. Peter Drucker states that the communicating ability is essential for success and is perhaps the most important of all the skills an individual should possess. In project management, Sievert emphasizes the importance of communication by stating that a high percentage of the friction, frustrations and inefficiencies in working relationships are traceable to poor communication.

Interpersonal Communication

Interpersonal communication is used to ensure messages are received and understood, two-way communication is necessary. When communicating in a project environment, both the sender and receiver have a duty to understand and to be understood. This is accomplished through feedback. Interpersonal communication is the process of sharing information with others. Three basic elements of interpersonal communication:

- The sender (or encoder) of the message.
- The signal or the message.
- The receiver (or decoder) of the message.

Goals of interpersonal communication include:

- Understanding the exact meaning and intent of others.
- Being understood by others.
- Gaining acceptance for yourself and/or your ideas.
- Producing action or change.

Process of interpersonal communication: (Wilbur Schramm)

- Sender determines what information to share and with whom and encodes the message.
- Sender transmits the message as a signal to the receiver.
- The receiver receives the message.
- The receiver decodes the message to determine its meaning and then responds accordingly.
- Communication is successful if the decoded message is the same as the sender intended.
- Utilizing experience, the sender anticipates how the message will be decoded and encodes the message, accordingly.

Methods of Interpersonal Communication

Project managers must have the ability to think logically and communicate effectively. The three forms of communication are verbal, non-verbal and written communication.

Verbal Advantages:

- Timely exchange of information
- Rapid feedback
- Immediate synthesis of message
- Timely closure

Verbal Disadvantages:

- Technical jargon especially in complex projects may make verbal communication difficult for non-technical people and other stakeholders.
- No paper trail.

Three stages of effective verbal communication and presentation:

1. The introduction: Tell them what you're going to tell them.
2. The explanation: Tell them.
3. The summary: Tell them what you just told them.

Non-Verbal

Encoding a message without using words. Includes gestures, vocal tones, facial expressions, environmental settings, manner of dress, and body language. Generally, a receiver's interpretation of a message is based not only on the words in the message, but also on the nonverbal behaviors of the sender. In an interpersonal communication situation in projects, nonverbal factors generally have more influence on the total impact of a message than verbal factors. Total Message Impact = Words (7%) + Vocal tones (38%) + Facial expressions (55%) (Albert Meharabian). Project managers may use nonverbal ingredients to complement verbal message ingredients whenever possible but must be careful that contradictory messages are not presented. Project managers should avoid sending ambiguous messages by "walking the talk" (mean what you say and say what you mean).

Written Communication

In a project environment, written communication includes reports, plans, proposals, standards, policies, procedures, letters, memoranda, legal documents, and other forms of information to be transmitted. The main aim of business writing is that it should be understood clearly when read quickly. The message should be well planned, simple, clear, and direct. Project managers and others can increase their personal power or influence by developing a "power" vocabulary when writing executive summaries, cover letters, bid proposals, project reports, marketing strategies, presentations, etc.

Major steps to writing:

- Establish the basic purpose of the message.
- Collect and organize material.
- Prepare draft.
- Check the overall structure.
- Send the message.

Determine when to put the message in writing. Written communication is effective in the following cases:

- When conveying complex information or data.
- When requiring future action from team members.
- When it is the receiver's preferred communication style.
- When communicating company policies or changes to policies.
- When conveying a message that could be misunderstood either accidentally or intentionally.

Macro-Barriers to Successful Communication

Macro-barriers are elements of the communication environment that hinder successful communication in a general sense. Such as the following:

- Lack of subject knowledge - Must have sufficient knowledge to send message. Must know level of understanding of receiver.
- Information overload - Keep messages simple and direct. Provide sufficient information - keep it simple and short.
- Cultural differences - Meanings and interpretations may vary among different cultures. Encourage team members to learn each other's cultures.
- Organizational climate - Minimize the differences associated with status and ego within the organization. Create an atmosphere of openness and trust by talking with people. Avoid talking down to people.
- Number of links - Reduce the number of transmission links. The more links, the more opportunity for distortion in the message. Be aware of entrophy. 23-27% of message is lost in upward communication.

Micro-Barriers to Successful Communication

Micro-barriers are elements of the communication environment that obstruct successful communication in a specific sense and include the following:

- Perceptions - Sender's view of the receiver: senders communicate differently depending on how they perceive the receiver's level of knowledge and ability to understand the message. Senders should be careful not to imply any negative attitudes towards the receiver through communication behavior. Receiver's view of the sender: How the receiver personally feels about the sender may influence how carefully the receiver listens. If negative, these feelings may cause the receiver to ignore the message. If overly positive, these feelings may inhibit the receiver's judgment.
- Message competition - Communicate only when you have the total attention of the recipient. Try to minimize noise or other factors contributing to message interference.
- Project jargon and terminology - Define project terminology used in messages. Be aware of the use of project terminology and the intended audience.

Types of Project Communications

- Interpersonal communication - Listening, self-presentation, problem solving, decision making, negotiating, and conflict management. Necessary skills for interacting with the project team and with the client on a daily basis.
- Communication with public and community - Includes all public relations efforts necessary to encourage community involvement, enhance public understanding of the project, break down resistance, gain acceptance, and be a project spokesperson. May involve public speaking, making presentations, dealing with media representatives, and producing written publicity or PR materials.
- Formal communication - Is carried out through traditional responsibility and relationship channels. Includes strategic plans, project planning systems, standards, policies, procedures, proposals, letters, etc. Most effectively done in written form.

- Informal communication - Done through informal groups in which relationships are dependent upon common ties such as interests, hobbies, kinship, friendship, social status, etc.

Project managers must identify the strengths and limitations of informal communications and explore strategies to increase overall project effectiveness through informal communications.

Managing Meetings Effectively

Meetings provide a means to exchange and share messages, ideas and information. Meetings require a great deal of time and effort and therefore should be called only when necessary. Meetings should not take the place of project managers resolving problems and issues by working individually with the team members via the telephone, personal discussion, or e-mail. Avoid calling a meeting just for the sake of calling a meeting. Meetings should be productive.

Guidelines for effective meetings:

- Before the meeting: Determine purpose, set ground rules for discussion, determine necessary attendees, notify participants in advance of location and agenda, start and end on time.
- During the meeting: Identify the specific objectives of the meeting, gather input from participants, stick to the agenda, use visual aids to illustrate points, periodically summarize the results of the discussion, assign action items as appropriate, and stick to the specified time limit.
- After the meeting: Follow up on individual action items, distribute concise minutes and use the minutes at the next meeting to measure results.

Communication Channels and Links

The project manager must recognize and understand the project's formal communication channels. Three basic channels of communication in the project environment:

- Upward communication (vertically or diagonally) - Information provided to upper management for their purposes of evaluating the overall performance of the projects for which they are responsible, or to refine organizational strategy. Project managers may use the "by exception" format for project status. This feedback helps top management assess priorities and make organizational modifications to effectively meet project goals and objectives and be more effective in the future.
- Downward communication (vertically or diagonally) - Provides direction and control for project team members and other employees. Contains job-related information focusing on scope and definition, quality, schedule, implementation, and evaluation and feedback. May include statements of organizational philosophy, policies, project objectives, schedules, budgets, and constraints, position descriptions and other written information relating to the importance, rationale and interrelationships and interactions of various departments projects, and jobs in an organization.
- Lateral communication (horizontally) - Information exchange between the project manager and his/her peers: functional managers, staff personnel, contractors, other project managers, etc. Involves negotiating resources, schedules, and budgets; coordinating activities between groups, as well as developing plans for future operating periods. Is vital to the success of a project and is also the most important factor for

survival and growth in a highly competitive and turbulent environment. Requires diplomacy and experience. If managed properly, it creates a harmonious, cooperative environment based on trust and respect for one another. If poorly managed, it may lead to conflict, blame, and failure to meet project objectives.

High Performance Communication

A project manager's performance depends upon how well he/she works with the project team in planning, implementing, coordinating, interfacing, integrating, and controlling the project. Project managers must be aware of their own communication strengths and weaknesses. The project manager achieves project objectives by using effective communication to inspire high team performance.

Key requirements for achieving high team performance include:

- Openness in communication
- Development of trust (so that accuracy of communication is achieved)
- Continuous support and counseling

Effective Listening

Effective listening is one of the most important skills for a project manager to acquire and practice. It is essential for successful project management and improves communication and helps develop mutual respect, rapport, and trust among project participants.

Verbal Listening Behaviors

Verbal listening behaviors in such things as asking questions to clarify and gather more information. Questions should be probing and constructive. Summarizing at intervals what the speaker has said to confirm what you have understood. Asking the speaker for examples. Ascertaining the speaker's feelings and acknowledging them. ("You seem angry."). Directing the speaker to the most appropriate listener. ("George can best help you with that.") Or, just listen if the person needs to let off steam.

Non-Verbal Listening Behaviors

Are actions that reinforce the message or undermine it. Some examples includes:

- Making eye contact. (indicates honesty and openness)
- Being expressive and alert. (indicates interest - motivates speaker to be open)
- Moving closer to the speaker. (establishes friendly environment)
- Listening for the intention behind the speaker's communication. (sometimes the real message is not what's said, but how it is said)
- Facial expressions, touching, use of personal space, use of time.
- Body language (a subset of non-verbal) accounts for 55 percent of communication) It includes facial expressions, touching, and body positioning.

Barriers to Effective Listening

The mismatch between our speed of talking (100-400 words per minute) and our speed of thinking (approx. 600 words per minute) makes effective listening tough. Some of the personal and environmental barriers that influence the overall effectiveness of communication include:

- Poor listeners - people do not talk freely when they know the audience isn't listening. This inhibits effective communications.
- Resistance to the message - people don't like to listen to something that is contrary to their preconceived ideas. When they should be listening, they are concentrating on their response or defense, instead.
- Physical distractions - telephone calls, people coming in and out of office/meetings, etc. Also, environments that create feelings of inequality in status discourage effective listening.
- Perceptual differences - can influence the behavior of people which in turn can affect communications. For example, when perceptual differences occur, people tend to:
  - Jump to conclusions
  - Confuse facts with opinions
  - Make frozen evaluations (those that cannot be easily changed)

Project managers must be aware of these barriers to effective listening that might be caused by interpersonal conflict, distractions, management response to new ideas or the overall project climate.

Project managers should try to minimize barriers by nurturing better understanding and good working relationships necessary to effective communication among project participants. Use of "I" messages instead of "you" messages assists the speaker with delivery of a nonjudgmental, non-critical message while still conveying the speaker's points.

Checking perceptions and asking for clarification from speaker of intended message helps facilitate effective communications.

Guidelines for Active Listening

Effective listening requires paying attention to the task, relationship and environmental dimensions of communication. Effective listening requires being genuinely concerned for the individual as a person, practicing neutrality, and taking an objective approach. It requires patience, mutual trust and respect. Active listeners empathize with the speaker, ask questions to clarify the message, and provide frequent feedback so that the sender can evaluate the accuracy of his or her message. Active listeners are equally aware of the influence of vocal tones, facial expressions and other nonverbal components in addition to the verbal component of communications.

Some practical guidelines for active listening include:

- Stop talking!
- Show the speaker you are ready to listen:
  - Silence: signals you are ready to listen.
  - Few distractions: shut the door, put the phone on hold, refrain from impatient mannerisms, etc.
- A receptive attitude: empathize with the speaker's point of view. Listen for total meaning, not just for points of opposition.

Communication Styles

The project manager uses communication more than any other skill set to manage the project throughout its life cycle and to ensure that team members are working cohesively and resolving problems.

Two dimensions of thinking and action include:

- The thinking and decision-making approach which varies from logical (sequential) to intuitive (random)
- The action style which varies from hands-on (concrete) to research based (abstract)

When the two dimensions are combined, the results are four major communication styles all of which are applicable at various times in the project life cycle. The styles are:

- Concrete-sequential: (Mr./Ms. Fix-it)
- Person likes to focus on ideas and tasks, thinks systematically and predictably.
- Person wants to complete tasks and minimize change.

Abstract-sequential: (Organizer)
- Person who relies on logical analysis and systematic planning to solve problems.
- These communicators are people and task-oriented, which makes them effect team builders.
- These communicators prefer to have all information before making a decision, and they know how to control resources and information.

Concrete-random: (Explorer/entrepreneur)
- Person relies on people and technology, finds practical use for theories and models.
- These communicators make decisions after thorough analysis and evaluation and excel at facilitating planning sessions, discussions, and changes.

Abstract-random: (Intuitive free thinker)
- Person views experiences from different perspectives and sees the big picture and the long-term vision.
- These communicators make good brainstormers because they can listen actively and enjoy the process of generating new ideas.

How Project Managers Spend their Time

Approximately 75-90% of project manager's time is spent communicating. Of the PM's time spent communicating, approximately 45% is spent listening. Another 30% is spent speaking. Approximately 10% is spent reading; another 10% writing, and 5% other. Project managers spend 50% of their time in meetings.

Risk Monitoring and Control (11.6)

Risk monitoring and control is the process of keeping track of all the identified risks and identifying new risks as their presence becomes known and residual risks that occur when the risk management plans are implemented on individual risks. The effectiveness of the risk management plan is evaluated on an ongoing basis throughout the project.

When a risk is apparently going to take place, the contingency plan is brought into place. If there is no contingency plan, then the risk is worked on an ad hoc basis using what is termed a workaround. A workaround is an unplanned response to a negative risk event.

The concern of the project manager and the project team is that the risk responses have been brought to bear on the risk as planned, that the risk response has been effective. Additional risks may develop, and additional responses may be necessary.

Risk management is a continuous process that takes place during the entire project from beginning to end. As the project progresses, the risks that have been identified are monitored and reassessed as the time that they can take place approaches. Early warning indicators are monitored to reassess the probability and impact of the risk. As the risk approaches, the risk strategies are reviewed for appropriateness, and additional responses are planned.

As each risk occurs and is dealt with, or is avoided, these changes must be documented. Good documentation ensures that risks of this type will be dealt with in a more effective way than before and that the next project manager will benefit from "lessons learned."

Contract Administration (12.5)

Contract administration is the formal verification that the contractor has fulfilled his contractual obligations. As part of contract administration, the project manager must make sure all project team members are aware of their responsibilities with regard to a contract.
During this step, the project manager—with help from the contracting specialists—monitors the seller's performance against the contract's specifications, performance standards, and terms and conditions. PMI® emphasizes that the legal nature of the contractual arrangement makes it imperative that the project team be aware of the legal implications of actions taken during contract administration.

Contract Document

At a minimum, the following items are usually documented in the contract:

- Delivery schedule
- Payment schedule - method for determining the price
- Handling of changes
- Warranties, insurance, inspections
- Delays termination
- Subcontracts, performance bonds

Contracts may have specific terms or conditions for completion and closeout. You should be aware of these terms or conditions so that project closure is not held up because you overlooked an important detail. If you are not administering the contract yourself, ask your contracts/procurement department if there are any special conditions that you should know about.

Standard Clauses

The use of standard clauses is encouraged where possible because they are legally sufficient for most contractual situations and because they cost less (customized contract language takes time and can sometimes be expensive to develop).

The following is a brief description of clauses specifically addressed in PMI's Contract Administration for the Project Manager.

Changes
- Changes to project scope constitute one of the major areas of cost growth
- Control of change
- Who initiates a change request
- How change is funded
- Final approval authority
- Configuration control
- Do not price changes on a cost-plus basis; use lump-sum

Warranties
- Establish a level of quality
- Express warranty: Contract explicitly states what the level of quality is
- Implied warranty: Contract describes "merchantability" or "fitness of use"

Doctrine of Waiver: the relinquishing of one party's contract rights because of a lack of enforcement of those rights

Delays
- Who caused it
- Nature of the interruption
- Impact

Bonds
- Performance bond: Secures for the buyer the performance and fulfillment of the contract
- Payment bond: Guaranteed payment to subcontractors and laborers by the prime or the guarantor

Breach
- Failure to perform a contractual obligation
- Measure for damage is the amount of loss sustained by an injured party
- Material breach: More serious than a contract breach

Nonfaulted party discharged from any further obligations: for example, when a contract stipulates that time is of the essence, failure to perform within the allotted time constitutes material breach and the project manager will not be required to accept late performance.

Elements of a Legally Enforceable Contract: Finally, you should be familiar with the elements of a legally valid (enforceable) contract:

- The agreement must be voluntary (there must be both an offer and an acceptance).
- The people signing must have the legal capacity to do so

- There must be sufficient cause to contract—"consideration" must be provided to both parties
- The contract must be for a legal purpose and must not violate public policy

Changes and Change Control

All contracts should define the process by which any changes to the contract (project) can be accommodated and should include the paperwork, tracking systems, and approvals necessary for authorizing changes. The system should cover who initiates a change request, how it is processed and funded, and who has the final approval authority. Changes made, whether they are approved or unapproved, must be reflected in the appropriate project documents.

Undefined Work

Undefined work becomes an issue when "time is of the essence." The parties would like to proceed with the project, but the price and other important terms and conditions of the contract have not been specified or agreed to.

This situation can arise either at the outset of a contractual relationship or as a result of significant changes to an ongoing contract. At the outset of a contract, a contractor will often proceed on the basis of a "letter contract," with the details to be worked out later. Obviously, a certain amount of trust exists in such a circumstance. When undefined work arises as a result of changes, contractors often proceed without a formal change order authorizing them to do so.

Review Questions

1. While the project is being completed, management requests a change. What is the first thing the project manager should do?

    (A) Comply with the request if possible.
    (B) Obtain a complete understanding of the scope of the change.
    (C) Tell the customer that a change will be coming.
    (D) Ask the team to accept the change.

2. In quality terms, one of the meanings of out of control is:

    (A) several data points fall on the same side of the mean within the upper and lower control limits.
    (B) a data point is within 1-sigma.
    (C) someone on the team is upset.
    (D) a data point on a control charts falls inside the upper or lower control limit.

3. The project is calculated to be completed four days after the desired completion date. You do not have access to additional resources. The project is low risk, the benefit cost ratio is expected to be 1.6, and the dependencies are preferential. Under these circumstances, what would the best thing to do?

    (A) Cut resources from a task.
    (B) Make more tasks concurrent.
    (C) Move resources from the preferential dependencies to the external dependencies.
    (D) Remove a task from the project.

4. From the project perspective, quality attributes:

    (A) determine how effectively the performing organization supports the project.
    (B) provide the basis for judging the project's success or failure.
    (C) are specific characteristics for which a product is designed and tested.
    (D) are objective criteria that must be met.

5. The previous project manager informed management that all was well on the project. However, the new project manager discovers that the project has a CPI of .89. What does this mean?

    (A) When the project is completed, 89% more than planned will have been spent.
    (B) At this time, it is expected that the total project will take 89% longer than planned.
    (C) The project is only getting 89 cents out of every dollar invested.
    (D) The project is only progressing at 89% of what was planned.

6. A company asks one of the project managers to lead a project to create a substantially improved version of one of the company's best selling products. The project manager is given total freedom of decision and resources, including whether to utilize contractor services and/or the company's resource pool. Under these circumstances, which of the following would be the best way for the project manager to build the team?

(A) She should contract the entire team utilizing a "cost plus incentive fee" type of contract.
(B) She should contract selected team members on an ad hoc and as needed basis utilizing a "time and materials" type of contract.
(C) She should choose her team from the top developers and fabrication workers in the company.
(D) She should create a team of company line workers and contracts the development services under a "cost reimbursable" contract with provisions to protect confidentiality.

7. Project coordination is enhanced through progress reporting, variance reporting, and cross-team meetings. These are all forms of:

(A) risk management and reporting.
(B) stakeholder management.
(C) communications management.
(D) quality management.

8. A client has asked you to add scope of work to the project. The project is under budget and a little ahead of schedule. What should you do?

(A) Let the client know the effects of the change on the project.
(B) Approve the change.
(C) Get approval from the configuration change board.
(D) Ask approval from the sponsor for making the change.

9. Which chart helps a project manager determine possible causes of potential problems and actual problems?

(A) A fishbone diagram
(B) The 50/50 rule
(C) A Pareto chart
(D) A control chart

10. The project manager on a large software installation project is working with her team on a critical set of tasks. They are working late on Saturday night. Circumstances create the situation wherein the project manager must decide to change the schedule that will push the end date of the project out two weeks. What best action should the project manager take next as a result of her decision?

(A) Scope creep has occurred.
(B) An emergency project change has taken place.
(C) Risk assessment failure has taken place.
(D) A status change to the implementation has taken place.

11. Where are control limits located on a control chart?

    (A) Above the statistical independence point.
    (B) Near the assignable cause.
    (C) Above the normal curve.
    (D) Within the specification limits.

12. A functional manager meets with the project manager's boss to discuss a change to the acceptance criteria for a major deliverable. After the meeting, the boss contacts the project manager and tells him to make the change. What is the best thing to do?

    (A) Understand the change.
    (B) Make the change as soon as possible.
    (C) Tell the team about the change.
    (D) Supply management with a change form and ask management to complete and return it as soon as possible.

13. The project is mostly complete. However, the customer wants to make a major change to the scope of work. The project manager should:

    (A) ask the customer for a description of the change.
    (B) meet with the project team to determine if this change can be made.
    (C) inform management.
    (D) explain that the change cannot be made at this point in the process.

14. Which type of cost is team training?

    (A) Net present value
    (B) Direct
    (C) Variable
    (D) Indirect

15. While reviewing project performance, the project manager determines that the project is behind schedule. What is the best option?

    (A) Look for tasks that can be done in parallel.
    (B) Remove resources from the project to one that is not failing.
    (C) Let management know.
    (D) Tell the customer.

16. You must start construction tomorrow to meet the deadline. What type of contract should you sign to start construction?

    (A) Cost plus contract.
    (B) Fixed-price contract.
    (C) Time and material basis contract.
    (D) Cost plus primary fee contract.

17. Management wants to look at how a project is doing. To make a valid judgment, management should compare this project with which of the following?

(A) Flowcharts
(B) Benchmarks
(C) Trend analysis
(D) Gantt charts

18. Informing appropriate stakeholders of authorized project cost changes occurs during cost:

(A) estimating.
(B) management.
(C) control.
(D) budgeting.

19. Non-random data points that are grouped together on one side of the mean of a control chart are called:

(A) specification limits
(B) in control
(C) rule of seven
(D) 6-sigma

20. Risk owners can potentially have conflict with risk auditors because risk auditors:

(A) investigate the effectiveness of the risk owner.
(B) report to the project manager.
(C) report to the stakeholders.
(D) measure the effectiveness of the risk thresholds.

21. Your project has had a major defect and you have gotten the project team and the quality engineers involved in problem analysis. There are three different opinions of what the cause of the problem might be. In order to get to the root of the problem you decide to use a cause-and-effect diagram. Which of the following would best describe what the group is involved in?

(A) Quality planning
(B) Quality analysis
(C) Quality assurance
(D) Quality control

22. A customer has requested a change that requires you to obtain new equipment. You need to decide whether to lease or buy the equipment. The daily lease cost is US $150. The cost of purchasing the item is US $2,000 for the investment cost and US $50 for the daily cost. You will need to use the item for about 12 days. What should you do?

    (A) Buy it.
    (B) Lease it.
    (C) Lease it for only seven days to try to save cost.
    (D) Ask the customer for a US $2,000 change order.

23. A cause-and-effect diagram and an Ishikawa diagram are both:

    (A) fishbone diagrams.
    (B) flow charts.
    (C) Pareto charts.
    (D) control charts.

24. The best method to control costs is to:

    (A) estimate during the execution of the project and then manage each task to the budget.
    (B) estimate during the execution of the project and have management confirm the estimates.
    (C) estimate during planning and then re-estimate before each task begins.
    (D) estimate at the beginning of the project and then check costs against the baseline.

25. Which of the following is correct in regard to scope change control?

    (A) Controlling cost is the most effective way of controlling scope.
    (B) Scope change control is never integrated with other control processes.
    (C) Controlling schedule is the most effective way of controlling scope.
    (D) Scope change control must be integrated with other control processes.

26. The project team is working on an important and complex project that requires a lot of coordination. Under these circumstances, the best strategy is to:

    (A) have a war room.
    (B) hire a contractor.
    (C) hold more meetings to get the word out.
    (D) gain extra assistance from management.

27. A management team is trying to decide if it will continue working on a project that has to date cost $500,000. The original estimate for work completed to date was $200,000. The $300,000 difference between the actual cost and the original estimate is best described as a:

    (A) direct cost.
    (B) sunk cost.
    (C) customer cost.
    (D) indirect cost.

28. During a project team meeting, a team member suggests an enhancement to the scope of work that is beyond the scope of the project charter. The project manager points out that the team needs to concentrate on completing all the work and only the work required. This is an example of:

    (A) scope management
    (B) change management process
    (C) scope decomposition
    (D) quality analysis

29. The customer requests a change to the project that will increase the project risk. Which of the following should you do before all the others?

    (A) Include the expected value of the risk in the new cost estimate.
    (B) Talk to the customer about the impact of the change.
    (C) Analyze the impacts of the change with the team.
    (D) Change the risk management plan.

30. Your current project has a major defect and as the project manager, you have decided to involve both the project team and the process engineers in analyzing the situation. One of the groups says that the real fault is in the age of the equipment. Another says it is the lack of a material for the correct quality. To address the root of the problem you decide to use an Ishikawa diagram to assist the group. Which of the following best describes the step of the quality management process in which the group is involved in this situation?

    (A) Perform quality assurance
    (B) Perform quality analysis
    (C) Perform quality planning
    (D) Perform quality control

31. Which of the following is the most likely cause of poor risk management?

    (A) Lack of a prioritized list of risks.
    (B) Lack of detail in the scope statement.
    (C) Inadequate risk response planning.
    (D) Poor risk monitoring and control.

32. Non-random data points that are still within the upper and lower control limit of a control chart are:

    (A) in control
    (B) not enough information given
    (C) specification limits
    (D) out of control

33. The project manager invited many of the project stakeholders to help inspect quality on the project. Of the following, which would not be an output of this activity?

   (A) Quality improvement
   (B) Rework
   (C) Acceptance decisions
   (D) Quality management plan

34. A project is seriously delayed. Earned value analysis shows that the project needs to be completed 10% faster than the work has been going. To get the project back on track, management wants to add 10 people to a task currently assigned to one person. The project manager disagrees, noting that such an increase will not produce an increase in speed. This is an example of:

   (A) earned value
   (B) life-cycle costing
   (C) law of diminishing returns
   (D) fast tracking

35. Which of the following is true of inspections?

   (A) They may not be conducted by the project team.
   (B) They test future desires of prospective customers.
   (C) They can only be conducted on the final product.
   (D) They prevent errors from reaching the customer before delivery.

36. A project manager is trying to manage a complex project at a 6-sigma level with 15 people. The project manager decides to use a trend report because it will help him:

   (A) examine project results over time.
   (B) evaluate earned value.
   (C) determine the level of quality.
   (D) analyze the level of project complexity.

37. A project manager decides to bring expected future schedule performance in line with the project plan. Which of the following best describes the process performed by the project manager?

   (A) The project manager used corrective action.
   (B) The project manager used lessons learned.
   (C) The project manager did this as a result of performing scope verification.
   (D) The project manager did this as a result of performing scope planning.

38. A project manager has just been notified of a cost increase from a seller. The project manager should first determine if:

   (A) another seller can provide it at the original cost.
   (B) the task is on the critical path.
   (C) another task can save money.
   (D) there is enough reserve to handle the change.

Answers

1. B
2. B
3. B
4. C
5. C
6. C
7. C
8. A
9. A
10. B
11. D
12. A
13. A
14. B
15. A
16. C
17. B
18. C
19. C
20. A
21. D
22. B
23. A
24. D
25. D
26. A
27. B
28. A
29. C
30. D
31. A
32. D
33. D
34. C
35. D
36. A
37. A
38. D

Chapter 8
Closing Process Group

The last major Process Group of a project's life cycle is the project Closing Process Group. Project closeout is performed after all defined project objectives have been met and the customer has formally accepted the project's deliverables and end product or, in some instances, when a project has been cancelled or terminated early. Project closeout is fairly routine, but it is an important process. By properly completing the project closeout, organizations can benefit from lessons learned and information compiled at closure.

The Closing Process Group is comprised of two processes: close project and contract closure. These are depicted in the figure below.

Figure 26 - Closing Process Group Processes

Some of the key elements to project closeout are:

- Completion and closeout of any contractual agreements with suppliers or providers
- Formalizing customer acceptance
- Closeout of any financial matters
- Preparation of the project's final performance report
- Conducting a project review
- Documenting lessons learned
- Completing, collecting and archiving project records
- Celebrating project success

Close Project (4.7)

The inputs into the close project process include the project management plan, contract documentation, enterprise environmental factors, organizational process assets, work performance information, and the deliverables. The project plan and contract documentation have been described several times already in this book.

The enterprise environmental factors include the organization's culture and structure. Standards, as established by the industry or government regulations, are also part of the enterprise environmental factors.

The people available for the project are a major part of the internal environmental factors, as are the personnel administration guidelines set up by the company. Another important internal environmental factor is the stakeholder risk tolerances, which will determine how you will manage the risks that occur in the execution of projects.

An external factor in the enterprise environment will be the marketplace conditions. These conditions are outside the control of the organization but will still influence how the project is executed and will probably influence whether the project is actually chosen in the first place.

The work performance information will come from the various performance reports that are done throughout the project, and your job, as outlined before, is to manage the variances between the planned and the actual in the execution of the project.

The outputs of the close project process are the administrative closure procedures. These will be the guidelines that are needed in order to bring full administrative closure to the project, and they should be clearly recorded and kept throughout the project. Without these, the project will go on and on and on... The procedures must be agreed upon early in the project, and then as the end of a project phase or the project itself approaches, the procedures should be implemented to make sure that the project is successfully closed from an administrative standpoint.

Contract Closure (12.6)

Contract closure is the formal verification that contractors have completely and successfully fulfilled their obligations to a project. During contract closeout, all paperwork and electronic files used during the project must be updated and filed in a database for future reference. Most often, the contract will specify how the contract and project should be closed.

Contract records are very important and include the contract itself and other relevant documentation such as progress reports, financial records, invoices, and payment records. These are often kept in a contract file, which should be part of the complete project file. The contract file is a complete set of index records.

Contract documentation is also important should a procurement audit be initiated. Such an audit is a structured review of the procurement process from procurement planning through contract administration. The purpose of the audit is to identify success and failures that warrant transfer to other procurement items on the current project or future projects.

The person or organization responsible for contract administration should provide the seller with formal written notice when the contract has been completed. The contract should define the requirements for formal acceptance.

Organizing for Contract Management

According to PMI® a company can assign project contracting responsibility in a centralized or decentralized manner.

Centralized Contracting

With centralized contracting, a single function within the company is responsible for the entire contracting process for all projects. Contracting procedures typically are stringent and standardized. This form works best in functionally organized companies.

Advantages of Centralized Contracting

- More economical.
- Easier to control overall contracting efforts.
- Higher degree of contracting specialization.
- Orders can be consolidated across several projects.

Disadvantages of Centralized Contracting

- The contracting office can become a bottleneck if several projects have heavy needs at once.
- Less attention is given to the special needs of individual projects.

Decentralized Contracting

With decentralized contracting, each project manager controls the contracting process for his or her project. This form works best if companies follow the projectized organization

Advantages of Decentralized Contracting

- Project manager has more control
- Contracting personnel are more familiar with project needs
- More flexible and adaptable to project needs

Disadvantages of Decentralized Contracting

- Duplication of contracting efforts across projects
- Higher costs
- No standard contracting policies

Force Majeure

Force Majeure literally means "greater force." These clauses excuse a party from liability if some unforeseen event beyond the control of that party prevents it from performing its obligations under the contract. Typically, force majeure clauses cover natural disasters or other "Acts of God," war, or the failure of third parties—such as suppliers and subcontractors—to perform their obligations to the contracting party. It is important to remember that force majeure clauses are intended to excuse a party only if the failure to perform could not be avoided by the exercise of due care by that party.

When negotiating force majeure clauses, make sure that the clause applies equally to all parties to the agreement—not just the licensor. Also, it is helpful if the clause sets forth some specific examples of acts that will excuse performance under the clause, such as wars, natural disasters, and other major events that are clearly outside a party's control. Inclusion of examples will help to make clear the parties' intent that such clauses are not intended to apply to excuse failures to perform for reasons within the control of the parties.

Privity of Contract

Privity of contract is a legal term that recognizes that the contractual relationship exists between a buyer and its prime contractor. No contract exists between the buyer and the subcontractors, and it is legally improper for a buyer to bypass a contractor and deal directly with a subcontractor(s).

Beyond the legal issue, there are other reasons for a buyer to be cautious about dealing with subcontractors. In doing so, the buyer may inadvertently relieve the prime contractor of certain responsibilities. For example, if a buyer informs a subcontractor that things might work better if the subcontractor would "try the following approach . . ." and the subcontractor runs into trouble, the prime contractor may rightfully claim that the buyer's interference caused the problems.

Review Questions

1. A company and its seller are in the middle of a long dispute over the costs of terminating the contract. The project manager determines that the only way to resolve the problem is to have it heard and resolved by a neutral party. To accomplish this, the project manager should use a(n):

    (A) functional resource manager.
    (B) conflict solution expert.
    (C) arbitrator.
    (D) lawyer.

2. A company is making an effort to improve its project performance and create historical records of past projects. What is the best way to accomplish this?

    (A) Creating project plans.
    (B) Creating lessons learned.
    (C) Creating network diagrams.
    (D) Creating status reports.

3. A contract has just been signed with a construction company to complete a remodeling project within three months. Due to force majeure, the project will be delayed by an additional three months. The construction company has asked for an early termination of the contract due to lack of resources. What is the appropriate thing to do in this situation?

    (A) Complete contract closure.
    (B) Re-negotiate the contract.
    (C) Seek legal advice.
    (D) Complete administrative closure.

4. A project is considered closed when the:

    (A) lessons learned are completed.
    (B) client accepts the product.
    (C) contract is finished.
    (D) archives are completed.

5. A project manager has just reached the end of a project. Which of the following documents will the project manager need for closure of the project?

    (A) Change requests.
    (B) Documents that describe the product of the project.
    (C) Documents that describe the project status.
    (D) Trend analyses.

6. A project manager has finished the project. He knows that all the scope has been completed and is within cost and time objectives set by the sponsor. The sponsor, however, says that the project is a failure, because the original schedule was for 27 weeks and the project was completed in 33 weeks. If the project baseline was 33 weeks, the project is a success because:

   (A) it only had six weeks of changes.
   (B) it was completed within the baseline.
   (C) there were so few changes.
   (D) there was good communication control.

7. A project manager for a large international bank has a project team that just implemented an electronic funds project involving four large vendors. The project manager struggled through every phase of the procurement process since the bank had a weak internal contracts department. What would be the MOST appropriate thing to do to ensure the problems are resolved for future projects?

   (A) Address this through contract change control.
   (B) Conduct a procurement audit.
   (C) Document all of the issues in a memo and schedule a meeting with the head of the contract office.
   (D) Include an agenda item in the project closedown to discuss these issues in a non-threatening manner.

8. A project manager is finalizing a project that has had repeated problems with cost conformance. He is concerned about what management will say. Which of the following types of information would be best for the project manager to use to evaluate performance?

   (A) Cost performance index (CPI)
   (B) Schedule variance (SV)
   (C) Cost variance (CV)
   (D) The project budget (PB)

9. A project manager you are mentoring comes to you for help because he is about to face his first procurement audit. You might explain that he should not worry about such an audit because it:

   (A) makes sure the contract is being followed.
   (B) identifies successes and failures that warrant transfer to other procurements.
   (C) makes sure the seller is following the contract.
   (D) makes sure costs are in line with the project.

10. A project team has completed all the technical project deliverables, and the customer has accepted the deliverables. However, the lessons learned required by the project office have not been completed. What is the status of the project?

    (A) The project is incomplete until all deliverables are complete and accepted.
    (B) The project is complete because the project has reached the due date.
    (C) The project is complete because the customer has accepted the deliverables.
    (D) The project is incomplete because the project needs to be re-planned.

11. All of the following are required to bring a project to closure except?

    (A) Perform project feedback with the team.
    (B) Obtain sign off from the customer.
    (C) Review project documentation for completeness.
    (D) Update the project plans.

12. An advisor to a new project manager tells the project manager to create lessons learned at the end of a project. What does a lessons learned include?

    (A) Reports from management.
    (B) All the plans used in the project.
    (C) Variances and their causes.
    (D) Reports from the customer.

13. At the end of a project, a project manager determines that the project has added four areas of functionality and three areas of performance. The customer has expressed satisfaction with the project. What does this mean in terms of the success of the project?

    (A) The project is unsuccessful because it was gold plated.
    (B) The project was successful because the team had a chance to learn new areas of functionality and the customer was satisfied.
    (C) The project was unsuccessful because the customer being happy means they would have paid more for the work.
    (D) The project is an unqualified success.

14. Contract closure and administrative closure both involve:

    (A) creation of the scope verification plan.
    (B) quality assurance activities.
    (C) product verification.
    (D) kick-off meetings.

15. Company procedures require the creation of a lessons learned. For which of the following is a lessons learned used?

    (A) Planning record for the current project.
    (B) Historical records for future projects.
    (C) Informing the team about the project plan.
    (D) Informing the team about what the project manager has done.

16. At the end of a two-year project, the key stakeholders agree that the project has met all its goals and objectives outlined in the project charter and further defined in the scope and statement of work. The project is within budget and has finished on time. The management of one of the functional areas is quite upset because over half of his staff quit during the project citing long hours and lack of management support. What is the most correct statement about this project?

   (A) The project was within budget and time and achieved its objectives. Upper management is responsible for providing adequate resources, and the project manager successfully managed the project with available resources.
   (B) The project should be measured against how successfully it met its charter. This was not done during this project.
   (C) The project manager did not obtain adequate resources and did not set a realistic deadline based on resources available.
   (D) The functional manager is responsible for his staff and obtaining adequate resources to meet the schedule once it has been set. The project and project manager achieved all of its goals set forth in the charter.

17. Documentation on a contract should include all of the following except:

   (A) Inspection reports.
   (B) Approvals.
   (C) Customer's meeting minutes.
   (D) Correspondence.

18. During project closure a project sponsor complains that the project did not increase the department's knowledge of Java programming and therefore, the project is not complete. The customer has accepted the project. The project manager determines that all stated objectives and deliverables have been met. He does not find evidence that Java programming was an objective. A review of project correspondence shows no mention of the deliverable. The project manager should:

   (A) meet with the team to discuss the issue and find a resolution.
   (B) get the project stakeholders involved to help resolve the issue.
   (C) begin project closure.
   (D) re-plan the project to include the new objective.

19. From the seller's point of view, the contract is considered closed when:

   (A) the archives are completed.
   (B) final payment is made.
   (C) scope of work is complete.
   (D) lessons learned is complete.

20. Of all decisions the executive sponsors must consider during an end-of-phase review meeting, the most difficult is:

    (A) canceling the project.
    (B) decreasing scope to maintain the budget.
    (C) authorizing scope change for the next phase.
    (D) authorizing budget increases for the next phase based on scope changes.

21. Part of the project objectives for your company was to acquire additional expertise completing a large scale project. The project is mostly completed when your client terminates the contract. A change in their business means the work is no longer needed. What is the most effective thing to do?

    (A) Complete the project, but do not charge the client for the time.
    (B) Stop work immediately.
    (C) Move on to project closure.
    (D) Tell the client that work will stop after it is completed.

22. Project archives are best described as:

    (A) Documentation of the project's product.
    (B) Lessons learned on the project.
    (C) A complete set of indexed project records.
    (D) Maintained only on an organization's most significant and complex projects.

23. The final deliverables have been sent to the client and have been formally accepted. All the balance of closure activities has been completed, when a procurement audit turns up a problem. The project is considered to be:

    (A) complete.
    (B) incomplete until the problem is resolved.
    (C) incomplete until formal acceptance is accomplished.
    (D) still to be in closure until the problem is resolved.

24. The first phase of your project has come to an end. Before beginning the next phase, you should ensure that:

    (A) the project's progress is comparable to its baselines.
    (B) the resources are available for the next phase.
    (C) corrective action(s) are taken to bring project results in line with project expectations.
    (D) the phase has reached its objectives and formally accepts its deliverables.

25. The project is completed and the final deliverable has been sent to the customer, but the customer refuses to give final acceptance on the project. It is most important for the project manager to:

    (A) ask the team for assistance.
    (B) inform management of the situation.
    (C) initiate legal proceedings.
    (D) document the situation.

26. The scope of work is completed on a project. However, the customer is not happy because they want additional work to be completed. In light of this, what should be done?

    (A) Tell the customer it is too late to make a change.
    (B) Add to scope of work and proceed with additional work after obtaining management's agreement.
    (C) Begin closure on the contract and sign a new one for the additional work.
    (D) Change to a cost reimbursable contract.

27. What is the main purpose of the procurement audit?

    (A) Validate that costs charged to the contract are valid and correct.
    (B) Loosely review the project.
    (C) Identify the successes to transfer to other procurements.
    (D) Acknowledge substantial completion.

28. What phase is a project in when the project team has completed all the work specified in the contract scope of work and the final deliverable transferred to the client?

    (A) Completion
    (B) Closure
    (C) End of execution
    (D) Scope verification

29. When is the earliest time administrative closure should be completed?

    (A) At the end of each project phase.
    (B) At the end of the project.
    (C) Whenever a deliverable is complete.
    (D) Whenever a new project manager takes over a project.

30. Which of the following would be considered the best option to ensure proper contract closure?

    (A) Procurement audits
    (B) Contract documentation
    (C) Formal acceptance
    (D) Scope change control

31. With a clear scope of work, a seller completes work as specified, but the buyer is not pleased with the results. The contract is considered to be:

    (A) incomplete.
    (B) waived.
    (C) complete.
    (D) null and void.

32. You are closing out a minor contract on a major project when you discover that a deliverable has not been received. Your manager wants the problem resolved as soon as possible without much trouble. What should you do?

    (A) Deduct the cost of the deliverable from payments.
    (B) Deduct the deliverable from the cost of the project.
    (C) Deduct the deliverable from the scope of work.
    (D) Require that the deliverable be done.

33. You have just completed a major deliverable on a project when you realize that the seller did not perform the required inspection. What should you do?

    (A) Deduct the cost of the inspection from payments.
    (B) Deduct the inspection from the scope of work.
    (C) Require that the inspection be completed.
    (D) Report the seller to the state agency in charge of inspection.

34. You have just completed the design phase for a client's project and are about to enter the implementation phase. All of the following need to be done except?

    (A) Formal acceptance
    (B) Completion of the product of the project
    (C) Lessons learned
    (D) Updating records

35. You have just finished most of the work on a new systems integration project when the seller comes to you with detailed procedures for closure of the contract. The contract included closure procedures. What should you do?

    (A) Get a change order.
    (B) Revise the closure procedures after getting management's approval.
    (C) Assess the quality of the seller's new detailed procedures, and if they are better than the current procedures, use them.
    (D) Create new procedures that are more complete.

36. You have just started administrating a contract when management decides to terminate the contract. What should you do first?

    (A) Go back to solicitation planning.
    (B) Go to contract closure.
    (C) Finish contract administration.
    (D) Go back to solicitation.

37. Your project is performed under a cost reimbursable contract, has finally entered closure. What must the buyer remember to do?

    (A) Decrease the risk rating of the project.
    (B) You need to reimburse the non-team member's department and pay the vendor at an overtime rate.
    (C) Evaluate the fee it is paying.
    (D) Make sure that the seller is not adding resources.

38. Your seller on the project has not performed and you are terminating the contract. Which of the following is your best option?

    (A) Meet with the seller, explain the problem, and obtain the seller's agreement on termination.
    (B) Follow the contract closure procedures.
    (C) Report the seller to the state agency in charge of inspection.
    (D) Review change requests.

Answers

1. C
2. B
3. A
4. D
5. B
6. B
7. B
8. A
9. B
10. A
11. D
12. C
13. A
14. C
15. B
16. C
17. C
18. C
19. B
20. A
21. A
22. C
23. A
24. D
25. D
26. C
27. C
28. B
29. A
30. A
31. C
32. D
33. C
34. B
35. A
36. B
37. B
38. B

Chapter 9
Professional Responsibility

The PMP® exam covers more than just the PMP® code of professional conduct in regard to professional responsibility. Many of these topics have been covered in communications and human resources. The main areas of professional responsibility are:

- Ensuring integrity and professionalism
- Contributing to the project management knowledge base
- Enhancing individual competence
- Balancing stakeholders' interests
- Interacting with team and stakeholders in a professional and cooperative manner
- Specific knowledge areas and skills have been identified in the Role Delineation Study for each of these tasks.

These questions will be based on situations or scenarios that require an understanding of the Project Management Professional Code of Conduct and the importance of professional ethics, awareness of legal issues, cultural sensitivity, and managing conflict of interest.

Example of Professional Responsibility Topics
The project manager's job is to ensure individual integrity and professionalism. This task requires knowledge of legal requirements, ethical standards, and understanding community and stakeholder values. It also requires skill in exercising appropriate judgment.

Each of these items can be related to specific knowledge areas of the PMBOK® Guide. For example, legal requirements can be related to the area of Project Procurement Management.

Ethical standards and stakeholder values can be associated with Human Resource Management and Communications Management.

The key is in understanding the relationship between the tasks identified in the Professional Responsibility Domain with the nine knowledge areas and the processes described in the PMBOK® Guide.

Ensure Integrity and Professionalism

As a project manager, your primary professional responsibility is to ensure integrity of the project management process that is outlined in the PMBOK® Guide. This applies not only to the project and product, but also in your own conduct.

A project has integrity if its product is sound and can be used by the stakeholders. If you follow the PMBOK® Guide and practice the proper project management processes you will help ensure that both the project and product will have integrity.

Personal integrity means adhering to the ethical code set forth by PMI® and that you will adhere to the PMP® Code of Professional Conduct. You should clearly understand this code because once you submit your application to PMI® you are agreeing to adhere to this code. The Code of Conduct is as follows:

As a PMI® Project Management Professional (PMP®), I agree to support and adhere to the responsibilities described in the PMI® PMP® Code of Professional Conduct.

I. Responsibilities to the Profession
   A. Compliance with all organizational rules and policies
      1. Responsibility to provide accurate and truthful representations concerning all information directly or indirectly related to all aspects of the PMI® Certification Program, including but not limited to the following: examination applications, test item banks, examinations, answer sheets, candidate information and PMI® Continuing Certification Requirements Program reporting forms.
      2. Upon a reasonable and clear factual basis, responsibility to report possible violations of the PMP® Code of Professional Conduct by individuals in the field of project management.
      3. Responsibility to cooperate with PMI® concerning ethics violations and the collection of related information.
      4. Responsibility to disclose to clients, customers, owners or contractors, significant circumstances that could be construed as a conflict of interest or an appearance of impropriety.

   B. Candidate/Certificant Professional Practice
      1. Responsibility to provide accurate, truthful advertising and representations concerning qualifications, experience and performance of services.
      2. Responsibility to comply with laws, regulations and ethical standards governing professional practice in the state/province and/or country when providing project management services.

   C. Advancement of the Profession
      1. Responsibility to recognize and respect intellectual property developed or owned by others, and to otherwise act in an accurate, truthful and complete manner, including all activities related to professional work and research.
      2. Responsibility to support and disseminate the PMP® Code of Professional Conduct to other PMI® certificants.

II. Responsibilities to the Customers and the Public
   A. Qualifications, experience and performance of professional services
      1. Responsibility to provide accurate and truthful representations to the public in advertising, public statements and in the preparation of estimates concerning costs, services and expected results.
      2. Responsibility to maintain and satisfy the scope and objectives of professional services, unless otherwise directed by the customer.
      3. Responsibility to maintain and respect the confidentiality of sensitive information obtained in the course of professional activities or otherwise where a clear obligation exists.

B. Conflict of interest situations and other prohibited professional conduct
   1. Responsibility to ensure that a conflict of interest does not compromise legitimate interests of a client or customer, or influence/interfere with professional judgments.
   2. Responsibility to refrain from offering or accepting inappropriate payments, gifts or other forms of compensation for personal gain, unless in conformity with applicable laws or customs of the country where project management services are being provided.

Another important area discussed in the Professional Code of Professional Conduct is conflict of interest. A conflict of interest is when your personal interests are put above the interest of the project or your stakeholders. Although not always easy or clearly definable, you must put the interest of the project over your own interest. If a conflict of interest should arise from such things as membership association, vendor gifts, or undue stakeholder influence you must inform the project sponsor at once of the conflict, failure to do so could result in legal action from the stakeholder and loss of your PMP® certification.

Contribute to Knowledge Base

Contributing to the knowledge base is taking any opportunity available and helping educate or train others in the field about correct project management skills, techniques, and current project management practices. This includes not only team members, but also management and current stakeholders. Learn how to communicate and transfer knowledge effectively, as a coach and mentor, and to use available research strategies.

Part of your commitment to PMI® is that you will stay current on project management practices, theories, and techniques. To do this effectively you should set up a network of other project management professionals in your area. The first place you may wish to visit is the local PMI® Chapter in your state. (To find out more about this subject matter, please visit, http://www.pmi.org/info/GMC_ChaptersOverview.asp).

Balance Stakeholders Interest

As you are aware, projects are undertaken at the request of a stakeholder. Most often, these stakeholders will have different needs and interests, and your job as the project manager is to try to balance the needs of the stakeholders with the projects. To do this you will need to understand the various competing stakeholders' interests and needs. Not all stakeholders have the same knowledge or work in the same department; because of this, your stakeholders will have competing needs. An example is that one stakeholder may want a software application that is easy to install, while another wants a word processing program that has an expandable dictionary. As project manager, it is your job to balance the two.

You will need to comprehend certain conflict resolution techniques in order to handle differing objectives. You need to remember to be fair in resolving conflicts during this period; the idea is to come up with a solution that is win-win for all parties involved.

Interact with Team and Stakeholders

As the project manager you are the so-called "ring leader" and must learn to interact with the team members and stakeholders in a professional and cooperative manner. You need to also understand cultural diversity and make sure that your team members also understand this diversity. You must be able to show flexibility toward diversity, tolerance, and self-control.

More and more projects and project managers are working in a global situation. It is important to understand and respect that cultural differences do exist and not to impose your beliefs onto others. Realize that when you or your team members are working overseas that culture shock does occur. This can be true if you or your team goes overseas or if you have overseas visitors working in your office. Training and education are both good ways to provide information on cultural differences. It is extremely important to take the time to build solid relationships with others. Once a feeling of trust is established, the project planning process will go much smoother.

Defining Culture and Its Norms

We define culture in as general terms as possible because culture is so broad and encompassing. It is simply everything human that a group shares among its members. It includes thought processes, belief systems, rules for behavior, rules governing families and marriage, and how one should set priorities—me first or the group first. It can make a project very successful or doom it despite all other reasons for success.

Every culture faces the same common problems. It is how cultures approach and solve these problems (food, shelter, marriage, communication, government, trade) that make them different from each other. Many of the outward actions that we see are based on internal values we do not see, but are part of the psyche of the person we are communicating with across a cultural divide. We can see and experience a foreign language, music, costumes, and folk stories. The values that underlie these require much greater study and where the majority of friction often exists in international projects.

Study of culture is possible because every culture must be learned by its members. Everything from language to etiquette to beliefs and values are learned from childhood. Cultures are not static—they constantly react to changes around them and are impacted, in both good and bad ways, by this change. Even within single countries we find multiple cultures that vary from the stereotype that foreigners expect to find upon arrival.

Culture must be learned and we can therefore learn multiple cultures if we apply ourselves to that endeavor. But why bother? The reason is simply economics. The global network is already upon us and the successful projects will involve those who can adjust and make things happen globally.

A first step to understanding other cultures is to understand your own. You must understand your own background and realize your own biases to be able to overcome them. The second step is to realize there are no good or bad cultures—only different ones. In fact, cultures are constantly learning and borrowing from each other ideas created in foreign cultures. Due to international exposure, your project will, most likely, find solutions to problems that can be adopted for all future projects.

Consider This Example – When You Woke Up This Morning

Shaving first (a practice created in India and considered by other cultures as a very strange masochistic act), you then dress choosing a shirt made from Egyptian cotton that is one of your favorites. Your shoes and belt were made in Mexico. Maybe you probably had coffee, from Latin

America, or chose tea, from China, while you watched for reports on traffic on a television made outside the United States.

Later, you heard news reports broadcasting live from around the world—something that your parents would have considered science fiction only decades earlier. You may have many friends living abroad that you have met, either physically or virtually on the 'Net, so news in those locations peaks your interest. You don't realize that you know many more people outside your town than in your own neighborhood.

Then you probably drove to work—most likely in a car manufactured by a foreign manufacturer or comprised of foreign parts (at least you know your tires were made in Japan). Or maybe you took a train that was manufactured in Germany or Austria. You pass billboards advertising new products by company names you might have problems pronouncing, but you understand the products and think about buying them regardless. The Czech crystal looks especially nice with Christmas, a celebration of a religion originating in the Middle East, is just around the corner. As you pass the airport, an aircraft manufactured in France, flown by a foreign airline, and arriving from a Canadian airport lands right on schedule.

While at work, you spend the morning reading emails from foreign offices that are now closed. With these updates you talk long distance to foreign suppliers about a change predicted and an existing order that will need adjusting. During lunch, you choose to eat at a restaurant that specialized in Italian food that you love and have adopted as a regular practice. In the afternoon, you update your project files and send out new tasks to your team in India and Singapore, knowing that they will receive and complete them later while you are sleeping.

After work, you pick up your children at school and go straight to their soccer practice, a fairly recent cultural adoption of a traditionally European sport. Your children's heroes are soccer stars from foreign countries, while you still follow tennis. Every year, you watch the big matches such as Wimbledon in England. On the way home, you pick up some take-out from a Chinese restaurant. You opt for chopsticks and show your kids how to use them successfully during dinner at home.

You spend the evening watching a travel show about the best beaches in the world that gets you thinking about a vacation with your wife reminding you she wants to vacation someplace where she can get a tan. She has a professional conference coming up soon in Acapulco or maybe another trip to the Caribbean. You explore the currency exchange rates on the Internet to come with some ideas. Then you check a Web site about international trade conferences that coming up soon. Comments from different sides' debate the impacts of new deals speculated. You make a couple of notes of things to look into tomorrow at work—the possibility of impacts on your domestic operations and on your exports.

Then you help with homework over math (using Arabic numerals we take for granted) and history lessons about wars where cultures came into conflict in centuries past. Some issues seem to be the same as today; the problems were never solved. Later, you read your youngest child a bedtime story from an old fairy tale that originated in Germany.

Before going to bed, you brush your teeth with a toothbrush made in China, wash your face with soap made in France, and put on silk pajamas you bought a few years ago when on business in Japan.

Face it, this is not the same world that your parents grew up in—and it won't be the same world next year.

Cultural Values

A culture develops values based upon common factors of:

- Environment - defeat nature or surrender to nature as a supreme force
- Time - focused on task accomplishments or on relationships
- Action - rapid decisions and action or contemplation forecasting all impacts carefully before proceeding
- Communication - direct or indirect, formal or informal, low content (just the facts!) or high content that requires emotion and personal contact to deliver the message as intended
- Space (personal versus public) - how physically close people are
- Power - shared or focused
- Individualism - collective or individual emphasis
- Competitiveness - highly competitive or not
- Structure - very structured and organized, or loose and very flexible
- Thinking - linear or circular logic, or long-term or short-term goals

Verbal Communication

Communication between cultures is basically the same as within a culture. It is the degree of understanding and the impacts of common misunderstandings that create a greater risk to international projects that are less dramatic with domestic projects. All communication consists of both verbal and nonverbal cues to transmit encoded messages to a receiver who must interpret the message through their own cultural biases to understand that message.

Verbal communication, of course, is a language. Language is the first thing that is often realized as a barrier between cultures. Every culture has its own language even if it is a modification of another language through slang, technical terms, or other adaptations. For example, there are many confusing meanings between Americans and the British over the same words, each using a common language. In some cases, though, there may not be a common language.

In addition, many languages contain multiple forms that can lead to problems if not understood and applied in the proper fashion. Social stature is often measured by the formality and titles used in the very first words spoken or written in a project proposal. Mistakes here can insult the receiver and terminate a project immediately. In some cultures there are words that are used when addressing a man and other words for addressing a woman or a child. Misusing these words can create a range of responses from humor to disgust—all at your expense to your credibility as a project manager.

So the first challenge to the project manager is to decide on a common language to create the project documentation. Ideally the project manager will be able to converse in whatever foreign language is required for better communication. Many nations are much further ahead of the United States when it comes to being multilingual. For example, business managers in Denmark are generally fluent in at least six different languages! As you can imagine, interpreters are becoming more important in the business sector. The translation of many terms and even common phrases must be run through a quality-control process.

Nonverbal Communication

Nonverbal communication takes on an important role in many cultures outside of the American culture. In fact, nonverbal communication is believed to consist of more than 60 percent of any intended message; it is also the most misunderstood part of communication, leading to great project problems. Nonverbal communication is also called metacommunications, paralinguistics, second-order messages, the silent language, and, very appropriately, the hidden dimension of language.

Again, every culture places different emphasis on different things. In the Orient, silence following a presentation, rather than applause, is actually a sign of respect for the ideas and wisdom of the speaker as the audience contemplates the information. Likewise, an American will become impatient with prolonged silence and will attempt to get everyone talking again, which is insulting to Asians.

Nonverbal communication is the best way to communicate emotions, underscoring key points, and controlling the information presented. It takes many forms, but a few common ones include:

- Facial expressions
- Stature
- Gestures
- Eye contact
- Proximity distance between people and things (for example, the way furniture is arranged in an office ... is it welcoming, or not?)

Many authors have written extensively about how to interpret nonverbal cues. Caution must be taken to read the cues in the context of the culture, remembering that cultures are constantly changing so generalizations may no longer match the author's interpretation.

Cultural Noise in the Communications Channel

Many problems within the communication channel come from:

- Ethnocentrism - believing one's culture is superior
- False attributes - inserting your cultural interpretations of situations (especially nonverbal) while in a foreign context.
- Stereotyping
- Decorum - nonverbal behavior, proper time and place for certain subjects, taboo subjects never discussed, and protocol.

Overcoming the barriers requires action through:

- thorough preparation (studying, anticipation, contingency planning)
- study your feedback (absence is also feedback in itself)
- active listening in multicultural setting
- putting data into environmental and cultural contexts
- remaining polite but not ingratiating
- focusing on building relationships and trust for this and future projects

Negotiation Cross Cultures

The key to success in negotiation is through personal relationships and persuasion using common values and goals. When conflict arises, it is important to study the situation and determine the real source of the conflict. Understanding the values of the other culture in order to know better what they are feeling is one of the most important factors in a conflict. Select a location for the meeting and establish acceptable agendas and ground rules in advance.

During negotiations, listen and speak carefully while looking for all the cues. Use everyone on your negotiation team to watch from different angles, miss nothing, and confer frequently during breaks to discuss what is really being transmitted for your choice of action.

Negotiation Techniques

- Paradigm shift where you consciously flip your way of thinking to look at all angles and possibilities
- Brainstorming options and comparing to come up with an optimal and mutually acceptable solution.
- Fuzzy logic techniques to look into the gray areas to find better solutions and overcome obstacles.

Conflict Resolution

- Confrontation = Win / Lose
- Smoothing = Agree to disagree
- Avoiding = Withdraw from conflict
- Bargaining = Splitting the difference or meeting halfway
- Problem solving = Facing issues together for a solution

Common Negotiation Tactics

- Personal attack
- Ultimatums
- Good cop / bad cop
- Walk-out threat
- Piling on = last-minute "add-on items".
- Playing dumb (effort to gain more time)
- Bluff
- Information dump (hide bad news in details)

Ethics and Legalities

Ethics are the commonly shared organizational values that define correct behavior and determine to control incorrect behavior. Every culture has its own ethics and every corporation, as its own culture, has its own ethical code. Today, in dealing with a variety of cultural values, laws, and ethical codes the international project has a much more difficult problem determining the right course for project decisions.

Acceptable behavior norms are understood by all in every culture for:

- Self-interest versus organization
- Financial gains
- Relationships
- Society responsibility
- Morality and belief systems
- Laws

The Project Management Institute has created a professional code of ethics for project management professionals (PMP®), and failure to follow this international professional code can lead to dismissal.

The key points of the PMP® Code are:

- Truthful representations of yourself and your work to PMI® and to your customers.
- Reporting any violations witnessed to PMI®.
- Maintaining customer confidentiality (unless unlawful) and focusing on customer objectives in work.
- Avoiding conflicts of interest.
- Promoting professional ethics including support to any investigation.

Today, some corporations accept a social responsibility to do the right thing regardless of cost, while others may see a more important obligation to prevent financial losses as for their shareholders' best interests.

A project manager can receive sources of ethical behavior from many directions: her own cultural bias, the foreign culture where the project resides, laws of different countries, the PMI®, and her own corporate policies. Is there a way to make international decisions easier?

Legality

The legal systems of different countries vary extensively and this area should not be taken for granted by any project manager. Foreign laws may be much stricter and carry extreme penalties; in other situations, the laws may be without teeth.

The United States realized the problems and created the Foreign Corrupt Practices Act in 1977 to police US companies dealing in unethical practices in foreign countries—primarily in the payment of bribes to foreign officials. The Securities and Exchange Commission (SEC) is responsible for enforcement, and violations carry stiff penalties—$2 million fine to corporation, and each individual faces $200,000 fine and up to five years imprisonment. Still, critics cite that the law leaves a great deal of interpretation as to what constitutes a bribe and what is commonly accepted business practice with foreign governments. It does require standard corporate accounting practices, reports submitted to the SEC, and audits for all assets in a foreign country to identify irregularities in assets that may be transferred as bribes.

Global Project Manager Competency

There are several forces that drive organizations to develop competency for international project management:

- Markets - global branding, smarter global customers focusing on better and tailored products
- Competition - domestic markets shrinking and international competition easily enter to compete with every company
- Technology - improved communications make many international operations possible and more profitable than ever before
- Cost Savings - production and presence overseas can provide lower costs to local foreign customers through avoidance of tariffs and reduced unit costs using local supply chains and production facilities
- Government - some governments reward local presence that induce corporations to establish partnerships or establish presence in foreign companies
- Relationship Management - corporations must establish and encourage positive relationships with customers, suppliers, partners, and operations on a worldwide scale upon entry into the international market place.

Corporations are usually at one stage of international exposure and development:

- Domestic company - focused on domestic market with strong domestic knowledge, possible export/import involvement, focus on cross-functional teams, and international strategy for market changes is entry or withdraw from foreign markets ,
- International (Multinational) Company - domestic home market and international markets on a parity, moves toward global company to build international customer relationships, focus is upon cross-cultural teams, and international strategy for market changes is reprioritizing resources between foreign operational units,
- Global Company - focus is on serving one worldwide market, customizing products to fit local cultural norms, and management focusing upon international branding, and international strategy for market changes is a central strategic center supporting nearly autonomous foreign business unit operations through a free-flowing information network.

The future competitive advantage for corporations dealing in international endeavors or working with a foreign partnership focuses squarely on the management skills dealing across multiple cultures by project or program managers. The goal is a professional integrator that can transcend corporate and cultural boundaries to solve problems efficiently, and to keep projects on track. Key skills to develop and emphasize in training are:

- Communications skills - including foreign language, cultural interpretations, and nonverbal
- Personality - adaptable, analytical, open minded, empathetic
- Motivation - corporation must make foreign assignments and training a boost for career
- Family - personal support and adaptive to live in foreign assignments when required

- General skills - maintaining broad outlooks, juggle contradictions, experience "hands-on" in international teams and assignments, emotionally stable, can implement risk management

Specific skills for international projects:

- Leadership in chaos situations - ability to "think outside the box" and operating in uncertainty
- Ability to adapt "best practices" to fit a cultural situation by understanding the various contexts and completing detailed analysis of the culture
- Understanding of the historical perspectives from all angles that is often a critical basis in decision making in many cultures and can be used to sell new methods if affiliated with a historical link
- Developing subordinates into leaders and sharing power especially to present a diverse leadership perspective to all shareholders
- Focus on performance measurement for success versus relying on traditional management rules or procedures from domestic experience for success

Review Questions

1. You are working on a large construction project that is progressing within the baseline. Resource usage has remained steady, and your boss has just awarded you a prize for your performance. One of your team members returns from a meeting with the customer and tells you the customer said they are not happy with the project progress. What is the FIRST thing you should do?

    (A) Complete a team building exercise and invite the customer's representatives.
    (B) Meet with the customer to uncover details.
    (C) Change the schedule baseline.
    (D) Tell your manager.

2. You are the project manager for a large project under contract with the government. The contract for this two year, multi-million dollar project was signed six months ago. You were not involved in contract negotiations or setting up procedures for managing changes, but now you are swamped with changes from the sponsor and from people inside your organization. Who is normally responsible for formally reviewing major changes to the project/contract?

    (A) The contracting/legal department.
    (B) The change control board.
    (C) Senior management.
    (D) The project manager.

3. You are asked by the PMI® to provide information concerning the violation of the PMP® Code of Professional Conduct by your best friend. To save the friendship, you refuse to provide any information: You are in violation of the responsibility to:

    (A) Comply with laws governing professional practice.
    (B) Report violations to PMI®.
    (C) Provide accurate information.
    (D) Cooperate with the PMI® concerning ethics violations.

4. You are four months into a three year project when your project team makes significant discoveries on your project. What is the best course of action?

    (A) Make certain you mention them at the senior management meeting in two months.
    (B) Make certain you tell the other project managers involved in this program at the weekly meeting.
    (C) Make certain the discoveries are included in the project lessons learned.
    (D) Make certain the discoveries are in the monthly status report.

5. You receive a contract to perform testing for a client. After contract award, the customer provides you with the test matrix to use for your 10 tests. A vice president says that the customer's test matrix is wrong, and he wants to use a different test matrix, which should give better results. This is a violation to the SOW. Suppose your sponsor is also the vice president for engineering. You should do which of the following?

    (A) Use the customer's test matrix
    (B) Use the engineering test matrix without telling the customer
    (C) Use the engineering test matrix and inform the customer
    (D) Tell your sponsor that you want to set up a meeting with the customer to resolve the conflict

6. You are managing a project with an estimated BAC of $5 million. About two-thirds through the project, you estimate that the project will be concluded early and just about 35% under budget. The contract is structured so that you will actually make less profit if you finish early. What should you do?

    (A) Direct your project team to increase the quality of their work so it takes the planned amount of time.
    (B) Inform the project stakeholder/sponsor about your budget projections.
    (C) Do nothing and deliver the final project at the planned time and within the allowed budget.
    (D) Have a team meeting and gather input from the team on how to make the project last longer.

7. While reading a magazine article, you discover that there is a tool of project management that other companies are using, but that your company has never heard of. What should you do?

    (A) Talk to your colleagues and see if they know about it.
    (B) Review the benefits of using it in your company and present them to your manager.
    (C) Arrange a meeting with your manager to discuss it.
    (D) Copy the article and pass it around your company.

8. An example of a conflict of interest would be:

    (A) You and a functional manager disagree with a task cost estimate
    (B) Your personality conflicts with that of a key member of your project team
    (C) Your sponsor decides to cancel your project because it no longer supports the company strategy
    (D) As a public official you make a decision about a contract award that will benefit you personally

9. The customer responsible for overseeing your project asks you to provide a written cost estimate that is 30% higher than your estimate of the project's cost. He explains that the budgeting process requires managers to estimate pessimistically to ensure enough money is allocated for projects. What is the best way to handle this?

    (A) Create one cost baseline for budget allocation and a second one for the actual project plan.
    (B) Ask for information on risks that would cause your estimate to be too small.
    (C) Add the 30% as a lump sum contingency fund to handle project risks.
    (D) Add the 30% to your cost estimate by spreading it evenly across all project tasks.

10. A seller has withdrawn from a project midway though execution and another seller is taking over. The project manager meets with the replacement seller and his crew. In this meeting, what should the project manager do FIRST?

    (A) Introduce team members.
    (B) Communicate the objectives of the project.
    (C) Assert authority.
    (D) Create a communications plan.

11. One of your employees is up for promotion. If the promotion is granted, the employee will be reassigned elsewhere causing a problem for you on your project. You can delay the promotion until your project is completed. You should:

    (A) Ask the employee to refuse the promotion until your project is completed
    (B) Support the promotion but work with the employee and the employee's new management to develop a good transition plan
    (C) Tell the employee that it is his responsibility to find a suitable replacement so that the project will not suffer
    (D) Arrange to delay the promotion until the project is completed

12. A project manager discovers a defect in a deliverable due to the customer under contract today. The project manager knows the customer does not have the technical understanding to notice the defect. The deliverable technically meets the contract requirements, but it does not meet the project manager's fitness of use standard. What should the project manager do in this situation?

    (A) Note the problem in the lessons learned so future projects do not encounter the same problem.
    (B) Inform the customer that the deliverable will be late.
    (C) Discuss the issue with the customer.
    (D) Issue the deliverable and get formal acceptance from the customer.

13. Your project sponsor is extremely happy with the project performance to date. To celebrate, he wants to hold a party with dancing and liquor for the entire team. You are concerned because the company policy states that "no alcohol can be served at company events." What should you do?

   (A) Inform human resources that the sponsor is serving alcohol at a company function.
   (B) The project sponsor is responsible. Hold the event as a good team building experience.
   (C) You should suggest the event be held outside of working hours.
   (D) Tell the project sponsor that the party is a great idea, but no alcohol can be served.

14. Maximizing one's influence facilitates communication. This involves building and sustaining credibility. Which of the following is now a behavior that can help in this regard?

   (A) Being flexible and open to differences.
   (B) Being respectful.
   (C) Exhibiting expertise by the answers you give.
   (D) Being reliable and committed.

15. Which of the following is not a measure that determines whether a business practice used by another country is an unfair business practice?

   (A) It does not supply a decent wage for the country and the type of work.
   (B) It discriminates against women.
   (C) It hurts the right to physical movement.
   (D) It is a common practice in the other country.

16. A control chart shows the last eight pipes produced were all less than average weight. You need to tell management there is a problem because the situation violates which of the following?

   (A) Rule of eight.
   (B) Rule of seven.
   (C) 6-sigma rule.
   (D) 50/50 rule.

17. Another project manager in your company is having difficulty managing his project. You have found that he has not used a project charter and that is probably the cause of the problem. How can you help?

   (A) Develop a draft charter for his use.
   (B) Talk to him about his project and offer help in creating a project charter.
   (C) Provide him with a copy of an article about project charters.
   (D) Work with his boss to get him a mentor.

18. You find out that a fellow PMP® lied about his years of experience on his application for PMP® certification. You decide to overlook it because he is a friend of yours. You are in violation of the responsibility to:

    (A) Report possible violations of the code of conduct to PMI®.
    (B) Cooperate with PMI® concerning ethics violations.
    (C) Comply with ethical standards governing professional practice.
    (D) Support and disseminate the PMP® Code of Professional Conduct to other PMPs.

19. Name the ethical code you'll be required to adhere to as a PMP®?

    (A) Project Management Policy of Ethics
    (B) Project Management Professional Standards
    (C) Project Management Code of Professional Ethics & Standards
    (D) Project Management Professional Code of Professional Conduct

20. You signed an agreement with your client that the integration plan and other documents they provided would remain confidential. You needed these documents to complete the project. Another company contacts you because you're an expert in the field. They ask you for samples of integration plans, which they want to include in a book they are writing. They promise you a "thank you" and a payment of $500, but they need the information today. What should you do?

    (A) Say no.
    (B) Use the material provided by the customer, but remove all company specific references.
    (C) Create new material based on the confidential material.
    (D) Try to get permission from the customer.

21. The project manager is having a very difficult time keeping a project schedule on track. The project is 13 months long and requires 220 people to complete. All of the project problems have been fixed to the project manager's satisfaction, the SPI is currently .67, the CPI is 1.26, there are 23 tasks on the critical path, and the project PERT duration is 26. Under these circumstances, the monthly status report should say that the project?

    (A) Has too many people assigned to it.
    (B) Is behind schedule.
    (C) Cost is behind budget.
    (D) Is too risky.

22. As a PMP®, you will be required to comply with the project Management professional Code of professional Conduct. This code refers to all of the following except?

    (A) Reporting conflicts of interest
    (B) Reporting experience and PMP® status truthfully
    (C) Complying with stakeholder requirements
    (D) Complying with rules and policies of foreign countries

23. The disorientation experienced by people who suddenly find themselves living and working in a different environment is known as?

   (A) Culture shock.
   (B) Sociocentrism.
   (C) Temporal shock.
   (D) Ethnocentrism.

24. During construction of a new manufacturing facility in another country, one of your team members complains to you that the wage paid to the workers is below the acceptable wage in your home country. In this situation it is best to:

   (A) Pay the workers at the new facility the same wage as your country.
   (B) Pay the workers at the new facility a little less than the same wage as your country.
   (C) Pay the workers an appropriate wage for the country within which they work.
   (D) Ignore the issue as you have not heard the workers complain.

25. Although your company is not the lowest bidder for a project, the client has come to expect good performance from your company and wants to award the contract to you. To win the contract the client asks you to eliminate your project management costs. The client says that your company has good project processes, and project controls unnecessarily inflate your costs. What should you do under these circumstances?

   (A) Remove costs associated with project team communications, meetings, and customer reviews.
   (B) Eliminate your project management costs and rely on experience.
   (C) Describe the costs incurred on past projects that did not use project management.
   (D) Remove meeting costs but not the project manager's salary.

26. What is the ethical code you'll be required to adhere to as a PMP®?

   (A) Project Management Policy of Ethics
   (B) Project Management Professional Standards
   (C) Project Management Code of Professional Ethics & Standards
   (D) Project Management Professional Code of Professional Conduct

27. The integrity of the project manager is often challenged by stakeholders who attempt to use personal power or influence to change the scope of an agreed upon deliverable. In these situations the project manager's most appropriate response would be:

   (A) Contact the legal department and suspend all further project work.
   (B) Determine the risks and rewards for implementing the change before taking any action.
   (C) Refer the stakeholder to the process for change documented in the approved contract.
   (D) Agree to the change because customer satisfaction is the goal regardless of cost.

28. A large, complex construction project in a foreign country needs coordination to move equipment through crowded city streets. To ensure the equipment is transported successfully, your contact in that country tells you that you will have to pay the local police a fee for coordinating traffic. What should you do?

    (A) Eliminate the task.
    (B) Pay the fee.
    (C) Do not pay the fee if it is not part of the project estimate.
    (D) Do not pay the fee because it is a bribe.

29. Which of the following situations describes a violation of the PMP® Professional Code of Conduct?

    (A) Complying with laws and regulations of the state or province in which project management services are provided
    (B) Disclosing information to a customer about a situation that may have an appearance of impropriety
    (C) Accepting a gift that is within the customary guidelines of the country or province you are currently working in
    (D) Use of confidential information to advance your position or influence a critical decision

30. As project manager you are managing a project with a BAC of $ 5 million. About halfway through the project, you estimate that the project will be completed early and roughly 30% under budget. The contract is structured so that you actually make less profit if you finish early. You decide that you should?

    (A) Tell the project sponsor about your budget and schedule projections.
    (B) Hold a team meeting and let them decide what to do.
    (C) Direct your team to increase work time and quality of work in order to get back on schedule.
    (D) Continue working on the project and complete early.

31. You are a project manager working on a multimillion-dollar project. As the project has progressed, you become friends with the general contractor. You are working on a US $100,000 change request. She has offered to let you use her boat on Lake Superior this weekend while she is away in Mexico. What should you do?

    (A) Decline the offer.
    (B) Ask your boss to approve you use of the boat.
    (C) Decline the offer and report it to you supervisor.
    (D) Accept the offer with thanks

32. A client has told you that his company is in extreme financial difficulties, but tells you to keep it under your hat. You decide to tell your sales manager. You are in violation of the responsibility to:

    (A) Provide accurate information.
    (B) Respect confidentiality of sensitive information.
    (C) Protect intellectual property of others.
    (D) Disclose conflict of interest.

33. Your company wants to assign a resource that is not within the project scope to your project and asks you to bill that resource to the customer. This concerns you because you get a bonus for maximizing billings to the customer. Which of the following is the best course to follow?

    (A) Maximize customer billings in any ethical manner possible.
    (B) Ask for the customer's approval before adding the resource to the project scope.
    (C) Ask for clarification of the intent of adding the resource.
    (D) Remind the appropriate members of the billing organization that monetary compensation is not worth compromising the integrity of the individual or the organization.

34. You have just discovered an error in the implementation plan that will prevent you from meeting a milestone date. Which of the following options is the best course of action?

    (A) Remove any discussion about due dates in the project status report.
    (B) Educate the team about the need to meet milestone dates.
    (C) Develop alternative solutions to meet the milestone date.
    (D) Change the milestone date.

Answers

1. B
2. D
3. D
4. B
5. D
6. B
7. B
8. D
9. B
10. A
11. B
12. C
13. D
14. C
15. D
16. B
17. B
18. A
19. D
20. D
21. B
22. C
23. A
24. C
25. C
26. D
27. C
28. B
29. D
30. A
31. C
32. B
33. C
34. C

www.ingramcontent.com/pod-product-compliance
Lightning Source LLC
Chambersburg PA
CBHW051210200326
41519CB00025B/7062